AF352315

Studies of the Americas

edited by

James Dunkerley
Institute for the Study of the Americas
University of London
School of Advanced Study

Titles in this series are multi-disciplinary studies of aspects of the societies of the hemisphere, particularly in the areas of politics, economics, history, anthropology, sociology, and the environment. The series covers a comparative perspective across the Americas, including Canada and the Caribbean as well as the USA and Latin America.

Titles in this series published by Palgrave Macmillan:

Cuba's Military 1990-2005: Revolutionary Soldiers during Counter-Revolutionary Times
By Hal Klepak

The Judicialization of Politics in Latin America
Edited by Rachel Sieder, Line Schjolden, and Alan Angell

Latin America: A New Interpretation
By Laurence Whitehead

Appropriation as Practice: Art and Identity in Argentina
By Arnd Schneider

America and Enlightenment Constitutionalism
Edited by Gary L. McDowell and Johnathan O'Neill

Vargas and Brazil: New Perspectives
Edited by Jens R. Hentschke

When Was Latin America Modern?
Edited by Nicola Miller and Stephen Hart

Debating Cuban Exceptionalism
Edited by Laurence Whitehead and Bert Hoffman

Caribbean Land and Development Revisited
Edited by Jean Besson and Janet Momsen

Cultures of the Lusophone Black Atlantic
Edited by Nancy Naro, Roger Sansi-Roca, and David Treece

Democratization, Development, and Legality: Chile, 1831-1973
By Julio Faundez

The Hispanic World and American Intellectual Life, 1820-1880
By Iván Jaksić

The Role of Mexico's Plural in Latin American Literary and Political Culture
By John King

Faith and Impiety in Revolutionary Mexico: God's Revolution?
By Matthew Butler

Democratization, Development, and Legality
Chile, 1831–1973

Julio Faundez

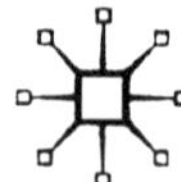

DEMOCRATIZATION, DEVELOPMENT, AND LEGALITY
Copyright © Julio Faundez, 2007.

All rights reserved. No part of this book may be used or reproduced in any manner whatsoever without written permission except in the case of brief quotations embodied in critical articles or reviews.

First published in 2007 by
PALGRAVE MACMILLAN™
175 Fifth Avenue, New York, N.Y. 10010 and
Houndmills, Basingstoke, Hampshire, England RG21 6XS
Companies and representatives throughout the world.

PALGRAVE MACMILLAN is the global academic imprint of the Palgrave Macmillan division of St. Martin's Press, LLC and of Palgrave Macmillan Ltd. Macmillan® is a registered trademark in the United States, United Kingdom and other countries. Palgrave is a registered trademark in the European Union and other countries.

ISBN-13: 978–1–4039–8406–7
ISBN-10: 1–4039–8406–9

Library of Congress Cataloging-in-Publication Data

Faundez, Julio.
    Democratization, development, and legality : Chile, 1831 to 1973 / Julio Faundez.
        p. cm. — (Studies of the Americas series)
    Includes bibliographical references and index.
    ISBN 1–4039–8406–9 (alk. paper)
        1. Democracy—Chile—History. 2. Chile—Politics and government. I. Title. II. Title: Chile, 1831 to 1973.

JL2681.F38 2007
320.983—dc22   2007003994

A catalogue record for this book is available from the British Library.

Design by Newgen Imaging Systems (P) Ltd., Chennai, India.

First edition: October 2007

10   9   8   7   6   5   4   3   2   1

Printed in the United States of America.

To Anne

Contents

Chapter 9
Legality Defeated   201

Concluding Comments   227

Acknowledgments

I am grateful to Warwick University for providing the environment that made possible the completion of this book.

I owe a special debt of gratitude to Alan Angell for his unflinching support and friendship during the long period of gestation of this project. I am also grateful to Tom Hervey, Iván Jaksić, John McEldowney, Sol Picciotto, and Ricardo Yocelevzky for their helpful comments and suggestions at different stages of this project.

I would like to thank Patricia Bruzzone from the *Biblioteca del Congreso* in Chile, who helped me locate critically important books and official documents.

As ever, I am especially grateful to Anne Faundez, my wife, who patiently read innumerable drafts and provided valuable critical advice on every aspect of this project. For these and other more important reasons, I dedicate this book to her.

List of Acronyms and Abbreviations

CAS	*Consorcio Agrícola del Sur*/Southern Agricultural Partnership
CDP	*Partido Demócrata Cristiano*/Christian Democratic Party
CERAS	*Centros de la Reforma Agraria*/Centers of Agrarian Reform
CIA	Central Intelligence Agency
CODE	*Confederación Democrática*/Democratic Confederation
CODELCO	*Corporación del Cobre*/State Copper Corporation
CORFO	*Corporación de Fomento de la Producción*/State Development Corporation
CRAC	*Confederación Republicana de Acción Cívica*/Republican Confederation of Civic Action
CTCH	*Confederación de Trabajadores de Chile*/Chilean Workers' Confederation
CUT	*Central Unica de Trabajadores*/United Workers' Federation
DIRINCO	*Dirección de Industria y Commercio*/Industry and Commerce Directorate
FOCH	*Federación Obrera de Chile*/Chilean Workers' Federation
ITT	International Telephone and Telegraph Corporation
JAPs	*Juntas de Abastecimientos y Precios*/Price Control Committees
MAPU	*Movimiento de Acción Popular Unitaria*/United Popular Action Movement
MNS	*Movimiento Nacional Socialista*/Nationalist Socialist Movement

POS	*Partido Obrero Socialista*/Socialist Workers' Party
PUMA	*Por un Mañana Auspicioso*/For a Better Tomorrow
PSA	Prices and Subsistance Agency/*Comisariato de Subsistencias y Precios*
SDG	Satute of Democratic Guarantees/*Estatuto de Garantías Democráticas*
SNA	*Sociedad Nacional de Agricultura*/National Agricultural Society

Introduction

Until the military coup of 1973, Chile's political regime was exceptionally stable. During the nineteenth century it managed to establish a strong state and a stable constitutional government. Presidents were regularly elected; the congress, representing different interests within the elite, had an increasingly important political role; and the military, under the control of civilian authorities, was often mobilized to suppress insurrections and to fight wars that resulted in a significant expansion of the territory. Stability within the framework of the constitution continued to be a feature of the political process during most of the twentieth century. Despite recurrent economic problems, political and legal institutions were stable and between 1932 and 1973 and they seemed to operate in accordance with the standards of developed Western democracies. Political and civil rights were generally respected; the press was free and lively; the judiciary was independent; the principle of legality was respected; and there were strict financial and legal controls on the activities of the state bureaucracy. These features of the political regime suggest that Chile had found a formula that even today eludes most developing countries. It achieved effective governance within a democratic framework that respected constitutionalism and legality.

Because of these features, the study of Chile's political system was popular among political scientists from Europe and the United States. In Chile they found a familiar milieu in which they could apply standard political science analysis to assess and predict political developments. Political parties had clearly defined programs with distinct constituencies; there were frequent elections; interest groups expressed their views through established channels; and the political organs of the state behaved very much like those in old established democracies. Thus, most observers of the democratic regime after 1932 tend to offer an optimistic appraisal of the political regime and compare it favorably with those of other countries. This optimistic appraisal was reinforced by the use of comparative political indicators. Indeed, in 1960 some empirical studies of democracy ranked Chile ahead of Switzerland and the United Kingdom and in 1965 ahead of the United States, France, and West Germany (Bollen 1980:387).

A special attraction that Chile had was that, despite its stability, the country's political process was neither dull nor entirely safe. Two of its main parties were Marxist and since the late 1950s had significantly increased their electoral appeal to become serious contenders in presidential elections. It also had two other strong parties, which, inspired, influenced, and often financed by social democratic parties from Europe, favored income redistribution and advocated the extension of rights to members of the subordinated classes. Thus, apart from academics with a genuine intellectual interest, some Chile-watchers had their own political agendas. European observers regarded Chile as a fertile ground for testing the possibility of implementing European style welfare policies in developing countries. Those from the United States were interested because the political process in Chile raised the specter that parties aligned with the Soviet Union would achieve power by electoral means, thus posing a threat to U.S. dominance in the Latin American region.

In the event, in 1970 Salvador Allende, a Marxist, won the presidential elections, but his period in office was short-lived. In 1973 he was deposed by a military coup that destroyed democracy and established a brutal dictatorship that was to last nearly two decades. The collapse of democracy generated a flood of books and articles that purported to explain the so-called lessons of Chile. Some welcomed the coup as a necessary step toward the restoration of democracy, while others attributed it to the undercover machinations of the U.S. government and multinational companies (Faundez 1975). Yet, neither critics nor apologists of the military coup raised any questions about the accuracy of interpretations depicting the former regime as an exemplary democracy fully committed to the principle of legality.

The collapse of democracy in 1973 suggests that, despite appearances, neither the democratic framework nor the legal system had the strength or resilience hitherto assumed. Optimistic assessments of the strength of democratic institutions (Gil 1966: Valenzuela 1994, 1978) focus mainly on variables such as the structure of the party system, levels of electoral registration and participation, ideological alignment, voting patterns and the role of unions, which can be easily observed or measured. Although these studies offer valuable insights into political behavior, they overlook facts that cannot be reconciled with the tranquil environment of established democracies. They either ignore or tend to gloss over the crucial role played by the military in the design of institutions during the period of intense political instability in the late 1920s and early 1930s. Also, they fail to take into account that during the period of coalition politics of the late 1930s and early 1940s, women were excluded from the franchise and their involvement in politics virtually had no impact until the early 1960s. Moreover, had these scholars examined, even superficially, the structure and operation of the law during that time, they would have noticed that many features of the regime were sharply different from those of well-established constitutional democracies. Thus, while the executive, with the acquiescence of the congress, consistently expanded the scope of its regulatory powers, the Supreme Court made no attempt to fulfill its role as guardian of the constitution. Further, the political elite consistently refused to establish an effective system of administrative justice. Most interpretations of Chile's political regime overlook these problems, as they tend to regard law and legal institutions as background factors that have little or no influence in shaping political outcomes.

Among the numerous scholars who have studied the evolution of state institutions, several have noted the shortcomings, as well as the virtues, of the country's institutional framework (Bauer 1975; Collier 2003; Drake 1989; Góngora 1986; Hirschman 1963; Loveman 1976; Pike 1963; Pinto 1973; Petras 1969; Silvert 1965; Sunkel 1959, 1965; Valenzuela and Valenzuela 1983; Véliz 1971; Zeitlin 1984). Yet, they have not developed their valuable insights into a comprehensive interpretation of the political regime. Maurice Zeitlin's seminal article on the evolution of state institutions in the late nineteenth and early twentieth centuries stands out as the most interesting and cogent (Zeitlin 1968). He attributes the stability and democratic nature of the system to the flexibility and self-confidence of the local elite, as well as to their relative independence from the two hegemonic powers in the region—Great Britain and the United States. Zeitlin's explanation of key structural features of the state in Chile is powerful and persuasive. Its shortcoming, however, is that it depicts the political process and the institutional framework as mere by-products of economic processes. As a consequence, he examines neither the influence that institutions have in the way political actors articulate their preferences nor the role of institutions in shaping political and social outcomes. Though the central importance of economic processes cannot be ignored, most scholars have neglected the complex interplay between economic policies and political and institutional outcomes. This oversight is regrettable as Chile was the pioneer of the policy of import substitution and also one of the first countries that sought, albeit unsuccessfully, to find market- and nonmarket-based alternatives to the policy of import substitution.

The shortcomings of prevailing interpretations are attributable not only to the methodology employed or to the absence of interdisciplinary approaches, but also to the complex and contradictory nature of the political regime. Indeed, though it is undeniable that the political regime had some outstanding features, it also had fundamental flaws. By the 1960s, the process of democratization had reached a high point, the polity had become more inclusive, the electorate significantly expanded, and governments were facing the dilemma of economic development. There were also imaginative attempts to promote new forms of political participation so as to effectively empower the subordinate classes, especially agricultural workers and the urban poor. Governments also began to implement comprehensive programs of economic modernization in the agricultural and mining sectors. But the political regime also had many unsavory features. Though the political elite consistently and effectively invoked the constitution and the law to legitimize their authority and thwart attempts to destabilize the regime, their commitment to constitutionalism and legality was neither straightforward nor orthodox. Indeed, while claiming strict adherence to the constitution, they often circumvented or ignored constitutional rules and crushed fundamental political rights. Throughout most of the period, agricultural workers were denied the right to form unions, and the exercise of their right to vote was severely curtailed through bribery and intimidation. Moreover, even workers whose right to organize was recognized by the constitution had no judicial protection when they were confronted with draconian state security measures that restricted their rights or curbed union power. Courts were reluctant to challenge policies designed to undermine basic constitutional and legal rights. They were indeed independent, but their independence was due more to their political irrelevance than to genuine respect for the principle of the separation of powers or any other constitutional principle. Meanwhile, the military, which was renowned for its respect for constitutional government, kept a close watch on political developments and, from time to time, made its presence felt in the political process.

The shortcomings of Chile's political regime are hardly surprising, as they are a feature of many developing countries. The political regime's achievements, however, cannot be ignored. Indeed, Chile made the transition in a relatively orderly and stable fashion from a largely rural economy in the nineteenth century to a fairly complex semi-industrialized country in the second half of the twentieth century. Moreover, in 1932, while most of the countries in the region were facing severe economic and political instability, there emerged in Chile a stable constitutional government that lasted for a little over four decades. Yet, the local elite were persistently haunted by problems that characterize underdeveloped economies. The dependence of the economy on a single export commodity, first nitrate and then copper, was a permanent source of concern and the cause of recurring waves of unemployment, inflation, and balance of payments crises. A stagnant agricultural sector combined with a rapid process of urbanization exacerbated economic difficulties. Given the magnitude of these problems, it is remarkable that throughout most of the period, 1831–1973, governments and other public authorities were almost invariably elected in accordance with the procedures established by the constitution.

The foregoing facts suggest that prevailing interpretations have failed to adequately explain crucial features of the political regime. Recurrent political crises have either been ignored or seen as exceptional in an otherwise consistent pattern of stability; legal institutions have been regarded as factors having no bearing on political and economic processes; and political outcomes have been regarded merely as by-products of economic policies.

This study while building on the vast academic literature on Chile seeks to supplement it. Its objective is to offer an interpretation of the evolution of state institutions and the political regime between 1831 and 1973, which takes into account the complex interaction of political, economic, and legal processes. Its approach is historical, its focus is on institutions, and the unifying thread is the concept of democratization. The historical approach helps to identify and trace long-term trends in political, economic, and legal processes. It is complemented by a focus on institutions, which make it possible to ascertain their impact on the political regime. Institutions are thus examined in their political and economic context. Thus, for example, in order to ascertain the impact of legal institutions on the evolution of the political regime, this study explains both the manner in which patterns of political development contributed to shape legal institutions, and the bearing of these institutions in shaping political choices and perceptions. Through an examination of the complex interplay among political, legal, and economic institutions, this study uncovers connections and interacting processes that available interpretations either ignore or misconstrue. Thus, for example, this approach helps to explain the key, but contradictory role of the Office of the Comptroller General (hereafter *Contraloría*) in developing a system of accountability that was generally regarded as an effective device for restraining the executive. It also makes it possible to uncover critical linkages between economic policies and political institutions. Instead of assuming that economic policies always determine political outcomes, this study explores the relationship between political and economic choices. Thus, for example, though prevailing interpretations regard the crisis of the import substitution model as an economic issue, a close analysis reveals that the crisis was far more complex. Indeed, the failure to find viable market-based as well as nonmarket-based alternatives to the policy of import substitution was caused as much by political as by economic factors. Likewise, on close inspection, the alleged economic incompetence of the Allende administration in the early 1970s had roots that had deeply penetrated the political regime. Indeed, the evidence suggests that, considering the peculiar evolution of the prevailing institutional framework, Allende's expectation regarding the regime's flexibility and its unlimited capacity to accommodate radical political and economic change was not altogether unreasonable.

This study employs as its unifying thread the notion of democratization, which, in turn, is loosely based on the conceptual framework developed by Charles Tilly (2000, 2004, 2007). He identifies four components of political regimes: breadth, equality, consultation, and protection. Breadth refers to the number of persons who are members of the polity. Equality denotes the extent to which polity members have similar access to government agents and societal resources. Consultation refers to the degree to which polity members exercise binding collective control over governmental agents, resources, and activity. Protection designates the extent to which members of the polity are shielded from arbitrary action by the government. Democratization, according to Tilly, obtains when there is a positive shift in these four components (2000:4–5, 2004:13–15, 2007:59–60). In other words, democratization is the result of a process that enhances the breadth, equality, accountability, and protection within the political regime. Tilly notes, however, that these components often change independently of each other and do not follow preordained sequences. In other words, high levels of participation (breadth) in the polity may coexist with low levels of protection or with profound inequalities. Moreover, he also points out that positive shifts of some of the components do not necessarily lead to an increase in the process of democratization.

Tilly's framework is helpful as it incorporates into the analysis political, economic, and legal factors, without assigning priority to any. This is especially pertinent to this study because, as what follows show, law and legal institutions are often so deeply entangled in the design and operation of political and economic institutions that ignoring them, or assigning them the role of background factors, distorts our understanding of the political process and trivializes the concept of law. The suggestion that shifts in the four components of democratization do not follow preordained sequences is especially relevant to the case of Chile, as some components of the regime, such as political accountability or consultation, developed at a relatively early stage, whereas others, such as the persistent discrimination against agricultural workers (breadth and equality), did not change throughout most of the period. The evolution of electoral politics is also a case in point. Though elections played an important role in the development of the political system, universal suffrage came at a relatively late stage. Initially, the president and members of the congress were selected by a narrow segment of the oligarchy. Although the electorate expanded in the 1870s, electoral participation did not become free, fair, and universal until the 1950s, when the suffrage was extended to women and electoral procedures were tightened so as to prevent widespread vote buying. However, though the extension of the suffrage constitutes an acknowledgment of formal equality among citizens (breadth), it does not guarantee that the political process takes into account their interests and demands (equality). Democratization thus requires that the members of the various groups and classes incorporated into the polity have the possibility of effectively engaging in collective action in defense of their interests. Although in Chile the incorporation of a segment of the subordinate classes into the political system, mainly workers in mining and manufacturing, occurred at a relatively early stage—in the 1930s—a large proportion of workers was excluded from the political system throughout most of the period. Similarly, although in the mid-nineteenth century some form of accountability of public authorities (consultation) became feature of the political regime, its evolution was not uniform, as there were relatively long periods when restraints on state authorities were either nonexistent (throughout most of the 1920s) or very weak (during the 1940s). An important dimension of accountability is the relationship between different state authorities (the well-known system of "checks and balances" that more recently has been described as "horizontal accountability"). In Chile, this dimension of accountability had peculiar features, as often the president and the congress appeared determined to circumvent it either by inordinately expanding the powers of the executive or by totally excluding the judiciary from important areas of public policy.

The protection of citizens against arbitrary acts of the government is an area where Chile's experience is bewildering. During the nineteenth century, the regime provided a stable framework through its political and judicial organs that facilitated and protected commercial activities in mining, agriculture, and the commercial sectors. The early codification of civil and commercial laws was explicitly designed to enhance the legal security of the business community. The protection of property and contractual rights was soon combined with the guarantee of political rights, which made possible first the emergence of political parties and later on, through a chequered and combative history, the emergence of unions and other associations through which citizens struggled to assert their interests and demand new rights. But, despite the early expansion of political rights, courts never developed the strength or the interest to adequately protect these rights. Although in many areas of legal practice, courts were efficient guardians of legality, they were unable fully to safeguard democratic rights.

In this study I use the term legality, rather than rule of law, because the latter is a highly contested normative concept associated mainly with established democratic regimes (Tamanaha 2004). By contrast, legality—defined, for the purposes of this study, merely as the practice of following rules—does not presuppose the existence of any particular regime. It is thus a useful analytical tool for studying legal institutions and practices in societies that are not fully democratic, as was the case of Chile during most of the period under study. This approach makes it possible to identify and trace the evolution of an array of complex institutional mechanisms that came into existence during the nineteenth century, when the process of democratization was incipient. These mechanisms allowed for the progressive parliamentarization of politics, restricted the powers of the president, and extended basic political and civil rights to an ever-increasing number of individuals. It also makes it possible to explain how and why, in the mid-twentieth century, Chile's political regime managed to combine a meticulous concern for administrative legality, a ruthless style of governance, and an absence of effective judicial remedies to protect citizens from abuse of power by the executive.

Law and legal institutions are essential components of political regimes long before political institutions become democratic, and the legal system develops specialized procedures to protect and defend the rights of individuals. The notion of the rule of law as a benevolent device designed to restrain government excesses captures only one aspect of the role of law in the long, arduous and bumpy road to democratization. Yet, it is crucial to note the close relationship between processes of democratization and the evolution of legal institutions. Indeed, it is through legal institutions that the aims and objectives of the process of democratization are achieved or, as it often happens, are frustrated. Thus, from this perspective, law is not merely an outcome of political and economic processes, but is also an independent factor that shapes social and institutional practices. Yet, the impact of legal institutions is not always easy to gauge. Although it often takes time to establish legal institutions, once established they cannot be easily discarded and they often sustain and justify social practices quite different from those that prompted their establishment. This attribute of legal institutions—which is also a general attribute of institutions—underscores the need to study them from a historical perspective, rather than by the snapshot methodology of decontextualized case analysis employed by traditional legal scholars. A historical approach to the study of legal institutions thus makes it easier to identify their practical and ideological impact.

The notion of legal culture is generally used to refer to the attributes and peculiarities of a legal system. One such attribute is the fact that Chile is part of the civil law tradition. As a civil law country, its legal institutions share most of the features generally attributed to those from this family of legal systems (Merryman 1969). For the purposes of this study, two of these features are of special relevance: first, the tendency to regard legislative enactments as the main, if not the only, source of law, even, occasionally, above the constitution; and second, the reluctance to accept that courts have a role to play in matters of political significance. Yet, as the contents of this book show, these two features are far too general to explain fully the interaction between legal and political institutions. At various moments during the period covered by this study, courts displayed considerable activist tendencies and resorted to various subterfuges in order to assert themselves and challenge decisions by the government or the legislature. Likewise, although governments were often ruthless in interpreting their regulatory powers, they were generally mindful of the views of the courts and, except for the final months of the Allende administration (1970–73), rarely sought a confrontation with the courts. Thus, while the fact that the legal system was part of the civil law tradition is not irrelevant, it does not provide more than a very general indication of the nature of the interaction between legal and political institutions. In order to understand this interaction, it is necessary to examine the evolution of legal and political institutions.

The notion of legal culture also has a wider connotation. It refers to ideas, attitudes, expectations, and opinions about law held by people in a certain community (Friedman 1975). It is reflected in the approach of judges to legal interpretation, in the prominent role played by public notaries, in the propensity of citizens to resolve their disputes through litigation, in the content and style of legal education, and in popular beliefs about the authority of law in general. Although this book is not intended to offer a systematic analysis of Chilean legal culture, it considers many features of the legal system that could well be regarded as part of the local legal culture.

Before concluding this section I should point out that while the focus of this study is the process of democratization, its aim is not to determine when Chile became democratic. Under a minimalist conception, political democracy arguably came into being after the Civil War of 1891, as, during that period, regular elections of the president and the congress were combined with a fairly active, though restricted, party system (Remmer 1984). If a stricter definition is to be used, democracy came into being only in 1938, following the second successive election of the president under the rules of the 1925 constitution, the expansion of the party system to include parties that represented the interests of an important segment of subordinate groups, and the widespread recognition of the right to form unions (Przeworski et al. 1996). On the other hand, some may choose a later date, as it was not until the mid-1950s that free and fair elections became a feature of the political system. Under an even stricter definition, it is arguable that full democracy did not begin until 1970, when the literacy requirement was dropped from the franchise (Rueschemeyer et al. 1992:185). The object of this study, however, is not to determine the exact moment of democratization, but to trace its evolution and its relationship with legal and economic institutions.

Structure of the Book

This book is divided into three parts, each containing three chapters. An overview of each of the parts follows.

Part I: State and Regime Building

The early consolidation of a stable political center under the rule of the constitution is one of the most outstanding features of the state during the nineteenth century. Indeed, in 1831, shortly after Chile achieved independence from Spain, a strong government evolved.

From 1831 until 1891, presidents were regularly elected and, over the years, became increasingly accountable to a more influential and active congress. Political stability enabled the local elite to develop the productive sectors of the economy, mainly agriculture and mining. Sustained economic growth was accompanied by a successful campaign for the extension of territory, which led, through war, to the conquest of vast mineral-rich territories in the North and, through internal colonization, to the incorporation of valuable agricultural land in the South. The remarkable political and economic success of the elite also enabled them to develop an early attachment to the notion of constitutional government and to the principle of legality.

The elite undoubtedly displayed enormous skill as they pursued the aim of consolidating a strong political center and establishing a national identity. They were also cunning, as evidenced by the way they successfully linked the principle of constitutional supremacy with their aim of securing political stability. However, they were not as successful in their efforts to design a political regime. Indeed, toward the end of the nineteenth century, as society and the economy became more complex, the elite proved unable to contain conflict. Despite their alleged gift for compromise and flexibility, in 1891 they were unable to avert a Civil War and the new regime was clumsy and ineffective. It turned its back on the emerging political forces and stubbornly refused to extend political and social rights to the emerging middle classes and working-class organizations in urban and mining centers. The failure of the political elite to effectively steer institutions toward a path of modernity brought about, in the 1920s, the collapse of the constitution, prolonged military intervention and political instability.

The three chapters in this part offer an overview of this process. Chapter 1 outlines the factors that explain the elite's success in establishing a strong political center. Its focus is on the constitutional arrangement, the nature of economic interests, the process of territorial expansion, and the prevailing conceptions of power and law. Chapter 2 explains why, despite their remarkable success in state building and their reputation for political flexibility, the elite, in 1891, were unable to prevent the breakdown of the political system and the costly Civil War that ensued. It also explains the impact that the emergence of nitrate mining as the mainstay of the economy had on the events leading up to the Civil War. Chapter 3 describes the nature of the regime that emerged after the Civil War and examines the factors that led to its collapse.

Part II: Party Democracy

The election of Arturo Alessandri in 1932 marks the beginning of 40 years of uninterrupted constitutional government. Alessandri implemented tough law and order policies, stabilized the economy, and in 1938 handed over power to an elected successor. It was the first transfer of power in accordance with the rules of the constitution in 18 years. The focus of this part is on the first three decades, from 1932 to 1964. I characterize this period as party democracy (Manin 1997:206–218). During this period, the party system became more inclusive and political parties emerged as the driving force of the political system. Parties had stable electoral constituencies. They also had well-defined and conflicting ideological positions. Despite their ideological diversity, they established broad government coalitions in which, at one time or another, all the political parties, including most notably the two Marxist parties, participated. During this period there were major advances in the process of democratization. The constitution acquired unexpected legitimacy, the military withdrew to the barracks, the political system became more inclusive, and governments became receptive to the needs and demands of an ever-increasing number of enfranchised citizens.

The chapters in this part focus on the political, economic, and institutional features of the regime. Chapter 4 examines the tension between the narrow scope of the political system and the limits of the prevailing economic policy. Initially, a limited consensus on a state-led policy of import substitution made constitutional government viable. Yet, this policy soon proved unsustainable, as it required the denial of social and political rights to a large proportion of the population. Then followed two attempts to restrict state intervention and shift the economy toward the market. Although these attempts failed, they brought about a process of political liberalization that radicalized the political process, and that was to mark the end of party democracy. Chapter 5 explains the paradoxical aspects of governance during this time, which combined a powerful executive with a unique mechanism of accountability that contributed to the reaffirmation of the principle of legality. Chapter 6 discusses the role of the Supreme Court during party democracy and explains how the Court responded to attempts by the political organs of the state to consistently sideline the judiciary from key areas of public policy.

Part III: Radical Democracy

Between 1964 and 1973 two successive administrations—Eduardo Frei (1964–70), and Salvador Allende (1970–73)—attempted to bring about major structural reforms. Their political slogans adequately summarize their objectives. While the Frei administration promised a "revolution in liberty," the Allende administration promised "a peaceful transition to socialism." These slogans record both the differences and similarities between them. The differences are important and are analyzed at length in chapters 7 and 8. Yet, the differences overshadow the fact that these administrations had a common aim: deepening the process of democratization through the inclusion and empowerment of subordinate groups. Accordingly, they both vigorously campaigned to increase electoral registrations, to further the unionization of urban and rural workers and to encourage the urban poor to establish mechanisms of political participation. They also launched ambitious policies of income distribution and comprehensive programs in health and education. Although they had different conceptions about the ultimate aims of these policies, they were both determined to break the mold of politics so as to accommodate the demands and interests of subordinate groups. Thus, for the prevailing political regime, the objectives of these administrations were unequivocally radical.

The Frei and Allende administrations achieved many of their objectives. During their tenure there was a massive increase in electoral registration, the rate of unionization, and the provision of health and educational services to the poorest sections of the population. Indeed, according to some observers during this period Chile finally achieved the status of a full democracy (Rueschemeyer et al. 1992:185). Yet, as this was also the period that brought about the collapse of democracy, it is necessary to explore the link between the undeniable expansion of the process of democratization and the destruction of the political regime. Three sets of questions arise from this exploration. The first concerns the conception of these administrations about the prevailing institutional framework. Did they misjudge the capacity and resilience of political institutions? Did their political programs lack coherence? Were they simply too ambitious or naive? The second set of questions concerns the relationship between their political strategies and the mobilization of subordinate groups. Did their policies effectively empower subordinate groups? Did electoral competition among left-wing parties undermine popular support for radical social and economic change? The third set of questions concern the role of legal institutions. What role did they expect legal institutions to play in the revolutionary changes they espoused? What impact did their policies have on legal institutions? Was the response of legal institutions consistent with prevailing practice? The chapters in this part attempt to answer these questions. Chapters 7 and 8 examine, in turn, the Frei and the Allende administrations. Chapter 9 explains the role of law and legal institutions in the process that led to the defeat of radical democracy.

Part I

State and Regime Building

Power can be stopped and still be kept intact only by power, so that the principle of the separation of power not only provides a guarantee against the monopolization of power by one part of the government, but actually provides a kind of mechanism, built into the very heart of government, through which new power is constantly generated, without, however, being able to overgrow and expand to the detriment of other centres or sources of power.

Hannah Arendt, On Revolution, 151–152

Chapter 1

Building a Strong State

Constitutional Framework

The turbulence that followed independence in 1818 came to an end in 1831. In that year, a coalition led by traditional landowners and the clergy inflicted a decisive military defeat on liberal groups advocating the establishment of a loose federation. Instead of a federation they established a unitary state. Instead of a liberal political system, they framed an authoritarian constitution that gave the president and the executive branch sweeping powers to suppress and repress dissent. Presidents, however, were also given extensive powers to facilitate and promote the activities of the emerging economic elite.

The constitution that presided over the establishment of the political regime was framed in 1833 and proved surprisingly flexible.[1] Although at first it served mainly as cover to legitimize the repression of political opponents, it had, by the middle of the century, become the focus of a lively political debate. As the process of political differentiation evolved, an assortment of groups enthusiastically and successfully campaigned for constitutional reform. The reforms that ensued significantly reduced the powers of the president and transformed the congress into the center of political deliberation and decision. Thus, by the end of the nineteenth century, a process of parliamentarization had begun to develop, which suggests that, as well as creating a strong state, the elite had also successfully established a viable and modern political regime.

After independence, there were four failed attempts at establishing a durable constitutional framework. While the constitutions of 1818 and 1822 were authoritarian and provided for a strong executive, those of 1823 and 1828 were liberal and they attempted to introduce principles of federalism. The 1828 Constitution was short-lived.

Following the first presidential elections held under its adoption, there erupted a civil war that was won by a conservative coalition of traditional landowners, the army, and the clergy. This winning coalition repudiated liberalism, depicting it as a foreign ideology unsuitable to the country (Bravo 1986:134; Encina 1934:242; Kinsbruner 1973:61–65). According to Diego Portales, the architect of the new political regime, the country was not ready for either liberalism or democracy. He advocated, instead, a republic with a strong central government run by men who were models of civic virtue and patriotism. Democracy, according to Portales, would be introduced at a later stage, and only after citizens had learned and practiced the principles of public morality. In the meantime, the only realistic alternative was a strong authoritarian regime (Bravo 1986:15). Portales's authoritarian views were eventually embraced by some of his fiercest critics. Thus, for example, in 1885, the prominent liberal president, Domingo Santa María, defended the authoritarian features of the constitution on the ground that citizens were still not ready for democracy (Castedo 1954:3:1985–88). His opinion serves to show that even liberals at the end of the nineteenth century regarded democracy as little more than an aspiration.

The 1833 Constitution faithfully reflected Portales's concerns and objectives. Its preamble read as follows: "[R]ejecting theories which are as hallucinating as they are impractical . . . [the drafters of the constitution] have concentrated their attention on establishing mechanisms which will forever ensure public order and tranquility" (Heise 1960:36). Such mechanisms included a president and a congress elected by a small group of property owners. The suffrage was restricted to males over 25 years of age, who were literate and owned property. Only a tiny group met this requirement. Until 1874 the number of registered voters was around 1.2 percent of the population (Valenzuela 1985:150). The president had sweeping administrative and legislative powers, including a broad legislative veto. He also had direct control over the judiciary, whose members were appointed by the Council of State, an advisory body established by the constitution and made up of members appointed by the president. Provincial government was entrusted to intendants, who, as personal representatives of the president, were accountable to him alone. The powers of the president were in fact similar to, if not greater, than those of the military governor (*Capitán-General*) during the colonial period. It is not a coincidence that the first two presidents of this period, Joaquín Prieto (1831–41) and Manuel Bulnes (1841–51), were both army generals, and Bulnes even resumed his military career, albeit briefly, upon completing his term in office.

Presidents were elected—through indirect elections—to a five-year term and could be reelected for a second term. The first four presidents each served two terms. The reelection of presidents owed more to their capacity to control the electoral process than to their popularity. Electoral intervention by the president made it possible for the executive to control the composition of the congress, thus making a sham of the electoral process. Indeed, 7 out of the 11 congressional elections held between 1833 and 1864 were virtually uncontested. The president's influence over the composition of the congresses was strengthened by the fact that members of the congress were allowed to hold jobs in the civil service. In 1843, two-thirds of the members of the congress had jobs in the civil service and were, thus, under the direct authority of the president (Collier and Sater 1996:57–58).

The president's emergency powers were equally broad and open-ended. A state of siege declared by the president had the effect of suspending the constitution in any locality identified by the president (Roldán 1913:321, 410–413). Given their concern with law and order, presidents made prolific use of their emergency powers. Thus, for example, in 1837, when Chile was at war with Perú and Bolivia, the congress approved a special emergency law authorizing the president to make use of all the powers he deemed necessary to enforce the emergency. This law remained in force for two years, and the president made full use of it, issuing scores of decrees on matters unrelated to state security (Roldán 1913:323–324). Similarly, in the 1850s, at a time when the government confronted two military insurrections, the country was placed in a state of siege for almost the whole decade (Schweitzer 1972:141).

Despite their exorbitant powers, presidents were neither military tyrants nor improvised political bosses. They were elected officials who, though initially not accountable through formal constitutional procedures, were nonetheless held to account by their electors, a small, but increasingly diverse group of oligarchs and property owners, including artisans and shop keepers. Government policies sought to balance the interests and expectations of this group. This process made possible the institutionalization of the office of the president, thus preventing the emergence of a *caudillo* tradition, so prevalent in other countries of the region at the time (Collier and Sater 1996:53).

The bicameral congress, though largely under the influence of the president, had jurisdiction in three key areas of policy. It had the power to approve the annual budget, to set land taxes, and to fix the size of, and expenditures for, the armed forces (Heise 1960:41). Over the years, these three policy areas provided the congress with a powerful leverage to reduce and control the powers of the president.

The authoritarian framework of the 1833 constitution left little room for judicial independence. Judicial appointments were made by the president upon a recommendation by the Council of State, an organ controlled by the president. Thus, it is not surprising that, during the three decades following the 1831 settlement, the courts did not challenge the behavior of the executive or the legislature. Although the constitution did not give courts the power to review the constitutionality of legislation, in 1848, the Supreme Court gave express assurances to the government that no judicial tribunal would ever contemplate declaring a law unconstitutional, as this would place courts above the legislature (Carvajal 1940:89).

The Economy

Before independence, Chile's leading export commodity was wheat, and its main market was Perú. After independence, at different intervals, new markets opened in England, Australia, and California. During the first half of the nineteenth century, a new group of dynamic entrepreneurs, made up of recently arrived European immigrants, emerged. These entrepreneurs, who, initially, had no links with the old landed aristocracy, developed the mining and financial sectors (Villalobos 1987:41–45). They discovered and exploited silver, copper, and coal, and were instrumental in bringing about an export boom.

Between 1820 and 1870, silver exports increased from 20,000 to 127,000 kilos, while copper exports increased from 3,000 to 45,000 tons (Collier 1985:595). By the 1860s copper exports represented nearly 40 percent of world production (Pinto 1973:26–27). The mining boom led to the establishment of export houses and financial institutions based mainly in Valparaíso. The boom generated further industrialization as cement plants, glass and bottle factories, as well as foundries and machine shops were established and some of these industries even exported their products to the United States (Zeitlin 1984:24–25). The export boom also led to the establishment of banks, insurance companies, and commercial houses.

Governments were, on the whole, responsive to the needs of the main economic actors. They facilitated the establishment of a national merchant marine, and, through a complex tariff structure, protected the interests of local manufacturing firms (Martner 1929:149). They built railway lines and roads, and provided exporters with special storage facilities that enabled them to weather unfavorable conditions in international markets (Cariola and Sunkel 1990:37). Governments also launched a major process of legal reform that led to the enactment of modern legal codes expressly designed to facilitate economic transactions. A special concern of most governments during this period was education, especially at the primary level.

Government intervention in the economy, however, was contentious. At issue was not whether the state should support economic activities, but, rather, who should benefit from state revenue. By the end of the century, state revenue was largely derived from duties levied on mining exports (Culver and Reinhart 1989:740). Mining enterprises based in the North and South of the country resented the central government for spending most of its revenue on projects aimed at benefiting Central Valley landowners and merchants in Santiago or Valparaíso. These economic grievances, in combination with other political and social factors, were the trigger for two major insurrections, one in 1851 and the other in 1859, against the central government in the midnineteenth century (Campos 1963:171–81; Volk 1993:92).

The landed aristocracy of Spanish origin enjoyed disproportionate economic, social, and political influence. They owned most of the productive land in the Central Valley, which, in turn, was heavily concentrated in a few large estates. According to tax records for 1860, approximately 850 landowners received two-thirds of the agricultural income from the Central Valley (Collier and Sater 1996:81). The power and influence of the landed aristocracy is underscored by the fact that, at the time, 80 percent of the population lived in the countryside and most of them were dependent on the large estates—the *haciendas*—for their livelihood.

The *haciendas*—as one observer has noted—came close to constituting a natural economy (Bauer 1975:35). Labor there was composed of service tenants—*inquilinos*—and seasonal workers. *Inquilinos* exchanged their labor for subsistence plots and a daily food ration. Seasonal workers, hired mainly during harvests, constituted a floating mass of over 50,000 workers (Bauer 1975:150). Service tenancy was a complex institution. As well as working for the *hacienda*, the *inquilino* was under obligation to supply one or more workers—often, family members—who generally received only a food ration from the landlord. Although neither the *inquilino* nor the rest of the workforce was under legal obligation to remain on the estate, they did so in practice as there was little else on offer (Kay 1977:104).

Life for the *inquilino* and other farm workers revolved around the *hacienda*, where relations with the landowner were paternalistic (Thiesenhusen 1966:20). Remuneration was mostly in kind and landowners settled disputes. Since the rural population was largely excluded from the market, social life revolved around the *hacienda*. Education—if any—was provided by schools within the *hacienda* and religious services were held in its chapel. Provincial cities, with the exception of the growing industrial centers of Valparaíso and Concepción and possibly, Talca, remained small and dilapidated (Bauer 1975:81).

While the *hacienda* system was an obstacle to modernization, landowners were not reluctant to venture into other sectors of the economy. Indeed, as absentee owners, for the most part living in Santiago, they often had a stake in urban-based investments. Easy credit terms enabled them to invest in commercial firms, insurance companies, and banking. While landowners ventured into other sectors of the economy, miners, merchants and bankers began to buy agricultural land (Pike 1968:209). With the abolition of entailments (*mayorazgos*)—the prohibition to alienate, divide, trade, or mortgage large estates—in 1852, the commercialization of rural property began, resulting in closer integration among the economic elite (Feliú 1951:222; Pregger-Roman 1983:49). Not surprisingly, most commentators of the nineteenth century remark on the extent to which the dominant sectors formed a cohesive group with common economic and political interests (Véliz 1971; Zeitlin 1968:232). By the turn of the century, as Frederick Pike notes, "urban and rural interests were crossed and crisscrossed to such a degree that the distinction was often meaningless" (1968:209–210). Henry Kirsch, a leading student of Chile's industrial development, arrives at a similar conclusion: "[O]ne of the strengths of the Chilean hierarchy has been its flexibility and ability to transfer its capital and talent among different areas of the economy in accordance with the relative opportunities offered by each" (1977:75). Money used in the purchase of rural estates did not, however, extend to modernizing agricultural production or altering social relations within the *hacienda*. The wealth derived from mining exports—as Bauer aptly puts it—"simply ran out on to the sands of a traditional countryside" (1975:181). Thus, by the end of the nineteenth century, although more diverse, the landowning aristocracy had lost none of its social and cultural prestige and still commanded significant influence over political developments (1990:236–238).

Territorial Expansion

Permanent Warfare

The elite's commitment to a strong state is evident in its foreign policy. It was based on the notion that, regardless of social or economic costs, the state had to be protected from any external threat, real or imagined. This policy led to a virtual permanent state of war and a determination to expand the territory, without regard for the principle of the sanctity of boundaries (Góngora 1986:37). During the five decades following the 1830 settlement, Chile experienced three major international conflicts. Between 1836 and 1839, it waged a successful war against the Perú-Bolivian Confederation. In 1865, it fought a brief war against Spain, and, later on, in 1879, it again successfully confronted Perú and Bolivia. This last war was to have a lasting impact on the country's development, as it resulted in the conquest of valuable mining territory in the north. There was also, during this time, an extended war against the indigenous Mapuche people.

The Perú-Bolivian Confederation was established in 1835 under the leadership of General Andrés Santa Cruz from Bolivia (Encina 1934:412–503). Its establishment was, undoubtedly, a source of concern, but it was not seen as a serious military threat (Burr 1965:33). At worst, the Confederation was a minor irritant. After the establishment of the Confederation, Perú repudiated a treaty that granted preferential treatment to products transported by vessels registered in Chile. This decision annoyed the Chilean government, but did not significantly affect its commercial interests (Burr 1965:35). Another source of concern was that Perú had granted political asylum to some of the military leaders defeated in 1830 and appeared to sympathize with their cause. Although it is likely that the establishment of the Confederation revived political ambitions among Chilean exiles in Perú, there was no imminent threat to the government in Santiago. Nonetheless, in December 1836, the Chilean Congress adopted a resolution formally declaring war on the Perú-Bolivian Confederation. Initially, ordinary citizens did not support the war. It was only after three years, following the battle of Yungay, which dealt a fatal blow to the Confederation, was there a major display of patriotism and public support for the war (Góngora 1986:34–35).

Chile's decision to wage war against the Perú-Bolivian Confederation reflects the elite's obsessive concern with stability. Their vision of the international role of the state is summarized by Diego Portales, the most influential politician of the 1830s, in his letter to

Admiral Manuel Blanco Encalada upon the latter's appointment to lead the naval expedition against the Confederation. Here, Portales argues that the Confederation had to disappear, both because it was disturbing the regional balance of power and was likely to upset domestic order in the country:

> The Confederation must forever disappear from the American scene. By its geographical extent; by its larger white population; by the combined wealth of Perú and Bolivia, until now scarcely exploited; by the influence that it would assert in the Pacific . . . by the greater intelligence—though lesser character—of its public servants . . . for all these reasons, the Confederation would soon suffocate Chile.
>
> The navy should act before the military . . . We must forever be the masters of the Pacific: this must be your objective now; and, hopefully, it should, at all times, be Chile's objective. (Góngora 1986:35–36)

While conceding that the Confederation did not pose an immediate threat to domestic political stability, Portales was, nonetheless, certain that its objectives were sinister. In his view, the Confederation would first act as a catalyst for political dissent among the exiled community; and then, after destroying Chile's social fabric, would force it to surrender (Góngora 1986:36). Thus, for Portales and the political elite, the mere existence of the Confederation posed a threat to Chile (Burr 1965:57).

Victory gave the local elite greater confidence in their political system. As Robert Burr explains, after the war,

> Chileans became aware of the extraordinary contrast between their own law and order and the chaotic turbulence of their neighbors. The more the Chileans learned about others, the more convinced they became that they were unique among Spanish American peoples in being able properly to govern themselves and to make orderly social and material progress. (1965:114)

By the mid-nineteenth century, national pride was flourishing. Newspaper articles proudly proclaimed that Chile had become "the England of South America" (Collier 2003:146). In 1853, Diego Barros Arana, a leading intellectual, wrote: "[F]orty years ago we were nothing in the eyes of the world or to ourselves, and today we call ourselves Chileans with pride and dignity" (Collier 2003:146). This level of self-confidence served the elite well during the War of the Pacific (1879–83) when Chile again defeated the combined forces of Perú and Bolivia and secured a massive expansion of territory. Self-confidence and arrogance was also on display during the brutal military campaigned against the Mapuche people.

Internal Colonialism

Pressure for land in the 1850s brought about the occupation of Araucanía, a vast territory south of Concepción, inhabited by the Mapuche people. Initially, a scheme was set up to allow speculators to buy land from the Mapuches, but when it failed the government launched a military campaign lasting nearly 15 years and resulting in the death of hundreds of Mapuche people, the destruction of their way of life, and the expropriation, without compensation, of agricultural land.

The Mapuche people lived in an area south of Concepción comprising approximately 50,000 square kilometers. They had their own political and social organization and owned and cultivated the land under traditional rules. In 1852, however, the government, resorting to its emergency powers, declared Mapuche territory to be a province of the Republic, the Arauco province, and began to establish military forts in key locations along the coast (Bulnes 1980:17). Military presence was combined with the establishment of a regulatory framework that required the intervention of government officials to validate any transfer of land (Bulnes 1980:19). The regulations did not achieve their objective. Because the notion of property among the Mapuches was based on customary usage, it was not possible to identify individual holdings. As a consequence, government intervention in the sale of land was ineffective. Instead, it served as cover to conceal the exploits of land speculators. Aware of the shortcomings of its approach, the government changed its tactics. A law enacted in 1866 effectively dispossessed the Mapuche people of their land and made provision for the sale of individual plots by the state to eligible buyers, a significant number of whom turned out to be military officers who had participated in the campaign against the Mapuches. Some of the Mapuches were granted smallholdings—called *mercedes*—while more than 30 percent had to leave the area to become farm laborers (Bengoa 1985:356, 377). This massive land expropriation strongly resisted by the Mapuche people became the cause of a protracted military confrontation.

All the main political groups supported the military campaign against the Mapuches. The means, however, were not universally approved, as the brutality of the army and paramilitary forces, acting in collusion with the army, was disproportionate to the resistance of the Mapuches. Thus, for example, in merely five months, between November 1868 and April 1869, while the army sustained 35 casualties, it killed 200 Mapuche people, taking 200, including women and children, into custody, and confiscating more than 10,000 heads of cattle (Bengoa 1985:221). This level of violence was a source of concern within some sections of the elite and was reflected in the editorials of some of the leading newspapers of the time. Thus, the Valparaíso daily, *El Mercurio*, though a staunch supporter of the military campaign against the Mapuches—which it described as "a civilizing process"—objected to the level of force employed "to contain the barbarians" on the ground that the "colonization" of the Mapuches could be effectively secured by other means (Bengoa 1985:223).

In 1883, the Mapuches were finally defeated. A year later, Chile completed its second, successful campaign against Perú and Bolivia, which led to its annexation of extensive nitrate-rich territory in the Atacama desert. Thus, by the mid-1880s, the self-confidence of the elite had seemed justified. They had undoubtedly managed to establish a strong state.

Power and Law

Limited Freedom

Given that one of the main objectives of the political elite during the early days of the Republic of Chile was to secure public order, it is not surprising that priority was given to the modernization of the legal system. Their concern with the legal system is consistent with the view that a comprehensive and robust legal system is an important component of a strong state. But, law also sets limits to the exercise of power, so there arises the question as to how the elite reconciled their concern for public order and stability with their interest in legal rationalization and legality. To answer this question, I will compare the views of two leading figures during this period: Diego Portales, the architect of the regime established in the early 1830s, and Andrés Bello, the main legal drafter and indefatigable advocate of codification. At one level, their approach to the relationship between law and power appears to be diametrically opposed. This view is reflected in the work of many historians of the period. While some depict Portales as a practical politician with nothing but contempt for constitutional or legal restraints (Villalobos 1989:116–125), others regard Bello as a legal purist with an uncompromising determination to restrain power through law (Encina 1934:271). On close inspection, however,

Portales's and Bello's approaches to law and power are not inconsistent, but complementary.

Portales undoubtedly had a healthy skepticism toward the law. Indeed, he states in a letter explaining why he was not interested in commenting on the draft of the 1833 constitution: "[A]s you know, no work of this kind is absolutely good or absolutely evil; neither the best nor any [constitution] will be of any use if the main spring of the machine is faulty" (Villalobos 1989:119). The phrase "main spring of the machine" refers to the institutional capacity and the political will of those who run state institutions. Portales skepticism about the law was combined with a conviction that neither the constitution nor ordinary laws should be allowed to restrain the government in fulfilling its overriding responsibility of maintaining public order (Jocelyn-Holt 1997:112–119).

An incident in 1834 exemplifies Portales's approach. While he was governor of Valparaíso, he uncovered a plot against the government. He informed his legal advisor that he intended to arrest those implicated. His legal advisor reminded him that, under the constitution, he did not have the power to order the arrest of any person, unless duly authorized by a court. To underscore his point, the advisor gave Portales a copy of a book on the right of habeas corpus. Portales was enraged by the legal advisor's response and in a letter to a close friend complained bitterly about it: "[W]hat the hell are constitutions and other pieces of paper good for if they are unable to stop an evil activity which is known to exist . . . As far as I am concerned, I can assure you that in extreme circumstances . . . that lady which they call the constitution should not be respected" (Villalobos 1989:121–122). Portales's commitment to the constitution was thus subject to the overriding imperative of maintaining public order by any means available.

Portales's views about public order were combined, however, with awareness that a well-designed legal framework is essential for achieving effective governance. In a letter written in 1832 to one of his cabinet colleagues he bitterly complained about the inefficiency of public officials, particularly of those in charge of maintaining public order. According to Portales, public officials did not properly perform their functions because they were ignorant of the law and unaware of their duties. He therefore proposed that his cabinet colleague should prepare a code, setting out clearly and in detail the powers and responsibilities of public officials (Guzmán 1988:79–81). Portales thus saw legal codification not primarily as a restraint on power, but as a means of ensuring compliance with legal rules.

Andrés Bello, the Venezuelan scholar and diplomat who arrived in Chile in 1829, played a leading role in the process of legal codification. Bello unequivocally supported the idea of a strong state. He wrote several newspaper articles in praise of the 1833 constitution. In one of these articles, he explains that the main objective of the constitution should be to combine a vigorous government with the full enjoyment of limited freedoms (*libertad arreglada*). According to Bello, limited freedom entailed giving the government ample powers to restrain the excesses of democracy. Although he acknowledged that procedures should be in place to protect individuals against despotism, he did not anticipate these procedures being used to restrain the government's insatiable appetite for order (Bello 1982:85–86; Jaksić 2001:178–179). In this respect, his notion of limited freedom is consistent with Portales's view that securing public order takes precedence over any right guaranteed by the constitution. Bello conceded that phrases such as "the good of the nation" are meaningless if individuals are not allowed to fully enjoy civil liberties guaranteed by an independent and technically competent judiciary (1982:620–625). Yet, Portales was also keenly aware of the crucial importance of having an efficient system for the administration of justice. Indeed, in 1837 he issued a decree requiring judges to give reasons for their decisions and to identify specifically the laws on which they based their decisions (Hanisch 1982:143). Portales's main concern was with public order, in particular, with what he regarded as the unacceptable leniency and inconsistency of judges in criminal cases (Guzmán 1988:43).

Legal Codification

Given the government's concern for order and stability, it is not surprising that Portales and his successors should have enthusiastically embraced the enterprise of legal codification. The process of codification, however, was also prompted by the chaotic state of the laws and regulations inherited from the colonial regime. Portales and his associates were keenly aware that the poor performance of courts stemmed largely from the fact that judges were often uncertain as to which laws were in force. The laws in force during the colonial period were fragmented, incoherent, and not easy to locate (Jaksić 2001:158). Courts, thus, had difficulties performing their functions and their interpretation of the law was not uniform. Soon after independence, attempts were made to rationalize the maze of legislation, but they were partial and failed to resolve the underlying problem (Borchard

1917:388; Matus-Valencia 1958:71). Concern about the chaotic state of the legal system prompted the government in 1831 to propose to the congress the appointment of a special law commissioner to identify and codify the laws in force. Although this proposal was not approved, the process of codification began thereafter, with the full support of the government. Throughout this process, there was a lively and well-informed debate both about the nature of the enterprise and about specific technical questions arising from successive drafts of the various codes (Guzmán 1982:61–71).

The entry of the economy into the world markets also contributed toward the need for a modern, well-designed legal system. By the middle of the nineteenth century, the economy had undergone changes as a consequence of the export boom in mining and agriculture. Moreover, prominent members of the educated classes uncritically embraced liberal economic doctrine, as popularized locally by Jean-Gustave Courcelle-Seneuil (Collier 2003:111). Thus, it is not surprising that the elite regarded legal codification as essential to securing economic prosperity (Fruhling 1978:21–32). Indeed, the objective of furthering certainty in legal transactions is strongly emphasized in the preamble to the civil code enacted in 1857. The preamble also points out that the implementation of the civil code would contribute to the reduction of lawsuits, thus indirectly helping to improve the administration of justice.

Work on codification began in the 1830s, and by the end of the century a comprehensive and well-systematized body of civil, commercial, and criminal law was in place. The first major code enacted was the civil code of 1857. The commercial code was enacted in 1867 and the criminal and judicial codes in 1875. The process of codification was completed early in the twentieth century, with the enactment of the codes on civil procedure in 1903 and the code on criminal procedure in 1907 (Borchard 1917). The most impressive achievement of the process of codification was the civil code drafted by Andrés Bello. It had a major impact in Latin America. It was adopted almost verbatim in Colombia and Ecuador, and it served as a model for the civil codes of Argentina, El Salvador, Nicaragua, Paraguay, Uruguay, and Venezuela. The main sources of Bello's civil code were Roman law, the French civil code (code of Napoleon) and Spanish law. It also drew upon other codes, such as those of Austria, Louisiana, Russia, and Sardinia (Bravo 1982; Matus-Valencia 1958:74).

Legal education and scholarship flourished during the process of codification. Teaching of law started at the University of San Felipe in the late eighteenth century. Upon independence, law was taught as a practical trade at the *Instituto Nacional*, but the University of San Felipe awarded law degrees. After 1842 the University of Chile started awarding law degrees. Law schools were later established in Concepción (1865), Valparaíso (1878), and a second law school was opened in Santiago, at the Catholic University in 1888 (Lowenstein 1970:80–83). Codification prompted the publication of books aimed at practitioners. Academic contributions to legal studies also appeared in the nineteenth century. Case reporting began in 1841 with the publication of the *Gaceta de los Tribunales*, and in 1903 the Law Society began publishing the *Revista de Derecho y Jurisprudencia*, both a law review and a law reporter (Insunza 1966:103–106).

Conclusion

During the nineteenth century, the elite established strong institutions that were widely respected both at home and abroad. Through war and diplomacy, the state created a distinct international presence and conquered valuable new territory. State resources were also used ruthlessly to complete the colonization of territory held by the Mapuche people. Thus, by the end of the nineteenth century the territory controlled by the state was nearly three times larger than in 1830 (Collier and Sater 1996:115). Given their success in state building, it is not surprising that the elite had a somewhat inflated view about the quality and strength of their political institutions. They were also fully aware that their political system was exceptional when compared with that of their neighbors. Thus, in an address to the congress toward the end of his term in office, President Joaquín Prieto boasted that Chile's social edifice had "serenely and majestically displayed its excellence in the midst of the storms that had wrought havoc in every other part of Spanish America" (Ortega 1985:154). The elite's level of success in establishing strong state institutions was not, however, matched in regime building. Indeed, despite their cohesiveness and reputation for pragmatism, by the end of the nineteenth century, the elite were unable to avert a major crisis that in 1891 led to a costly civil war.

Chapter 2

Political Liberalization and Civil War

Introduction

The Civil War raises puzzling questions that have long divided observers. Interpretations of the Civil War fall into two main groups: one concentrates mainly on political factors, while the other stresses the pervasive importance of economic factors. The first attributes the conflict to the stubborn and obstinate behavior of President Balmaceda (1886–91), who ruthlessly defied the authority of the congress and the constitution. According to this interpretation, those who opposed the president in the Civil War are depicted as upholders of the rule of law (Blakemore 1974; Campos 1963; Castedo 1954). Left-leaning and Marxist historians disagree with this interpretation. They regard Balmaceda as the victim of an unholy alliance between British investors and local oligarchs who, determined to defend their stake in the nitrate industry, destroyed the possibility of a genuine independent path to capitalist development (Ramírez 1969; Zeitlin 1984).

The Civil War has an important bearing on the theme of this book, as it had a major impact on the evolution of democratization. Indeed, the conflict contradicted the generally held view about the pragmatism and flexibility of the ruling elite, and its timing was baffling. The Civil War took place not long after the political elite had, in an exemplary display of civic consciousness, resolved major political differences. It also occurred at time of unprecedented economic prosperity. In the 1870s, the authoritarian regime established by Portales changed beyond recognition. Legal and constitutional reforms made the political system more inclusive and drastically reduced the hitherto arbitrary powers of the president. These liberal reforms modernized state institutions and seemed ideally suited to enabling the political regime to cope with the ongoing crisis of the export sector and, later on, with the social and economic changes brought about by the enormous revenue generated by nitrate exports. Given these auspicious conditions, it is not surprising that the violent collapse of the political regime should be a source of controversy and bewilderment. The Civil War is also important because it shaped the contours of the political regime during the first three decades of the twentieth century and it accounts for the strong state-centered policies pursued after 1932. These policies, embraced by most administrations until the collapse of democracy in 1973, were based on the widely shared perception that the laissez-faire policies espoused by the victors of the Civil War, squandered a valuable national asset, thus wasting a unique opportunity to set the country on course toward sustained economic development.

The debate over the Civil War is unlikely to subside. The aim of this chapter is not to resolve this debate, but to answer two related questions arising from it. First, why did the elite allow a seemingly unimportant dispute over the powers of the president develop into a full-blown armed confrontation? Second, if the elite were as flexible and closely integrated as most observers suggest, why did they slip into a costly and divisive conflict? To answer these questions it is necessary to understand the nature and evolution of political and economic processes in Chile in the second half of the nineteenth century. Accordingly, the first section of this chapter examines the evolution of the political process before the outbreak of the Civil War. It traces the emerging fractions within the ruling elite, shows how political groups evolved into parties, and explains the factors that brought about a major liberalization of the political regime through constitutional and legal reforms. Political liberalization and stability seemed set to open up a process of democratization. Yet, as the final part of this section shows, a dispute over the constitutional powers of the president led, in 1891, to the outbreak of the Civil War and the collapse of presidentialism. An interesting feature of the political and constitutional debate during this period is that it did not address issues of economic policy. The neglect of economic issues is surprising because, while the congress was busy debating the constitutional amendments, the economy was experiencing serious difficulties as export markets became more competitive and unstable. To cope with this situation, successive administrations were forced to take tough economic decisions that, naturally, favored some economic sectors and groups more than others. Yet, remarkably, they did not spark a debate on economic policy. In the event, the debate over economic policy became redundant as the annexation of extensive nitrate-rich deposits after the War of the Pacific (1879–83) instantly resolved the economic problems that had haunted the elite since the early 1860s. The second section of this chapter thus traces the tensions and disagreements over economic policy and explains why, despite their importance, they did not spill over into the political arena. As a consequence, when the abundant nitrate revenue gave the state a degree of autonomy from the economic elite, and President Balmaceda attempted to use this revenue to advance national development objectives, he found himself isolated. Depicting him as a tyrant who was in breach of the constitution, the elite opted for a model of development in which the role of the state was limited to the collection of export taxes and the maintenance of law and order.

The Political Process

By the middle of the nineteenth century serious divisions emerged within the coalition that supported the settlement of 1831. These divisions stemmed from conflicting views over the role of the church in society and led to a breakdown of the forces that supported the government. They also led to the emergence of political groups that, at least initially, defined themselves largely in terms of their position regarding this dispute. But the split within the ruling coalition also provided liberals and other critics of the regime with the opportunity to agitate for political liberalization. Thus there began a political process that led to major constitutional and political transformations that were to strengthen the role of the congress and provide the foundations for the development of a party system that soon extended to the entire country.

Republicanism versus Clericalism

Given the elite's determination to establish a secular state that would ensure public order and tranquility, it was inevitable that they would soon clash with the Catholic Church. The church supported the conservative forces in 1831, but was closely identified with the social, cultural, and economic interests of the old colonial power. In exchange for its support of the conservative forces, the church had obtained constitutional recognition of the union of church and state and a ban on the public worship of other religious faiths. The church, however, was deeply suspicious of the vigor with which the elite pursued their republican objectives, especially in the area of education (Campbell 1959:371–374). It regarded President Manuel Montt's (1851–61) efforts to establish a national system of state education as a deliberate attempt to undermine its influence in society. A law approved during the administration of President Manuel Montt had set a goal of having at least 1 primary school for every 2,000 inhabitants. Although this goal was not realized, Montt's achievements are, nonetheless, remarkable. Between 1851 and 1861, the number of pupils in primary education increased from 22,000 to 43,000, while the number of educational establishment nearly doubled (Castedo 1954:2:1197). The church was also alarmed at the tolerance displayed by the government toward other religious faiths (Castedo 1954:2:1097–1104; 1298–1300, 1343–1346).

The 1833 Constitution recognized Catholicism as the official religion and prohibited the offer of public worship by any other religion. The church, however, regarded the government's religious tolerance and its policies on education as a sign that the political system was falling under the influence of freemasons and atheists. Thus, influential clerics began seriously to reassess the relation between church and state. Their immediate target was the *patronato*, an established colonial institution. Under the *patronato*, the Spanish crown had granted the church religious monopoly and other privileges in its colonies, and in exchange the church gave the crown control over the appointment of senior clerics. The 1833 Constitution retained the *patronato* giving the president the powers once vested in the colonial authorities. These powers included the right to nominate clerics for the post of bishop and archbishop (Castedo 1954:2:1099; Scully 1992:31–33). Church authorities, however, were unhappy with this arrangement. Their views on this issue became public in 1845, when a Catholic publication demanded the abolition of the *patronato* and called for the separation of church and state. In that same year, the cleric, who was a leading advocate of church autonomy, was nominated by the government to the post of archbishop of Santiago, but he rebuffed the government by declining the nomination (Edwards 1932:1:134).

The controversy over the appointment of archbishop was resolved, but tension between the church and the government persisted. In an attempt to retain the *patronato*, the government decided, in 1855, to raise the issue directly with the Vatican. The negotiations, however, were unsuccessful. Instead of accepting the government's position, the authorities in Rome demanded that all educational establishments be placed under the direct supervision of the church. They also insisted that clerics should retain their traditional rights under cannon law. The government flatly rejected these demands, regarding them as a ludicrous attempt to expand the powers of the church and as an unacceptable challenge to the supremacy of the constitution (Edwards 1932:1:138,139).

The collapse of the negotiations with the Vatican exacerbated relations between the church and the Montt administration. Thus, not surprisingly, shortly thereafter, in 1856, a seemingly innocuous conflict blew up into a major political confrontation. The matter concerned two junior clerics dismissed from their duties in the cathedral. After exhausting legal remedies within the church, the clerics requested the Supreme Court to review the archbishop's decision as, under the *patronato*, the Court had jurisdiction (*recurso de fuerza*) to review some decisions by Ecclesiastical tribunals. The Court accepted jurisdiction and ordered the archbishop immediately to reinstate the clerics. The archbishop refused, claiming that the Supreme Court did not have jurisdiction over spiritual matters. Instead, he requested the president to intervene. But the president refused as he claimed that the decision of the Court was final (*res judicata*). While this exchange was taking place, the Supreme Court handed down yet another decision threatening the archbishop with penalties—including deportation—if he failed promptly to reinstate the clerics. In the end, the government persuaded the clerics to withdraw their complaint and the matter was laid to rest (Collier 2003:199–204).

This episode involving the Court and the archbishop had huge political repercussions. It caused a split within the government forces and brought about the establishment of a proclerical Conservative Party. The church, nonetheless, continued to oppose and criticize the government. Indeed, just before the congressional elections of 1858, the archbishop issued a pastoral letter, read in all the churches during three consecutive Sundays, claiming that a vote for the government was a vote for Protestantism and calling upon Catholics to support opposition candidates (Castedo 1954:2:1109). In the event, candidates who supported the government won a majority of seats in the congress, but the opposition, led by the proclerical Conservative Party, won 20 percent of the seats. Relations between church and state remained tense (Castedo 1954:2:1298–1300, 1343, 1346).

A further source of tension was the enactment in 1865 of a law that recognized the right of members of any religion to worship in private and to establish schools to educate their children (Campos 1963:311). Moreover, the controversy over the *patronato* resurfaced in 1878 when, following the death of the serving archbishop, the Vatican refused to appoint the cleric nominated by the government. This snub prompted the government to break off diplomatic relations with the Vatican. Thereafter, a series of legislative enactments, which included laws on civil marriages and lay cemeteries, continued to exacerbate the tension between the government and the church. The church's uncompromising position not only served to test the republican resolve of the elite, but also marked the beginning of a process of political differentiation that formed the basis for the emergence of political parties.

Political Divisions

As noted above, the conflict between the Montt administration and the archbishop brought about a split within the government forces. Those who remained loyal to President Montt came to be known as *Nacionales*, or the *Montt/Varista* party (after the surnames of the incumbent president and his senior minister). Those who withdrew from the government formed the proclerical Conservative Party. It must be noted that, although the *Nacionales* held strong republican views, they were not against the Catholic Church. They disagreed with the Conservatives on the role of the church in society, but at no time did they advocate a separation of church and state.

The question over the role of the church was not, however, the only source of discord. From the late 1840s, the ruling coalition had begun to face challenges from the regional elite, mainly mining entrepreneurs, dissatisfied with the economic policies of the government in Santiago and liberal intellectuals frustrated by the excessive powers of the president. In 1851, and then again, in 1859, these groups, together with disaffected military officers, rebelled against the government. The leaders of the 1851 insurrection called for the establishment of a constituent assembly to devolve power and provide adequate financial resources to the provinces (Campos 1963:171, 180). A similar objective inspired the 1859 insurrection, though in this case the rebels, couching their claims in the language of federalism, demanded self-government for the provinces. Although the insurrections were crushed, their leaders did not lose their economic influence and soon became prominent members of the elite and energetically campaigned for political reform.

During this turbulent period there also emerged a small group of intellectuals who, inspired by contemporary developments in France, disseminated utopian socialist ideas. The two most prominent members of this group, Francisco Bilbao and Santiago Arcos, established, in 1850, the Society for Equality, and vigorously campaigned for electoral liberalization, political equality, and social and economic reforms. In one of his writings, Arcos described the situation of the poor as intolerable and called for the establishment of a political party to represent the laboring masses (Galdames 64:289–304). The government did not take kindly to the Society's activities and soon disbanded it, sending its leaders into exile. But such harsh measures could not be used against the moderate liberal leaders who, in addition to being profoundly hostile to the political influence to the Catholic Church, demanded constitutional reform and enjoyed considerable support from regional economic elite. Prominent among these intellectuals was José Victorino Lastarria, who played a leading role in the establishment of the Liberal Party in 1857 (Bravo 1986:188). Lastarria became a parliamentarian and then a cabinet minister during the administration of President José Joaquín Pérez (1861–71).

In 1861 yet another party emerged: the Radical Party. It was formed by a group of disillusioned liberals led by Pedro León Gallo, a wealthy miner from the North who had played a prominent role in the 1859 insurrection. It was a liberal party, both in political and economic terms. It represented the interests of wealthy miners from the North and an emerging group of agricultural entrepreneurs from the South. It was thus a party that represented regional interests, but which soon developed a nationwide network and an important presence in Santiago. In 1864 five radical candidates were elected to the congress on a platform that included demands for constitutional and electoral reform, decentralization, and lay education.

The configuration of political forces brought about significant changes. It forced presidents to seek the support of the newly established political groups in the congress and prompted these groups to form broad coalitions. Thus, in 1861, clerical Conservatives and the core of the new Liberal Party joined forces and shared cabinet seats in the administration of President José Joaquín Pérez. This coalition supported the Pérez administration throughout its two terms in office and provided the basis for the election of a prominent liberal, Federico Errázuriz (1871–76). This Conservative-Liberal coalition broke down in 1873 over differences regarding the role of the church in education (Edwards 1932:2:224). Its collapse forced the proclerical Conservatives out of government, paving the way for nearly 20 years of Liberal-led governments (Aníbal Pinto (1876–81), Domingo Santa María (1881–86), and José Manuel Balmaceda (1886–91)).

The alliance between the Conservative and Liberal Parties enabled President Pérez to restore confidence in political institutions, which had seriously declined after the failed insurrection of 1859. The Pérez administration, however, did little to move forward the agenda of political liberalization. This neglect brought into being, in 1868, the *Club de la Reforma*, a loosely structured alliance of all the political forces that sought, above all, to reduce the powers of the president. It included members of the liberal and radical parties, as well as prominent members of the *Partido Nacional*, the party that supported the Montt administration. The *Club* also had close links with wealthy mining entrepreneurs. Indeed, two of the most prominent mining entrepreneurs, Pedro León Gallo and Jerónimo Urmeneta, were actively involved in *Club's* activities (Gazmuri 1998:143). One the most remarkable features of the *Club* was that it served both as a pressure group for constitutional reform and as a center to promote civic education and raise citizens' awareness of their rights and obligations (Estelle 1970:120; Gazmuri 1998:201). It established 15 branches throughout the country and organized regular conferences and discussion groups on constitutional topics (Estelle 1970:120–123). The *Club de la Reforma* played a decisive role in building a consensus that led to the approval in 1874 of constitutional reforms. In 1874, the *Club*, having accomplished its objective dissolved itself, and its members pursued their careers through the newly established network of parties.

Affirming the Separation of Powers

The broad coalition that advocated constitutional reform reflected the elite's deep-seated and long-standing dissatisfaction with the prevailing autocratic presidential regime. Indeed, long before the approval of the constitutional amendments, the elite, acting through the congress, had attempted to rein in the powers of the executive, thus bringing about an effective separation of powers. This process also served to give the judiciary, albeit indirectly, a measure of independence.

Concerns about the excessive powers of the president were expressed early on and, as already noted, account in part for the insurrections of the 1850s. These concerns were also reflected in parliamentary practices. Although there was no constitutional procedure to give effect to the principle of executive accountability to the congress, such a procedure was introduced through parliamentary practice long before the debate over constitutional reform became part of the political agenda. In 1846, Manuel Antonio Tocornal, a prominent member of the congress, drawing on the French model, introduced the practice of *interpelaciones*, or parliamentary questions to cabinet ministers (Edwards 1932:1:28). This procedure soon became established and in the 1880s was prolifically used to challenge President Balmaceda's policies. Efforts by the congress to influence government policy and have a say in the composition of the cabinet also predate the approval of the constitutional amendments. Indeed, in 1850, close to the end of President Manuel Bulnes's administration, the congress attempted to use its powers over the budget to influence government policy. The government successfully rejected this attempt (Edwards 1932:1:32). Seven year later, in 1857, President Montt faced a similar challenge. The majority in the senate, dissatisfied at what it regarded as the incompetence of some members of the Montt administration made approval of the annual budget conditional to changes in the composition of the cabinet. The president, a staunch defender of the constitution and of the presidential regime, regarded this pressure as unacceptable and sent a letter of resignation to the congress (Edwards 1932:1:158). The conflict was eventually resolved and the president withdrew his resignation. Two years later, government opponents again attempted to use the debate on the budget to secure policy concessions. This time, however, the government made full use of its majority in the congress, bringing the debate to an end. This decision, characterized as unconstitutional by government opponents, is regarded by some observers as one of the factors that sparked the insurrection of 1859 (Edwards 1932:1:173). Although in 1857 President Montt admitted that the congress had the right to scrutinize the activities of the executive, he resolutely rejected the notion that the congress could have any say on the composition of his cabinet (Edwards 1932:1:160).

Judicial independence also became part of the political debate long before the adoption of the constitutional amendments. In 1857 President Montt invoked the principle of judicial independence when he clashed with the church over the dismissal of two clerics. As noted above, on that occasion the Supreme Court, acting under the provisions of the *patronato*, ordered the archbishop to reinstate the clerics. The archbishop refused to comply with the order and, instead, requested the government to intervene. President Montt, however, declined the archbishop's request, claiming that under the constitution he was bound to respect the principle of judicial independence. While Montt's decision was, undoubtedly, prompted by political expediency, it did, nonetheless, also reflect the elite's determination to affirm the republican objectives embodied in the constitution. These objectives required respect for the secular nature of the state, as well as the principle of separation of powers.

The issue of judicial independence reemerged in 1868, when the chamber of deputies approved articles of impeachment against four members of the Supreme Court (Edwards 1932:2:43–84; Huneeus 1891:234). This incident also involved Manuel Montt, who, after completing his term as president, was appointed to the Supreme

Court and, at the time, was acting as its president (Anonymous 1868). The articles of impeachment claimed that Montt had used his influence as a member of the Supreme Court to secure the release from prison of a relative accused of murder. Although the objective of the impeachment was to embarrass Montt, it generated a lively debate in the congress and the media. The proceedings lasted nearly nine months, from August 1868 to May 1869, and focused mainly on issues regarding the role of courts in the constitutional order and the nature of the judicial function. In the event, the senate rejected the impeachment. This outcome, as well as the debate that preceded it, was widely regarded as a public endorsement of the principle of judicial independence (Edwards 1932:2:84).

It is likely that the controversy over the impeachment and the debate on the nature of judicial independence enhanced the Court's status within the political system. An exchange of notes in 1872 between the Supreme Court and the minister of war suggests that this was the case. The exchange began with a letter from the Court to the minister, in which the Court complained that, in the course of implementing emergency legislation, military officers had usurped the powers of ordinary courts. According to the Court, the officers had ignored the principle of the separation of powers and had thus committed a serious breach of the constitution. The government replied promptly, concurring with the Court's view that, even in the case of a state of emergency, state officials, including military officers, could not ignore the independence of the courts or tread on their jurisdiction. As the minister's statement reaffirming the principle of judicial independence was contained in a private communication, the Court suggested that the exchange of notes should be published so that public opinion could be informed about government policy on this important point. The government acquiesced. *El Araucano* published the exchange of notes on May 25, 1872. While this exchange did not have a dramatic outcome, the fact that it took place and that the Court demanded its publication was significant, as it shows that the Court was beginning to assert its rights under the prevailing institutional framework (Huneeus 1891:479–485; Roldán 1913:451).

The foregoing suggests that, at the time of the adoption of the constitutional amendments of the 1870s, the political regime had already undergone a major transformation. Presidents could not ignore the interests represented in the congress and could not treat courts as instruments of the executive branch. The constitutional amendments moved this process forward by formally reducing the powers of the president and expanding the powers of the congress.

Constitutional and Electoral Reform

The first constitutional amendment, approved in 1871 under the Pérez administration, prohibited the reelection of the president, thus effectively reducing the term of office from ten to five years. The amendments approved in 1874, under the Errázuriz administration (1871–76), were aimed mainly at curtailing the powers of the president. This was achieved by a restructuring of the Council of State, an organ responsible for judicial appointments and hitherto controlled by the president. Its membership was expanded to include a majority of members appointed by the congress. As a consequence, the executive lost influence over judicial appointments. The emergency powers of the president were also drastically reduced. The president's powers under the state of siege provisions were restricted to measures relating to personal freedom. The provisions on emergency legislation were also redesigned. While hitherto the congress could authorize presidents to indefinitely suspend the constitution, the amendment provided that emergency legislation could last only one year and could only restrict freedom of assembly, personal freedom, and freedom of the press. The amendments also strengthened civil and political rights. A new clause was added to the constitution recognizing, for the first time, freedom of assembly, freedom of association, and freedom of education. The constitutional amendments also introduced changes aimed specifically at strengthening the congress. In order to expedite the legislative process, the quorum required to take decisions in the congress was reduced to one-third in the senate and one-quarter of the members in the chamber of deputies. The senate, hitherto elected from a single national list, was transformed into an organ that represented groupings of provinces, thereby enhancing the political profile of the regions, while making it more difficult for the president to control the election of senators. Provisions on the impeachment of cabinet ministers were clarified. The congress could impeach cabinet ministers for the crime of treason, extortion, misappropriation of public funds, bribery, breach of the constitution, disregard of the laws, and for seriously compromising the honor and security of the state. A conviction upon impeachment brought about the removal from office, but did not always have the effect of disqualifying the person concerned from holding a similar office in the future. The person ousted from office by impeachment was subject to trial by ordinary courts. Finally, in order to safeguard the independence of the congress, its members were barred from holding presidential appointments, except for posts in the cabinet.

The constitutional amendments were complemented by major reforms to the electoral regime. Control over the electoral process was transferred from the municipalities to local committees of leading taxpayers. The objective of this measure was to reduce the influence of the president on the electoral process while encouraging political participation by regional elite. Legislation enacted in 1874 eliminated property qualifications. It provided that males over 25 years of age who could read and write were deemed to have fulfilled the property qualifications required by the constitution. (In 1888 the minimum age was reduced to 21.) The liberalization of the electoral system is a landmark in the process of democratization. It is important to bear in mind, however, that democratization was not the main aim of the forces promoting legal and constitutional reforms. Their main aim was to reduce the powers of the president. Throughout this period, the elite remained deeply suspicious of the notion of democracy. Thus, in 1885, the liberal president Domingo Santa María—echoing Portales's views—claimed that citizens were still not ready for democracy (Castedo 1954:3:1985–88). Other prominent liberals shared Santa María's skepticism about democracy. Indeed while liberal leaders were determined to shift the constitutional balance of power in favor of the congress, they were cautious on matters regarding the extension of the vote, as they feared that given the large rural population, the main beneficiaries of any major electoral reform would be the conservative landowners. Their unease on this issue is reflected in a pamphlet written in 1850 by Victorino Lastarria and Federico Errázuriz, who later became president and under whose presidency most of the reforms were adopted:

> We accept universal suffrage, but only when this universality is that of men (without distinction of class) who are capable of exercising political rights . . . All men are equal . . . But in the political order not everyone can have equal participation . . . In Chile, if the day-laborers and servants of the haciendas were to exercise the electoral right, the result of the election would be very different from the result of an election voted in by artisans of the towns and other citizens who are legally qualified to vote. In the first instance it is the landowners, the bosses of that multitude without a will of its own, who would do the electing; in the second case, the election would give us a free expression of the national will. (Collier 2003:133)

In 1850, Lastarria and Errázuriz described their brand of universal suffrage as "intelligent universal suffrage." Yet, despite their misgivings about the virtues of universal suffrage, the electoral reforms sponsored by the liberal administrations had an immediate impact on electoral registrations and participation. Thus, while in 1873 the number of registered voters was 49,000, representing 2.4 percent of the population, in 1876 this figure reached 106,000 or 5 percent of the population. Electoral participation during the same period increased from 26,000 in 1873 to 80,000 in 1876 (Borón 1971a:432). The expansion of the electorate did not, however, improve the quality of the electoral process. Indeed, since under the new electoral regime presidents could not rely on state agencies to manipulate electoral outcomes, the executive—and the opposition—resorted to violence and intimidation. Thus, the three liberal presidents who succeeded Errázuriz did not hesitate to use force to secure favorable electoral outcomes. So effective were liberal presidents in determining the outcome of elections that in 1882, not a single Conservative candidate was elected to the congress (Borón 1971a:402). As the opposition resisted intervention by the executive, electoral contests became bloody events. In 1886, for example, 45 people died and 160 were seriously injured as a consequence of electoral violence in Santiago (Valenzuela 1977:190). Despite these problems the constitutional amendments and the liberalization of the electoral regime brought about a shift in the balance of power in favor of the congress. Thus, not surprisingly, the leading constitutional textbooks of the period argued that the amendments had abolished presidentialism and brought about a parliamentary regime (Bravo 1986:211). This view, though technically incorrect, reflects the spirit that animated those who campaigned to secure the approval of the constitutional amendments.

Civil War and the Constitution

The question as to whether the political system had shifted from a strong presidential regime into a parliamentary one became a lively political issue in 1890. Indeed, the factor that ostensibly triggered the Civil War was a disagreement between the president and the congress about their respective roles in the political system. While Balmaceda's opponents claimed that he could not appoint cabinet ministers without the approval of the senate, the president argued that, under the constitution, he was entitled to do so. Given the extended, well-informed and responsible debates that surrounded the approval of the constitutional amendments, it seems astonishing that those involved in the reform process had failed to address this important issue. Yet, they had not. Under the constitution, the president had special and discretionary powers to appoint and remove from office cabinet ministers.[1] In 1874, the text of Article 82 (6) was slightly amended in order to reflect the changes made to the composition of the Council of State. The rest of this clause, however, remained unaltered. This suggests that those involved in the process of constitutional reform did not intend transforming the prevailing presidential system into a parliamentary regime. But while the constitutional text was unambiguous, political practice, on the eve of the Civil War, was not.

As already noted, the constitutional amendments significantly reduced some of the powers of the president. But presidents still retained enormous powers. The executive deployed this power to great effect between 1879 and 1883, during the war against Perú and Bolivia. Indeed, the constitutional reforms of the 1870s appear to have strengthened state institutions, as evidenced by the speed and effectiveness with which Chile responded to the challenge posed by a war against two countries that had superior military power and twice its population (Martner 1929:330). As Harold Blakemore notes, despite the economic problems that the country was facing when war broke out, Chile's "lack of preparation, economic weakness and uncertainty . . . looked like meticulous planning when compared to their adversaries"(Blakemore 1986:501). During the war, constitutional procedures were rigorously observed: there was an orderly transfer of power from one elected president to another and not once did the government have to resort to the use of emergency powers. Thus, not surprisingly, success in this war served to enhance the legitimacy of the government and, in particular, contributed toward the reinforcement of the confidence of the executive on its ability to run the affairs of the state.

Victory in the war also resulted in the acquisition of rich nitrate deposits that added a valuable asset to the country's economy. Aware of the importance of this newfound wealth, President Balmaceda embarked on a massive program of investments in infrastructure development and launched an ambitious program to further primary and secondary education. These interventionist policies, however, were singularly out of step with the laissez-faire views dominant among the political and economic elite. His determination to expand the economic role of the state was seen by his opponents as an attempt to revert to the style of presidency that prevailed before the constitutional reforms of the 1870s (Jocelyn-Holt 1997:49–51). Thus, not surprisingly, Balmaceda's opponents had no difficulties in depicting him as a ruthless politician determined to accumulate power at any cost. Differences between the president and the congress developed into a major constitutional conflict. The congress refused to approve the annual budget and Balmaceda responded defiantly, announcing that he would implement the budget approved for the previous year (Collier and Sater 1996:154). This threat prompted the congress to adopt a resolution deposing him. Balmaceda responded by issuing a decree that purported to close down the congress. These events marked the beginning of the Civil War.

The confrontation between the president and the congress was accompanied by an intense debate about the correct interpretation of the constitution. Balmaceda, relying on Article 82 (6), argued that the president did not need the explicit, or implicit, approval of the congress to determine the composition of the cabinet. His opponents disagreed. As noted above, in 1857 the congress had deployed this argument unsuccessfully against President Montt. From then on, presidents managed to neutralize the congress mainly through electoral intervention. During the Balmaceda administration, however, the president was unable to resist political pressure from the congress. As a parliamentarian, Balmaceda had endorsed the view that congress should have a say in the composition of cabinets. Thus, it is not surprising that, once in office, when confronted with strong congressional opposition, he repeatedly made changes to his cabinet in order to appease his opponents. But Balmaceda's tactics backfired, since his opponents in the congress interpreted his conciliatory moves as further evidence that, in practice, presidents required congressional approval for the appointment of cabinet ministers. Yet, the dilemma that Balmaceda's opponents faced was that, although the constitution had been recently amended, the president's power to appoint ministers without consulting the congress had not been altered. This dilemma is reflected in a pamphlet his opponents published in Washington in 1891, in which they sought to justify before international public opinion the uprising against the government (Montt 1891:6–8). In this pamphlet, they were unable to point to any specific provision to justify their claim that Balmaceda had ignored the constitution, on this point. In any event, the disagreement about the interpretation of the constitution was not the real source of conflict. The conflict was over the role of the state in the administration of the newly acquired nitrate wealth.

Economic Policy and Nitrates

Underlying the dispute between Balmaceda and his opponents over the nature of the political regime was a fundamental disagreement over economic policy. Balmaceda's attempt to use nitrate revenue to achieve general development objectives met with strong resistance from the political elite, including members of his own Liberal Party. Balmaceda's opponents regarded his policies as a departure from sound economic management and as a way of usurping the newly acquired powers of the congress. The Civil War resolved this conflict in their favor. Their victory brought into being a self-styled parliamentary regime that eliminated most domestic taxes, reduced import duties, and relied on the revenue collected from nitrate exports to fund the bulk of public expenditure.

The disagreement between Balmaceda and his opponents regarding economic policy is surprising. Indeed, hitherto the elite had managed to resolve serious economic differences through compromise and accommodation. The first part of this section explains why economic policy was not an issue among the elite, despite the numerous problems that plagued the economy during the second half of the nineteenth century. Balmaceda's ambitious policies challenged the prevailing consensus on economic policy and caused the breakdown of the political regime. Balmaceda, however, also had difficulties formulating a coherent policy. Thus, the second part of this section examines the problems that Balmaceda faced as he tried to develop a policy on the nitrate industry.

Crisis and Adjustment

From 1845 to 1861, the economy flourished as agricultural and mining exports expanded. Foreign trade grew at an annual cumulative rate of 7.9 percent, and the value of exports was three times larger than that of imports (Ortega 1985:154). The state played an important role facilitating economic activity. It simplified customs procedures, maintained an efficient system for the collection of duties, and provided basic infrastructure facilities (Cariola and Sunkel 1977:281). By 1860, however, these favorable conditions came to an end as successive administrations were forced to make policy adjustments. This task was not easy as the elite strongly resisted increases in domestic taxation and were reluctant to raise import duties.

Chile's agricultural exporters began to face problems when producers from America, Australia, and Russia began to compete in the former's traditional markets. As products from these countries pushed prices down, Chilean exports—flour, wheat, and cereals—lost ground with the result that by the late 1880s the agricultural sector went into a deep recession (Bauer 1975:65–71; O'Brien 1982:37). Mining exports, especially copper, were also affected as a consequence of protectionist policies in the United States, the Franco-Prussian War, and a general slowdown of the world economy. The decline of the export sector brought about a fiscal crisis. While before 1860, customs duties accounted for 60 percent of ordinary revenue, by 1878 this figure had dropped to 40 percent. During the same period, the annual growth of ordinary revenue declined from 6.3 percent to 4.1 percent, while public expenditure increased at a rate of 5.7 percent per year (Ortega 1985:157). As attempts to introduce taxes were strongly resisted, successive administrations were forced to meet the shortfall of public revenue with loans from domestic and international banks. Deficit financing led to a sharp increase in the national debt so that by the late 1870s the cost of servicing it represented nearly 40 percent of total expenditure (Ortega 1985:159). Eventually, in 1877, the government finally secured authorization from the congress to raise import duties on selected products. This measure gave a boost to local producers of textiles, footwear, paper, and furniture. But this protectionist measure was taken reluctantly, as it was considered to be inconsistent with sound economic principles. Senior government officials regarded import duties exclusively as a device to raise revenue and made it clear that any benefit to local artisans and industrialists was unintended (Ortega 1985:164).

The reluctance of the elite to provide incentives to local artisans and industrialists and their inclination to rely on deficit financing have generally been attributed to the overriding social and economic power vested in large landowners and local merchants (Bauer 1990:236; Zeitlin 1984:59). Claudio Véliz offers a complementary and more immediate explanation. He argues that none of the three main economic actors during this period—landowners, miners, and import-export houses—would have benefited from protectionist policies as they derived the bulk of their revenue from international trade. Thus, according to Véliz, free trade and disdain for protectionism was a natural option for the economic elite (Véliz 1971:232–240). Given their aversion to protectionism, it is not surprising that the elite were also devout followers of the laissez-faire doctrines disseminated in Chile by Jean-Gustave Courcelle-Seneuil, the French economist.[2] Evidence confirms that the elite were not especially concerned with the fate of local artisans, even though the government was aware of their plight. Indeed, in 1861 a delegation of artisans requested President Pérez to impose duties on selected industrial products, but their request was ignored (Collier 2003:244). Bauer notes, referring to textiles and flour milling, that government policy during the second half of the nineteenth century was characterized by indifference to local artisans and industrial entrepreneurs. As a consequence, he argues, they were not allowed to develop into proto-industries, as they were swamped by imports and enjoyed no protection from the government (1990:234–235).

Small artisans were not, however, the only neglected group. The government also neglected entrepreneurs involved in copper mining, even though their activities contributed greatly to state revenue. Between 1850 and 1880, Chile was a leading exporter of copper. Such was the importance of copper for the national economy that one observer has characterized this period as the age of copper (Fox-Przeworski 1980:118). Chile's copper production, both in relative and absolute terms was impressive. In 1870, Chilean output accounted for 42 percent of world total, with the United States and Great Britain accounting for 12 percent and 7 percent respectively. In terms of volume, production increased from 7,000 tons in 1840 to nearly 40,000 tons in 1860 (Culver and Reinhart 1989:726). By the mid-1870s, the copper industry accounted for 50 percent of the total value of exports (Fox-Przeworski 1980:9). Yet, by the early 1880s Chilean copper began to lose ground in world markets and production went into a steady decline. In 1882, it was less than 50,000 tons. By 1895, while production was reduced to just over half of this figure, Chile's share of world production dropped to a mere 7 percent (Culver and Reinhart 1989:726).

Some observers attribute the decline of copper to the inability of local entrepreneurs to keep up with the technological developments in the industry (Mamalakis 1976:40). Zeitlin disputes this view, pointing out that the decline of the industry began long before technological advances were introduced. Instead, he attributes the decline to high fuel and transport costs and to the absence of adequate infrastructure (1984:144, 194). This interpretation suggests that the right mix of policies would have succeeded in arresting, and even reversing, the decline of the industry. Benjamín Vicuña McKenna, a prominent nineteenth-century intellectual and politician, complained bitterly about the government's failure to support the copper industry (Culver and Reinhart 1989:731). Local mining entrepreneurs strongly lobbied the government to secure changes to the mining code and improvements in infrastructure. Mining legislation, based on old colonial regulations, established cumbersome and costly procedures aimed mainly at maximizing tax receipts rather than production (Culver and Reinhart 1989:731; Volk 1993:73). The new mining code approved in 1888 made things worse, as it strengthened surface land rights and introduced a tax based on production rather than profits

(Culver and Reinhart 1989:739). The government's response to the miners' demand for infrastructure improvements, in particular, transport, was even more disappointing. Indeed, while the government borrowed money in London to build railway lines to provide landowners in the Central Valley with easy access to the port of Valparaíso, mining entrepreneurs had to build private railway lines to access ports in the North (Fox-Przeworski 1980:118–119). Thus, as most observers agree, the decline of copper was a failure of policy caused by the inability of copper mining entrepreneurs to overcome the indifference of the government (Culver and Reinhart 1989:731; Fox-Przeworski 1980: 251; Zeitlin 1984:198).

It is important, however, not to overstate the implications of the government's neglect of the copper industry. While entrepreneurs involved in copper mining had reasons to be dissatisfied with the policies of the government, mining entrepreneurs in other sectors, such as coal and nitrate, did not. Indeed, the events that led to the 1879 War of the Pacific suggest that mining interests played a key role in shaping state policy. Indeed, the main factor that triggered the war was the protection of the interests of local mining entrepreneurs with investments in Perú and Bolivia. From the mid-1860s, Chilean entrepreneurs had begun investing in nitrate mining in Bolivia (Antofagasta) and Perú (Tarapacá). In addition to direct investment, there was also a large flow of migrant workers from Chile into Bolivia and Perú to work on the newly established enterprises. Indeed, so intense was this migratory movement that on the eve of the war nearly 90 percent of the population of Antofagasta was Chilean, while in Iquique, the main urban center of Perú's Tarapacá province, Chileans accounted for 70 percent of the population (Cariola and Sunkel 1990:72). Thus, not surprisingly, Chile claimed that the objective of the war was to protect foreign investment and the well-being of its nationals. But, as is generally the case in international relations, the legal justification concealed other objectives. In this case, the objective was annexation of territory. Before and during the war, the policy of annexation was openly advocated by leading liberal politicians, including Domingo Santa María and José Manuel Balmaceda, both of whom were to become presidents. Moreover, Domingo Santa María, as well as half of the members of President Pinto's cabinet, which took the country to war, were also shareholders of the *Compañía de Salitres y Ferrocarril de Antofagasta*, the main Chilean company affected by Peruvian government policies (Ortega 1984:362, 372, 374). It must also be noted that Gibbs and Son, a British-owned company operating in Valparaíso, held more than a third of the stock of *Compañía de Salitres y Ferrocarril de Antofagasta* (Ortega 1984:348).

The foregoing shows that despite the serious problems facing the economy from 1860 onwards, the adjustment process was relatively painless. The elite refused to take hard economic decisions. They refused to cut public expenditure, resisted raising domestic taxes, reluctantly raised import duties, and relied on loans to cover the growing deficit in the public sector. Although the government neglected the interests of some important economic players, such as copper mining entrepreneurs, it did not ignore the interests of core economic actors, as evidenced by its response in defense of Chilean nitrate investors in Perú and Bolivia. The War of the Pacific, however, not only resolved the immediate problem faced by nitrate investors, but it also revived the export sector and stimulated domestic economic activity. These circumstances explain why differences between the government and segments of the economic elite—such as copper mining entrepreneurs—did not spill over into the mainstream of the political debate. Thus, after successfully resolving the problems that had troubled the economy since the 1860s, it is not surprising that the elite should have welcomed a return to the good old days when domestic taxes were low, and export revenue funded the bulk of public expenditure and provided ample resources to pay for luxury products imported from Europe. Given these expectations, it is not surprising that the elite regarded Balmaceda's attempt to shift the direction of economic policy not only as unacceptable but also tyrannical.

Disagreements over Nitrate Policy

The acquisition of nitrates resolved the impending economic crisis and added a new asset that appeared to guarantee indefinite growth and prosperity. After the War of the Pacific, nitrate became the mainstay of the economy, replacing copper and silver as the leading mining export. The abundant revenue derived from nitrate exports also compensated for the decline of agricultural exports. The introduction of new production methods reduced labor costs and brought about a significant increase in output. Between 1880 and 1886, nitrate exports doubled, reaching 451,000 tons a year (O'Brien 1982:63). The economic boom brought about by nitrate stimulated the development of manufacturing industry and expanded the national market for the ailing agricultural sector (Kirsch 1977:14). The state, which already had considerable experience in collecting export duties and ruthlessly enforcing law and order, thus assumed an important role in the transfer of resources from the mining sector in the North to the elite in the urban centers and landowners in the Central Valley and the South. Yet, formulating a coherent policy on nitrates proved difficult.

The first policy decision facing the government was the question of ownership of the nitrate deposits. The Peruvian government had expropriated the foreign-owned nitrate deposits and, instead of paying compensation in cash, had issued certificates redeemable in two years. Perú refused to honor the certificates and when the war broke out their value plummeted. The certificates were subsequently acquired by a group of British speculators led by John Thomas North on the expectation that Chilean victory would bring about a shift in policy in favor of foreign investors (Blakemore 1986:20; O'Brien 1982:26). Their expectation, based on inside knowledge of the views of Chilean government officials, proved correct (Osgood 1949:71). A committee appointed to advise the government on the future of the nitrate industry rejected the option of state ownership. Characterizing state ownership as dangerous, the committee recommended that the government should "observe and reaffirm the golden rule of economic policy that rejects any form of state intervention in the economy"(Cariola and Sunkel 1977:290). Given that the War of the Pacific was waged to vindicate private rights trampled by the alleged arbitrary acts of the governments of Perú and Bolivia, the committee's recommendations are not surprising. In 1881 the government turned over the nitrate fields to the holders of Peruvian government certificates. The main beneficiaries of this self-styled privatization were British investors who, by 1895, were controlling more than 60 percent of nitrate production (Collier and Sater 1996:165).

When President Balmaceda took office in 1886 he was determined to make good use of the newly acquired state revenue and thus launched an ambitious program of reforms. He established a Ministry for Public Works and Industry and used nitrate revenue to modernize the infrastructure of roads and railways, to build hospitals, prisons, and government offices. He also significantly increased expenditure in education and achieved impressive results. In less than four years, school enrolment nearly doubled (Blakemore 1974:31–32). But Balmaceda's enthusiasm for national development projects was not widely shared. Indeed, even before Balmaceda took office the elite had shown no interest in using nitrate revenue to further public investment. Their attitude is reflected in changes made to the tax system: domestic taxes and import duties were drastically reduced and export taxes on copper and coal were virtually eliminated. With these changes the elite were clearly signaling their determination to use nitrate revenue to ease their tax burden and increase their consumption of imported goods (Bowman and Wallerstein 1982:446).

Balmaceda's problems did not, however, stem exclusively from the elite's fiscal irresponsibility. Although his program of public expenditure was clear, his nitrate policies were not. His main objective was to achieve greater participation by Chilean interests in the production of nitrate. Yet, it was unclear whether he intended to increase local participation through public or private investment. His foreign investment policy was also ambiguous. He strongly opposed the monopolistic practices of foreign investors—such as John Thomas North's attempt to extend his control over the railways in the area. Yet, he was keen to encourage investment by U.S. firms, although in his speeches he often complained about the preponderant role of foreign capital in the industry. Thus, while Balmaceda was determined to ensure that nitrate revenue should contribute to national development, he was unclear as to the role that the state should play in securing this objective. While he did not wish to restrict the role of the state to that of a mere tax collector, he offered no clear alternative (Blakemore 1974:85–91; Zeitlin 1984:102–108).

Balmaceda's dilemma was further complicated by the fact that the structure of the industry made it difficult to find allies even among those who would have benefited from his policies. The involvement of foreign investors in the industry was prompted largely by growing international demand for nitrate, both as a fertilizer and as a component in the manufacture of explosives. By the 1880s, technological and capital requirements were making it difficult for local entrepreneurs to effectively compete with foreign investors. Between 1879 and 1886, average capital investment per nitrate enterprise (*oficina*) doubled, while the number of *oficinas* dropped from 164 to 42. Despite these economic trends, Chilean-owned enterprises still accounted for nearly 10 percent of production (O'Brien 1982:74). However, given their subordinate position, it was unlikely that local entrepreneurs would have become Balmaceda's allies in increasing local investment. Moreover, Balmaceda's objective of increasing output clashed with the interests of investors—both foreign and local—as their concern was to avoid overproduction in order to keep prices at reasonable levels. To this effect, they had entered into a variety of restrictive agreements and were thus not in a position to support Balmaceda. As a consequence, even those who stood to benefit from Balmaceda's nitrate policies resisted them.

Conclusion

At the outset I raised two questions. Why did the elite allow a relatively unimportant political dispute to develop into a full-blown, armed confrontation? And why, if the elite were as flexible and closely integrated as most observers have noted, did they slip into such a costly and divisive conflict as the Civil War? The contents of this chapter show that, while, on paper, the constitutional reforms of the 1870s foreshadowed a strong commitment to political liberalization and democratization, the objective of the main advocates of reform was more limited. Rather than extend the vote and include more citizens into the political sphere, they simply wanted to ensure that the congress would decide key political and economic decisions. Thus, after the reforms, the congress undoubtedly had a major say on matters of economic policy. The sluggish response of successive administrations to the chronic economic crisis that developed after 1860 reveals not only the values and objectives of the economic elite, but also that state policy was firmly under their control. Likewise, the brisk and efficient response of the state to the plight of Chilean companies and workers in Perú and Bolivia illustrates the overwhelming influence of the economic interests represented in the congress. Thus, Balmaceda's attempt to assert a more direct control over the economy contradicted the spirit underlying the constitutional amendments of 1874, which was to ensure that the congress retained control over key policy decisions. From this perspective the dispute over the nature of the presidential regime was neither trivial nor pedantic. It was an issue of the gravest importance to the economic elite, who were also the main players in the political system.

The foregoing analysis also answers, in part, the question as to why such cohesive and closely integrated elite so readily slipped into such a costly conflict. Indeed, it was precisely because the economic elite were so closely integrated that Balmaceda's attempt to redirect state policy was so out of step with the dominant views. It must be noted, however, that the cohesiveness of the elite was not spontaneous. It had been achieved through a bitter struggle that involved both force and compromise. The decisive military defeat of the two insurrections in the 1850s was followed by the integration of most of the defeated leaders into the ruling circles. It must also be noted that not all members of the economic elite had equal access to political and social influence, as evidenced by the government's neglect of the copper industry. Thus, though the integration of the elite made it difficult to establish the identity of its various segments, landowners clearly emerged as the leading group. Evidence from an 1882 survey of the 59 wealthiest people in Chile highlights the preeminent role of large landowners. Among them, 20 had made their fortune in agriculture. The remaining 39 were miners, merchants, and bankers. But remarkably, these 39 individuals had all reinvested their earnings in rural estates (Bauer 1990:243). The economic integration of the elite was thus tilted in favor of agricultural interests and, not surprisingly, contributed to prolonging the seigniorial social relations that prevailed in the countryside (Zeitlin 1984:29).

The dominant role of agricultural interests was reflected in the composition of the congress. In 1875, 50 percent of the members of the congress included a large estate on the list of their main assets. A quarter of a century later the proportion of large landowners with seats in the congress had increased to 60 percent (Bauer 1990:242–243). Thus the hegemony of landowners made it difficult for Balmaceda to find reliable allies in his struggle to modernize the economy. Moreover, as any attempt to modernize it would have required a commitment to developing a national market that would have threatened the survival of seigniorial relations in the countryside, landowners were among Balmaceda's fiercest opponents. Balmaceda's defeat thus had negative consequence for national economic development and it kept landowners socially and economically in power (Bauer 1990:243). The Civil War thus marks the end of the elite's drive toward democratization and political liberalism. After the war they refused to extend rights to subordinate groups, concentrating their energies on sterile parliamentary maneuvering in a congress that had turned its back on social and economic developments.

Chapter 3

Transition to a Modern State

Introduction

The victors of the Civil War established a self-styled parliamentary regime that lasted a little over 30 years. The central role of the nitrate industry during this period accounts for not only the relative stability of the regime, but also its decay and eventual collapse in 1924. Stability, however, was deceptive. Although presidents and members of the congress were regularly elected, the regime stubbornly refused to include the emerging middle and working classes into the political system. The political exclusion of the most dynamic social groups prompted sporadic, but effective public protests and the consequent use of strong law and order measures. It also brought about the emergence of a union movement hostile to state institutions and skeptical of political democracy. The malaise of the political regime was reflected in widespread vote buying and favoritism regarding appointments to the public service, the judiciary, and the army. The nitrate industry was also the main cause for the regime's collapse. By the mid-1920s, nitrate revenue had become unstable, bringing about a breakdown in the political system. This was followed by nearly a decade of political and economic dislocation. The growth of nitrate industry was responsible for important social and economic transformations. It was accompanied by a major shift in population from the countryside to the cities. The population became more literate, the service and manufacturing sectors grew, and there was a major expansion of roads and railways. The elite, however, failed to respond to the challenge posed by economic and social modernization. Their failure to tackle these issues was further complicated by international developments beyond their control. Thus, not surprisingly, it took the elite more than a decade to restore a semblance of stability after the collapse of the political regime in 1924.

Between 1924 and the restoration of stable democracy in 1932 there were 15 administrations. During this period, there were several attempts to adapt the political and constitutional order to the changes that had taken place since the Civil War. Under the watchful eye of the military, a new constitution and a comprehensive system of labor regulation were introduced. There was also a determined attempt to modernize state institutions and to stimulate domestic investment and growth through a process of import substitution. As working-class organizations became more militant, the middle classes also began to assert themselves and play an important role. Although many of the laws and policies launched during this period were not fully implemented or their implementation was partial or biased, they all had a decisive impact on the development of political and legal institutions during the 30 years that followed.

This chapter is divided into two sections. The first examines the nature of the regime that emerged after the Civil War and explains the factors that led to its demise in 1924. The second section provides a brief outline of the chaotic developments between 1924 and 1932 and assesses the blend of authoritarian and populist policies implemented during this period.

A Gentle Anarchy: 1891–1924

Reaffirming the Rule of the Constitution

Constitutional government was promptly restored after the Civil War. The 1833 Constitution remained in place and the groups that had run the country before the war continued in charge. Even the party that had supported Balmaceda—the Liberal Democrats—soon returned to the political arena, and by 1894 had elected four of its members to the congress (Edwards 1972:176). Thus, after the war, the government promptly recovered its "regularity, civility and respect for public law and legal forms" (Edwards 1972:264). Yet, despite signs of continuity, the political regime was novel. Although known as the parliamentary republic, this regime did not have the features typical to a parliamentary system. While the congress had the power to bring cabinets down, the president did not have the power to dissolve it. Moreover, although the congress could remove ministers, it could not remove the president. The system thus did not have an effective mechanism to settle conflicts between the president and the congress (Reinsch

1909:514). As a consequence, there were 121 cabinet reshuffles during this period, while there had been only 31 in the preceding 55 years. The average length of service of the 530 ministers appointed during this period was 4 months (Heise 1960:77). Because of chronic cabinet instability, parliamentarians spent most of their time plotting parliamentary maneuvers. As a consequence, the legislative output during this period was low and there was virtually no policy innovation (Remmer 1984:206–208, 220). Government bills languished in the congress for several years. They were discussed at great length, but never approved, as was the case with a bill that purported to reform the educational system (Millar 1972:16). The complacency of the political regime was partly a consequence of the abundant revenues generated by nitrate exports.

Revenue Windfall and Economic Modernization

After the War of the Pacific, nitrate mining became the main economic activity, providing the bulk of the country's foreign exchange. Chile was in an enviable position. It was the sole supplier of natural nitrates. Nitrate exports increased from 6.3 million dollars in 1880 to a peak of 90 million dollars just before World War I, representing around 70 percent of the country's exports between 1900 and 1914 (Meller 1996:24). Between 1895 and 1920, taxes on nitrate-related activities accounted for 50 percent of total tax receipts (Cariola and Sunkel 1990:89). The abundance of revenue from nitrate and other exports led to the progressive dismantling of direct and indirect taxes and to a complete erosion of fiscal discipline (Meller 1996:28). The reduction of the internal tax burden also brought about a sharp increase in the national debt (Remmer 1984:146).

The nitrate boom had a major impact on all sectors of the economy. It boosted infrastructure development, created a significant domestic market for agriculture, and strengthened local industries. Between 1891 and 1894, public expenditure fell by 47 percent, but later rose sharply so that by the turn of the century, it had overtaken the levels reached during the Balmaceda administration. At the outset, a large part of this increase in expenditure was devoted to the military because of fears of war with Argentina. Later on, a sizeable portion of it was spent on education and infrastructure development, mainly on the railways (Bowman and Wallerstein 1982:432–437). The network of state railways increased from just over 1,000 kilometers in 1890 to nearly 5,000 in 1920 (Cariola and Sunkel 1990:142). The agricultural sector also benefited. While between 1870 and 1900 agricultural exports fell sharply from 30 percent to 6 percent of total exports, the demographic changes brought about by the nitrate industry opened up a vast new domestic market for agricultural produce (Remmer 1984:40). Between 1895 and 1920, the population in the mining areas and cities of the North increased from just over 100,000 to 300,000 (Cariola and Sunkel 1990:81). During this period, the proportion of the population living in cities with more than 5,000 inhabitants increased from 23 percent to nearly 40 percent (Remmer 1984:42). This demographic shift was concentrated in two cities: Santiago and Valparaíso. Between 1865 and 1925, Santiago's population grew from just over 100,000 to more than 500,000 and that of Valparaíso trebled, reaching nearly 300,000 (Kirsch 1977:9). The growth of urban centers brought about an expansion of primary and secondary education. The number of pupils in state educational establishments increased from 150,000 in 1869 to 500,000 in 1925 (Cariola and Sunkel 1990:92). Expenditure in education was reflected in an increase in the literacy rate from 29 percent in 1885 to a little over 50 percent in 1920.

With the exception of education—a priority area for most governments since the middle of the nineteenth century—governments showed no interest in developing policies to favor less privileged groups (Remmer 1984:208). Although the process of urbanization expanded the market for agriculture produce, the agricultural sector failed to modernize. The average yield per acre fell during this period by nearly 40 percent (Pike 1963:100). Inefficient local producers were protected by legislation that excluded cheaper food imports, mainly from Argentina. Thus, commercial policy continued to favor agricultural interests (Remmer 1984:151). The nitrate boom also provided an impetus to manufacturing industry. Although the government afforded protection to some industrialists, it did not have a coherent policy to support industrial development. The elite's main concern was to protect their insatiable appetite for luxury imports. Indeed, the import bill for luxury products during this period—jewels, champagne, silks, and perfume—was twice as much as that for industrial goods and agricultural machinery (Pike 1963:100). Despite the absence of a policy on industrial development, by 1930, the manufacturing, construction, and service sectors were employing 50 percent of the workforce (Atria 1983:204). During this period employment in the state also increased, rising from 3,000 in 1880 to 13,000 in 1900, reaching 27,000 in 1919 (Cariola and Sunkel 1990:141). Thus, by 1920, the sums spent on wages and salaries in the public sector had become equal to the entire state budget for 1900 (Remmer 1984:146).

Limits of Political Competition

Throughout this period governments were regularly elected under the rules established by the constitution. There was intense electoral competition and lively political debates in the congress. The electorate expanded from 134,000 in 1888 to 370,000 in 1920. As a proportion of the population, the number of registered voters increased from 5 percent to almost 10 percent. Elections, however, were marred by widespread corruption (Reinsch 1909:515, 525). The rate of electoral abstention was also high, reaching 54 percent in the 1920 presidential elections. The three major parties represented in the congress—the Conservative, Liberal, and Radical—drew their support from a narrow constituency and most of their leaders came from the upper classes. Only a few were from the medium and lower end of the socioeconomic scale. Large landowners continued to dominate the political establishment. They controlled 40 percent of seats in the Senate and 20 percent of the seats in the chamber of deputies. Thus, as Remmer argues, party competition during this period not only failed to equalize political opportunities, but also may have enhanced the importance of wealth and social status as mechanisms to achieve political influence and power (1984:131).

Political competition and contestation are widely regarded as the most positive features of this period (Loveman 1979:216; Valenzuela 1977:210–214). The congress was the main center of political activity. It was where parliamentarians aired their differences with dignity, ability, and decorum (Reinsch 1909:509–510). Political parties, however, lacked cohesion and did not offer distinct policy alternatives. The never-ending cabinet reshuffles—an average of one every four months—were the result of shifting factional interests within the parties, rather than substantive disagreements over public policy. The absence of major political disagreement is confirmed by the fact that nearly three quarters of the divisions in the congress were "open issues;" that is, decisions over questions in which parliamentarians had a free vote, for, political parties had no interest in their outcomes. Congressional majorities were thus unstable and party loyalty inherently weak. As a contemporary observer noted, party government did not exist and the congress was little more than a council of the governing classes (Reinsch 1909:509, 527, 533).

Given the shortcomings of the regime, it is not surprising that the elite showed little concern for the plight of the laboring masses.

Although from time to time members of the Conservative and Radical Parties, drawing attention to the harsh working conditions of the poor, sponsored the enactment of paternalistic social legislation, there was no coherent response from the political system (Alvarez and Poblete 1924). Only a small circle of intellectuals took this issue seriously, but was unable to bring it to the forefront of the political agenda (Pike 1963:103–107). The dominant political parties did not even take into account the interests of the emerging middle classes. This neglect prompted the establishment in 1919 of a pressure group that called itself the Middle-Class Federation. This group, however, did not seek to form an alliance with the subordinate groups. Instead, its objective was to become part of the oligarchy. In 1930, *El Mercurio*, the mouthpiece of the dominant classes, warmly acknowledged this fact when it noted, with satisfaction, that whenever public order was threatened the middle classes invariably took the side of the upper classes (Pike 1968:211–212).

Except for the tiny Democratic Party, established in 1887 to defend the interests of the working class, subordinate groups virtually had no voice within the political system. As the Democratic Party had supported Balmaceda, it was banned after the Civil War and it only managed to elect a deputy in 1894. In 1912 it elected four deputies and one senator, but was not a serious challenge to the established parties and never became part of a government coalition (Remmer 1984:67–69). In the absence of proper channels of representation, strikes, and other forms of protest proliferated. Governments, distracted by the permanent threat to cabinet instability, were unable to respond to protestors' and strikers' demands other than through repression. The most violent repression was handed out to the nitrate workers in Antofagasta and Iquique. Thus, for example, in Iquique in 1907, a peaceful protest in support of a miners' strike led to a massacre in which more than 200 people—men, women, and children—were murdered by security forces who were following orders from the government in Santiago (Fernández: 2003:104; Morris 1966:98–99). Massive popular demonstrations also took place in Valparaíso and Santiago. A key issue prompting these demonstrations was the soaring price of food as a consequence of duties imposed on Argentinian livestock. This protectionist measure benefited local landowners, but had devastating consequences for the urban poor who spent nearly 50 percent of their income on food (Wright 1982:100). The demand for lower food prices was backed by public rallies, which in October 1905 led to a week of riots in Santiago following a spontaneous demonstration of approximately 50,000 people. Demonstrators demanded higher salaries, the establishment of health services, and an end to police brutality (Izquierdo 1976:90–91). The ensuing riots of October 1905, known as the Red Week, left about 300 dead and 1,000 injured (De Shazo 1983:113–142, Wright 1982:103).

Failure to accommodate the demands of the new social forces greatly contributed to shaping the emerging workers' movement in the mining areas of the North and the industrial centers in Santiago and Valparaíso. Initially, workers' organizations were mainly mutual aid societies. By the middle of the 1910s, however, they had evolved into unions and they came together to form a powerful labor confederation known as the *Federación de Obreros de Chile* (FOCH). FOCH was soon closely identified with the just then established Socialist Workers' Party, created by a faction of Democratic Party dissidents. In 1922, after the Socialist Workers' Party joined the Third International and changed its name to the Communist Party, the FOCH embraced the party's anticapitalist ideology. Thus, by the early 1920s, despite neglect by the official political system, the labor movement had developed an institutional base that was closely identified with the Communist Party. Workers' organizations in Santiago and Valparaíso were also influenced by anarchism and syndicalism (De Shazo 1983:112, 212–218: Drake 1978: 50, 57). According to government statistics, the number of workers affiliated to unions in 1925 was 205,000, about three quarters of whom belonged to unions affiliated to the FOCH. Nitrate workers were the most highly unionized, with a rate of about 60 percent, followed by metal, and railway workers (Poblete 1926:Anexo 5).

Politicians in the congress did not fully appreciate the significance of developments taking place at the grass roots. The contrast between the sophisticated political maneuvering in the congress and political reality is admirably captured by Alberto Edwards. According to Edwards, politicians during this period had no contact with the people and controlled elections with their check books. The political process was, in his view, a "gentle anarchy" (1972:264). This gentle anarchy was sustainable so long as revenue from nitrate exports poured regularly into the coffers of the state. But as nitrate exports began to fluctuate, the regime began to fall apart. Sharp swings in the price of nitrate, combined with the closure of some markets and competition from synthetic substitutes, had a dramatic economic and social impact. Employment in the nitrate industry oscillated from 56,000 in 1918 to 25,000 in 1922, and 60,000 in 1925 to 35,000 in 1927 (Loveman 1979:226). While the decline of public revenue was offset with international loans, the political and social unrest that ensued could not be ignored.

Arturo Alessandri, a member of the Liberal Party, capitalized on the growing political discontent. Running on a platform that called for major social and economic reforms, he won the presidential elections of 1920, thus opening a new and turbulent chapter in the evolution of the political system.

Between Populism and Authoritarianism

Alessandri's victory in the 1920 presidential election is generally regarded as a watershed that marks the incorporation of the middle and working class into the political system (Borón 1971b:50; Serrano 1979). This interpretation is correct insofar as Alessandri's political platform largely reflected the interests and aspirations of middle-class voters. Alessandri, however, did not seek to incorporate the working class into the political system (Pinto and Valdivia 2001:19–22). Indeed, as soon as his administration began to experience difficulties, he turned his back on his working-class supporters and sought help from the armed forces (Aylwin and Alamos 1979). His expectation was that the military would help him impose discipline among workers and restore the presidential regime abolished by the Civil War. The military responded swiftly to Alessandri's approach and not only helped him secure approval of part of his legislative program, but also soon forced him out of office. Thus, Alessandri's election in 1920 marks the beginning of 12 years of instability that brought about the collapse of the 1833 Constitution. During this period, the political regime oscillated between populist and authoritarian rule. Had Alessandri been a genuine leader of the emerging middle class he would have attempted in the 1920s what the Radical Party was to achieve in the late 1930s: the establishment of an alliance between middle- and working-class parties.

Upon taking office Alessandri attempted to persuade the congress to approve several bills designed mainly to regulate labor and restore trust between workers and employers (Pinto and Valdivia 2001:19) But the congress, in characteristic fashion, debated his proposals at great length, and took no action. Instead, parliamentarians preferred to concentrate on their favorite pastime of bringing down cabinets. Between 1920 and 1924, Alessandri was forced to reshuffle his cabinet 16 times (Pike 1963:175). Frustrated, Alessandri focused on winning a majority in the general elections of 1924, while calling at the same time for a constitutional amendment to strengthen the powers of the president. His efforts were partly rewarded. His party—the

Liberal Party—and its allies won an overall majority in both houses of the congress. But Alessandri was unable to persuade the liberals to approve his legislative program. Although he had a large following among workers, artisans, and members of the emerging middle class, Alessandri did not appeal for their support. Instead, he turned to the military. His decision to rely on the military was not accidental. Despite his inflammatory rhetoric, Alessandri was a conservative politician, who, in 1914, had advocated restricting the suffrage in order to contain the excesses of democratic politics (Valenzuela 1977:214–215). Aware of the obstacles that his reform proposals would encounter, he had maintained close relations with the military from the beginning of his administration. Thus, not surprisingly, in 1924 scores, of young officers accepted his invitation publicly to express their discontent with the behavior of the congress. (Haring 1931:6). They attended a public session of the congress and demanded the immediate approval of government bills, including one that gave them a substantial pay increase. This unprecedented military intervention was successful. In less than 24 hours the congress approved all the outstanding government bills (Gil 1966:58).

Alessandri had no difficulties persuading the military to side with him. Discontent within the military had been brewing for some time. Senior officers were alarmed at the growing popular unrest, which they regarded as the main cause for the deterioration of the economy (Strawbridge 1968:68). Junior officers had specific grievances. Between 1912 and 1920, as inflation soared to 80 percent, the salaries of the military remained unchanged (Millar 1972:45). Alessandri enthusiastically supported its claim for higher salaries, but could not persuade the congress to act. The military was also frustrated because there were no clear rules for promotions and no compulsory retirement age. Moreover, politicians had so corrupted the promotion process that officers often needed the sponsorship of a member of the congress to secure advancement in their careers (Millar 1972:51).

Political meddling in military appointments was a consequence of the Civil War. As the army had remained loyal to President Balmaceda, it was subjected to massive restructuring after its defeat. As a consequence, most senior officers during the parliamentary republic were political appointees, with little or no formal military training. In 1924, only 10 of the 40 highest-ranking officers had completed a full course of study at the military academy, 13 had had no military training whatsoever, and the remaining 17 had completed only part of their formal training (Millar 1972: 33–34). By contrast, junior officers were well trained, but were underpaid and had virtually no career prospects.

They were thus keen supporters of military intervention and they played a decisive role in political events after 1924.

Given the discontent among military officers, it is not surprising that Alessandri's attempt to rely on them backfired. Indeed, once they became aware of their power, the military closed down the congress and dispatched Alessandri to Italy on an extended leave (Silva Bascuñán 1963:2:51). Thus, a bloodless military putsch brought down the parliamentary regime and the much-revered 1833 Constitution. Military intervention did not, however, bring about stability. Policy disagreements soon broke out among the military, and Alessandri emerged as the only politician capable of resolving the political impasse and so the military then invited him to return from exile to complete his period in office (Fernández 2000:140). He accepted the invitation on condition that the military should return to barracks and that a constituent assembly should be elected to draft a new constitution that would restore the presidential regime (Silva Bascuñán 1963:2:52). His conditions were accepted, and in March 1925 he resumed his presidency. Upon his return, however, the military continued to take a keen interest in politics as by then they had regarded themselves as the sole guardians of good governance (Strawbridge 1968:70). Alessandri presided over the drafting of the new constitution, but, unable to withstand pressure from the military, he again resigned from office in October 1925.

On December 23, 1925, Emiliano Figueroa was elected president. The reestablishment of constitutional government, however, was brief. After two years in office, the new president also resigned. Figueroa's frustration stemmed from the behavior of the parties in the congress and persistent pressure from the military, which he opposed. The three main parties—Conservative, Liberal, and Radical—continued to behave as if they were still under the parliamentary regime. They questioned the legitimacy of the constitution, claiming that it had been imposed by the military, and refused to endorse the government's legislative program, including its annual budget, claiming that the government was dominated by the military (Donoso 1976:318). The military, through Colonel Carlos Ibáñez—Figueroa's minister of war and later minister of the interior—considerably influenced the formulation of government policy. Ibáñez skillfully exploited the behavior of the political parties. Echoing the frustration of large sections of the public, he repeatedly reminded the congress not to indulge in the parliamentary maneuvers that had brought down the previous regime and called upon politicians to address the real problems of the nation, rather than focus on narrow party interests (Donoso 1976:314). In the event, President Figueroa's resignation was prompted by Ibáñez's clumsy attempt to eradicate corruption from the judiciary. Initially, the president had agreed to a partial purge of the judiciary. But he changed his mind when Ibáñez demanded the resignation of the president of the Supreme Court, who happened to be the president's older brother (Haring 1931:22; Vergara 1954:393–400).

Following Figueroa's resignation, Ibáñez was elected president in a hastily arranged election in which he, the sole candidate, polled nearly 90 percent of the vote. Once in office (1927–31), although he reaffirmed his loyalty to the constitution, he did not observe it. He persecuted political opponents, repressed workers' organizations, and manipulated congressional elections (Nunn 1970:127, 167). On the economic front he established several institutions that, ten years later, were to provide the foundations for the development of a comprehensive policy of import substitution. His administration, however, was unable to withstand the economic consequences of the Great Depression. In 1931, following several demonstrations by middle-class professionals and university students, he was swept from office and was forced to flee to Argentina. After Ibáñez's departure, there were 11 administrations, including one that was democratically elected under Juan Esteban Montero, and 4 military juntas, one of which was a self-styled Socialist Republic that lasted 12 days in office. Constitutional stability was not restored until December 1932, when, once again, Arturo Alessandri was elected president.

Designing New Institutions

The political and economic turmoil that prevailed between 1924 and 1932 forced the numerous administrations of this period to address three key tasks: the design of a new constitution; the establishment of a system for the regulation of labor, and the search for a new economic policy. This section examines, in turn, how they approached this task.

A New Constitution

One of Alessandri's main aims upon his return from Italy in 1924 was to restore presidentialism. His original intention was to convene a constituent assembly, but, as he became aware that the main political parties did not share his enthusiasm for presidentialism, he changed his mind. He entrusted the task of drafting the new constitution to a committee of approximately 122 members. This committee, in turn, appointed a drafting committee of 15 that was chaired by Alessandri (Gil 1966:89; Gómez 2004:101–102). The military welcomed Alessandri's commitment to presidentialism and took a keen interest in the drafting process. In a statement to the drafting committee, General Mariano Navarrete reminded its members that the objective of the military intervention of 1924 had been to stamp out the corrupt practices of the parliamentary regime and warned them that the military would not accept any outcome other than the restoration of presidentialism (Donoso 1976:274, 280). Pressured like this, it is not surprising that the committee promptly produced a draft constitution restoring presidentialism.

The conditions surrounding the drafting and enactment of the new constitution were unpromising. The constitution was drafted under the auspices of a government closely watched by the military. It was approved in a hastily convened referendum boycotted by the main political parties and in which less than half of those eligible to vote participated. The Conservative Party opposed presidentialism, fearing that the new regime would become a breeding ground for populists and demagogues. The party was also strongly against the separation of church and state proposed by the new constitution. The Radical Party, which had come into prominence during the defunct parliamentary regime, also opposed presidentialism. Even the just then established Communist Party rejected presidentialism, despite its misgivings about the virtues of parliamentarism (Donoso 1976:282, 283). The only parties in favor of the restoration of presidentialism were the small left-leaning Democratic Party and the old pro-Balmaceda Liberal Democratic Party. The rejection of presidentialism by the leading political parties is not surprising. In their experience, strong presidents were associated with electoral intervention, political patronage, and hostility toward the congress. They also feared that the enthusiastic endorsement of presidentialism by the military was prompted more by their authoritarian inclinations than by their commitment to constitutional democracy. Ibáñez's behavior during the Figueroa administration and during his elected dictatorship (1927–31) suggests that the political parties had a point. Thus, from the perspective of the parties, presidentialism was tantamount to political suicide.

The overriding objective of the drafters of the new constitution was the restoration of presidentialism. The drafting process thus concentrated almost exclusively on the rules governing the powers of the president and of the congress. Concern with this issue led them to focus on the separation of powers, thus indirectly strengthening the position of the judiciary. The rest of the constitution—with one or two exceptions—followed almost word for word the 1833 Constitution (Gil 1966:88–128; Silva Bascuñán 1963:2:60–62).[1]

Under the new constitution executive power was vested in the president, who was the head of the government and chief administrative authority. The president was elected to a six-year period by direct popular election and could not stand for reelection. Cabinet members were appointed by the president and were directly accountable to him. They could not be removed from office by the congress on political grounds. The president also had broad regulatory powers to implement legislation. Presidential power was strengthened by the major role assigned to the president in the legislative process. The president had exclusive power to initiate bills in financial and administrative matters and had a broad power to veto legislation. He was also given a form of guillotine privilege to ensure the speedy approval of legislation. Moreover, the president was entitled to convene the congress into session that would last six months and set its agenda.

Although the president was meant to play a dominant role in the political system, the role assigned to the congress was no less important. The congress had two chambers: the chamber of deputies and the senate. Members of the congress were directly elected through a system of proportional representation. The chamber of deputies, representing about 30 electoral districts, was composed of 150 deputies elected for a 4-year term. The senate had 50 members elected for an 8-year term, 5 representing each of the 10 provincial groupings. Members of the congress were not allowed to hold cabinet or other government posts, thus underlining their independence from the executive. Bills could generally originate in either chamber and members of the congress could initiate bills on most matters, except for those reserved for the president. Although the congress did not have the power to remove cabinet ministers on political grounds it had several means available to control members from the other branches of the state. The chamber of deputies was charged with the task of scrutinizing executive action and making representations to the president on any matter arising from the exercise of his office. To this effect, the chamber of deputies had broad powers to set up committees of inquiry. The congress also had the power to impeach the president, cabinet ministers, the Supreme Court and court of appeals judges, the comptroller general and other senior officials.

In contrast with the 1833 Constitution, the new constitution formally recognized the principle of judicial independence and conferred upon the courts exclusive jurisdiction in criminal and civil cases, explicitly enjoining the president and the congress from exercising judicial functions. The Supreme Court, made up of 13 judges, was the governing body of the judiciary. As a court of cassation its main function was to review decisions by courts of appeal to ensure that the law was correctly applied. The purpose of the cassation powers was to achieve uniformity in the interpretation of the law. The constitution also gave the Supreme Court the power to declare a law inapplicable in particular cases, as violating the constitution. Declarations of inapplicability could only refer to specific sections of the relevant law and never to an entire act. A declaration of inapplicability had no binding effect beyond the immediate case in question.

The new constitution reaffirmed the civil and political rights already recognized by the 1833 Constitution. Thus, it recognized the principle of equality before the law and basic freedoms such as freedom of expression, assembly, and association. It also introduced several provisions reinforcing the right to physical liberty and gave constitutional status to the right of habeas corpus and to the principle that there should be no criminal penalty without prior legal authority. In the area of religious freedom, the constitution also introduced important changes. Under the old constitution, Catholicism was recognized as the religion of the state and the offer of public worship by other religions was forbidden (Guerra 1929:38). The constitution brought about the separation of church and state and guaranteed freedom of worship and religious freedom.

The protection of property rights was the object of close scrutiny as some members of the drafting committee advocated the introduction of a clause to allow the expropriation of agricultural land. Despite a lengthy debate on this point, the property right clause finally approved was not significantly different from that of the 1833 Constitution (Avila 1971:88). It provided that no one could be deprived of property except by judicial decree or by an expropriation decree on grounds of public utility determined by the law. Full compensation had to be paid prior to taking possession of the property. A reference to the social function of property was introduced as a gesture toward the members of the drafting committee who advocated a more radical approach to property rights (Guerra 1929:12–132). Thus, Article 10 (10) provided that the exercise of the right of property was subject "to the limitations or rules demanded by the maintenance and advancement of the social order and, to that end, the law may impose obligations or servitude of public policy in favor of the general interests of the state, the health of the citizens, and public welfare." Over the years, this reference to the social function of property provided the basis for validating several laws and regulations that restricted the scope of property rights.

A major innovation of the constitution was the establishment of a system of proportional representation. Article 25 called for the introduction of an electoral system that would yield a proportional representation of the views of all political parties. To give effect to this provision, the legislature adopted the system designed by Victor d'Hont and introduced in Belgium in 1899. As it turned out, the d'Hont system seemed to have been especially designed to favor large established parties—Conservative, Liberal, and Radical—and to underrepresent smaller parties (Parrish et al. 1970:257).

Labor Regulation

In 1924 Alessandri proposed to the congress a legislative package, regulating aspects of labor relations. This proposal was a belated acknowledgment that workers' organizations had a role to play in the political system. Indeed, it was submitted to the congress more than a decade after the labor movement had established itself as a force within the political arena. The congress, under pressure from the military, approved this legislative package in 1924. Several years later, in 1931, Ibáñez consolidated labor and social security legislation into a single Labor Code. Both Alessandri and Ibáñez endorsed the new legislations, as they sought to achieve the same objectives: containing labor unrest and eliminating the political influence of Marxist and anarchist groups within the union movement. But Ibáñez went one step further. He established a network of state-controlled unions and attempted to transform them into a political movement that would back his administration. His objectives became clear in 1930 when, after rigging the congressional elections, he assigned 14 seats in the chamber of deputies to members of the *Confederación Republicana de Acción Cívica* (CRAC), the umbrella organization under which the state-sponsored unions had been established (Urzúa 1984:31).

The Labor Code, though ostensibly designed to extend rights to workers and their organizations, was in fact deliberately designed to fragment unions and insulate them from the influence of left-wing parties. It prohibited the establishment of confederations of union—thus instantly turning the powerful FOCH into an illegal organization. Provisions on the right to form unions were exceedingly formalistic and restrictive. Unions could be established only by private sector workers and only if they worked in enterprises employing at least 25 persons. Workers' freedom of association was thus severely restricted.

Provisions on collective bargaining and strikes were also restrictive. The Code set out in detail the main components of individual and collective contracts of employment, leaving little room to negotiate. The provisions of the Code determined minimum holiday entitlement, dismissal procedures, family allowances, and minimum wages. Although there was some room to negotiate pay levels and fringe benefits, anti-inflation legislation had the effect of further restricting the scope of collective bargaining (Angell 1972: 64; Morris 1966:20). The Code also set out detailed and complex procedural steps to deal with disputes. These steps had to be meticulously followed before a strike could be called. Participation in an illegal strike was a criminal offense, punishable by up to 60 days in prison. The Ministry of Labor had the power to also cancel the registration of unions involved in illegal strikes.

While the Code placed in the exercise of labor rights a stifling array of procedural obstacles, the government was given sweeping powers to repress and contain labor unrest. A provision in the Labor Code also gave the government the power to break strikes whenever a strike was deemed to pose a threat to public health or general economic welfare. Under this provision, the minister of labor could bring a strike to an end by issuing back-to-work orders (*decretos de reanudación de faenas*) that required workers to return to work and to submit their dispute to compulsory arbitration. While arbitration was pending, the enterprise concerned was placed under the administration of a government appointed official, who was often a military officer (Yávar 1972).

Incipient Import Substitution

In addition to the introduction of a framework to regulate labor relations, there was a determined effort during this period to diversify the economy so as to reduce the excessive dependence on nitrate. The first indications that the elites were searching for a new economic policy became apparent shortly after the outbreak of the First World War. Although the war caused a brief surge in the demand for nitrate because of its use in the manufacture of explosives, it also led to a sharp decrease in the value and quantity of imports. The restriction of imports gave a boost to local manufacturing. The end of the war, however, marked the beginning of a more determined search for a policy to make the economy less vulnerable to the volatility of world commodity markets (Palma 1985:322). Between 1914 and 1929, various measures were introduced to stimulate domestic production. Tariff rates were raised and new fiscal policies were introduced to make the state less dependent on export taxes. A progressive income tax was established and several indirect taxes were introduced (Drake

1989: 05; Mamalakis 1976:113). Besides, during this period, successive currency devaluations made imports less attractive, thus further stimulating domestic production (Palma 1985:322).

Ibáñez endorsed this economic policy shift and complemented it with an ambitious program of institutional reform. His administration introduced a modern system of statistical reporting and financial controls designed to improve the efficiency of public administration. It also established several institutions, including the Central Bank and the Office of the Comptroller General, that greatly strengthened the capacity of the state to formulate economic policy and promote economic growth, (Drake 1989:92; Palma 1985: 323). Ibáñez's efforts to revamp the economy were strengthened by the reappearance of copper as the country's main mining export. As noted in chapter 2, Chile dominated world markets in the mid-nineteenth century, but by 1910, however, its share of world copper production had dropped to a mere 4 percent (Mamalakis 1976:40). However, because of the abundance of nitrate revenue, the decline of copper was hardly noticed. In the early 1900s, however, American investors successfully revived copper mining and by the 1920s the value of copper exports had become equal to that of nitrate. By 1932, copper had overtaken nitrate to become the country's main export.

The policies launched by Ibáñez had a positive impact on the economy. Between 1927 and 1929, industrial production and building activities underwent significant expansion (Ellsworth 1945:4–5). The Great Depression, however, had a devastating impact on the economy. Contemporary reports indicate that Chile was the country worst affected by the Great Depression (Palma 1985:328). In 1932, the value of exports and imports dropped to about 20 percent of their 1929 value; unemployment increased from 6,000 in 1929 to 55,000 in 1932. Thus, not surprisingly, despite Ibáñez's efforts to overhaul the economy and improve the efficiency of state institutions, his administration was blamed for the consequences of the Great Depression, and, in 1931, it was swiftly removed from office.

The onset of the Great Depression cut short Ibáñez's term in office. Yet, had he been allowed to remain in office, it is unlikely that his project to transform the union movement would have been successfully achieved. Although CRAC-affiliated unions had a respectable following of approximately 50,000 members, he was unable to gain the trust of union leaders, as his policies were aimed at suppressing, rather than empowering, workers. Indeed, although he encouraged the establishment of unions loyal to the government, he violently repressed independent, communist, and left-leaning unions. Ibáñez's behavior toward political parties was also contradictory. Though he was a severe critic of political parties, he did not attempt to replace them. Instead, he successfully manipulated the old established parties and even persuaded them in 1930 to accept a scheme to rig the congressional elections. The scheme involved nominating as many candidates as there were seats available, thus making the election unnecessary. Needless to say, he vetted the names of the candidates. As Haring notes, the leaders of the old established parties went along with this astonishing electoral fraud because they feared that an open and fair contest would bring about a resurgence of social unrest (1933:198). This travesty of the democratic process enabled Ibáñez to handpick a tame congress, but he could not count on the loyalty of his docile parliamentarians. Indeed, as soon as his administration began to confront serious economic difficulties, even the parliamentarians who had benefited from the electoral fraud turned their back on him and joined those who demanded his resignation (Nunn 1970:156).

Conclusion

After the Civil War, the reputed flexibility of the elite was put to test and was found wanting. Under the self-styled parliamentary regime, the congress occupied a prominent place within the political system. Yet, instead of becoming a focus of serious political deliberation and a forum to further the process of democratization, the congress remained little more than a debating club of the economic elite. It was an urbane and sophisticated assembly, but it showed little or no concern for the plight of the emerging middle class, the mining and industrial proletariat, and rural workers. The regime that emerged after 1891 also failed to make good use of the abundant revenue generated by nitrate exports, focusing instead on satisfying the short-term appetites of the groups represented in the congress. Thus, not surprisingly, by mid-1920s, as nitrate revenue became unstable and the political system collapsed, there followed nearly a decade of political and economic instability during which a succession of civilian and military governments unsuccessfully attempted to restore presidentialism, resolve the economic crisis, and forge an alliance with organized workers in mining and manufacturing.

The instability that followed the collapse of the constitution in 1924 is not surprising. The majority of political parties rejected presidentialism either because they associated it with authoritarianism and arbitrary government, or because they were reluctant to give up the privileges they had enjoyed during the parliamentary period. Moreover, the mix of authoritarian and populist policies implemented by successive administrations during these chaotic years was short-lived, as it did not enjoy widespread support and was swept away by the instability prevailing in the world economy. The main reason for the failure of these policies was that they sought to subdue the emerging social forces rather than acknowledge them as equal interlocutors in the political process. Yet, as the contents of the second part of this book show, the policies and institutions devised during this period provided the inspiration for policies that, in the late 1930s, gave new impetus to political and legal developments. Thus, the new constitution, discredited because of its association with the military, acquired unexpected legitimacy during the subsequent four decades. The failed attempts to diversify the economy provided solid foundations in the 1940s for the development of a relatively successful policy of import substitution. Labor regulation, despite its rough edges, provided the framework for the development of a lively and heavily politicized labor movement. Yet, all these policies flourished only after the political system gave voice and power to the parties and groups that hitherto had been forcibly excluded. It was thus that party democracy came into being.

Part II

Party Democracy

We should not search for a single set of circumstances or a repeated series of events that everywhere produces democracy. Nor should we look for actors having democratic intentions, seeking to discover how and when they get chances to realize those intentions. We should look instead for robust recurrent causal mechanisms that combine differently, with different aggregate outcomes, in different settings.

Charles Tilly, *Contention and Democracy*, 9

Chapter 4

Relative Autonomy—Politics and Economics

Coalition Politics

Political Realignment 1932–38

Arturo Alessandri's main achievements were his success in restoring confidence in the economy and his imposition of discipline on the armed forces. His success in these two areas brought about a realignment of political forces that facilitated the emergence of a consensus on economic policy, which, in turn, resulted in the consolidation of the constitutional regime.

Alessandri succeeded in restoring economic confidence by imposing strict fiscal discipline and by offering selected incentives, complemented by strategically targeted employment creation programs. He imposed strict controls on public expenditure, sharply raised taxes, and successfully eliminated the enormous deficit caused by the Great Depression. The introduction of special incentives to stimulate construction brought about a building boom that helped to drastically reduce unemployment. Between 1932 and 1935 unemployment was reduced from 129,000 to a mere 8,000 (Ellsworth 1945:23–32). These achievements were complemented by his determination to restore army discipline. He removed from office most of the senior officers involved in political conspiracies hatched during and after the Ibáñez administration. The purge of the armed forces was relatively easy, as the military was weak and deeply divided, as evidenced by the four chaotic military administrations that followed the collapse of the Ibáñez administration. Moreover, since public opinion blamed the military for the economic consequences of the Great Depression, Alessandri's purge of the army enjoyed widespread support.

Alessandri did not scrupulously respect the constitution. He violently repressed strikes and imprisoned scores of union leaders and left-wing politicians. As he did not entirely trust the army, he also encouraged and supported the activities of the Republican Militia, a 15,000 strong paramilitary organization established by right-wing sympathizers in 1932 to resist the short-lived Socialist Republic. The Republican Militia worked in partnership with Alessandri, thus creating a buffer between the military and the newly established civilian administration. Under these conditions, the government was able to undertake a major restructuring of the military purging Ibáñez supporters and restoring army discipline. After the military was safely returned to barracks, the Republican Militia was disbanded and their arms handed over to the government (Deutsch 1999:147–155; Gómez 2004:148; Joxe 1970:72).

Despite his lack of concern for constitutional niceties and his harsh treatment of trade unionists and left-wing politicians, Alessandri, in the end, did respect basic political freedoms as evidenced by the opening of the political system and the major realignment of forces that took place toward the end of his administration. The main beneficiaries of this realignment were the left-wing parties and the union movement. Shortly after Alessandri's election, there emerged in 1933 a new Marxist party, the Socialist Party, led by an assortment of middle-class social democrats, anarchists, retired left-wing military officers, and intellectuals (Drake 1978:139–151). What united this heterogeneous group was their rejection of the pro-Moscow orientation of the Communist Party. They were also open to forming alliances with other parties. Although, initially, the electoral strength of the Socialist Party was negligible, it soon acquired a solid working-class base made up of the remnants of the legal unions established by Ibáñez. The establishment of the Socialist Party was followed in 1936 by the creation of a new labor confederation—the *Confederación de Trabajadores de Chile* (CTCH)—that brought together socialist- and communist-controlled unions. Meanwhile, the Radical Party became more responsive to the demands of the middle classes and began to distance itself from the right-wing parties and the Alessandri government. These events led, in 1936, to the establishment of the Popular Front, an electoral alliance that included the Radical, Socialist, and Communist Parties (Stevenson 1942:57–71). The Popular Front was the first alliance between a middle-class party and parties representing working-class constituencies. Its political importance was underscored by the fact that the CTCH was also recognized as a member of the Popular Front (Drake 1978:177).

In 1938, Pedro Aguirre, the Popular Front candidate, won a narrow victory in the presidential elections. Aguirre's program was ambitious: it called for sweeping economic reforms, including a radical revision of the tax laws, the introduction of national economic planning, and strict controls over foreign investment (Stevenson 1942:83–85). The Popular Front administration, however, did not have the political strength to implement such a radical program. Its main achievement, however, was that it put in place an economic policy that became the basis for the development of a system of coalition politics that lasted just over a decade. During this period the Radical party presided over two further administrations. One led by Juan Antonio Ríos (1942–46), elected with the backing of the Socialist and Communist Parties and a faction of the Liberal Party, and the other led by Gabriel González (1946–52), elected with the vote of the Radical and Communist Parties. The coalitions that voted these administrations into office soon collapsed, to be replaced by an endless round of shaky alliances in which every party represented in the congress had the opportunity to form part of the government. In order to understand the institutional consequences of this process, it is necessary to explain the nature and limits of the economic policy consensus.

Import Substitution

Import substitution, as noted in the preceding chapter, had been tried before. During the 1920s several administrations were forced to develop import substitution policies in response to the instability and eventual collapse of revenue from nitrate exports. The Aguirre administration, however, launched a systematic policy of import substitution. It used a variety of instruments to stimulate domestic production, such as tariffs, import licenses, quotas, multiple exchange rates, and production subsidies. But the key institution driving the import substitution policy was the *Corporación de Fomento de la Producción* (CORFO), a state development corporation established during the Aguirre administration. CORFO was entrusted with the task of drawing up a str ategy to ensure balanced growth. It was given broad powers to implement policies, including the establishment of industrial and commercial enterprises. CORFO also acted as a development bank channeling financial resources to the private sector. CORFO took its entrepreneurial role seriously. It assumed direct control of 6 industrial enterprises and had equity interests in 24 more during its first 4 years (Muñoz 1968:107). As the government did not interfere in its day-to- day activities, CORFO soon developed a reputation for technical and managerial efficiency. Its popularity within the business community stemmed largely from the fact that it did not seek to replace the private sector, but merely to complement and support it (Ellsworth 1945:93–94).

The new economic policy had the backing of all the major parties represented in the congress, the leading business associations and organized labor. Its scope and limits were defined during the political bargaining that led to the approval of the CORFO bill. The government had proposed that CORFO should be given broad powers to promote projects in every sector of the economy and that its activities should be funded through domestic savings. The business community welcomed the idea of state support to key sectors of industry, but opposed the notion that CORFO should have a free hand to intervene in every sector of the economy (Cavarozzi 1975:120). Instead, it proposed that CORFO should circumscribe its activities only to the manufacturing sector and, in particular, that it should have no involvement in the agricultural sector. The business community also rejected the proposal to fund CORFO through domestic taxes. Instead, it proposed the introduction of a 15 percent tax surcharge on copper exports. Moreover, in order to ensure that CORFO did not run out of control, it demanded that five seats on CORFO's board should be reserved for representatives of the leading business associations (Menges 1966:357). As the Conservative and Liberal Parties sided with the business community, the government had no choice but to give in to these demands.

CORFO was thus barred from intervening in two crucial economic sectors: agriculture and large scale copper mining. The surtax on copper exports became a guarantee that CORFO would not extend its entrepreneurial activities to this strategic sector, controlled at the time by U.S. mining companies. The agricultural sector, inefficient and in desperate need of modernization, was also excluded form CORFO's purview. The exclusion of the agricultural sector from the import substitution policy had devastating effects. Between 1932 and 1952, agricultural output dropped by 16 percent and, consequently, the government had to divert scarce foreign exchange to compensate for the food deficit. It has been estimated that about 65 percent of food imports between 1945 and 1959 could have been produced domestically (Thiesenhusen 1966:9). As one observer has noted, while governments were busy implementing import substitution policies in manufacturing, a rapid process of import desubstitution was taking place in the agricultural sector as the country was importing agricultural produce that it could have produced at home (Behrman 1977:27).

The exclusion of the agricultural sector from the scope of CORFO's activities was combined with a reaffirmation of the long-standing policy of denying union rights to agricultural workers.

Reluctant Democrats

The consensus on economic policy, as embodied in the approval of the CORFO bill, provided the basis for a succession of heterogeneous coalition governments between 1941 and 1952. All these coalitions were led by the Radical Party and, as I explain in the chapter that follows, they transformed the strong regime into a hybrid that had many features of a parliamentary regime. These coalition governments also contributed to legitimize constitutional procedures, as they were all duly elected and they respected the political authority of the congress. Yet, at the outset, neither the right-wing nor the left-wing parties fully accepted the implications of participating in a democratic system.

That the right-wing parties readily accepted Aguirre's victory in the presidential elections, despite the fact that their candidate had been defeated by the narrowest of margins—50.26 percent against 49.33 percent—may suggest a strong commitment to constitutionalism and the democratic process. On close inspection, however, their reason for conceding defeat was that they had no alternative. They could not have relied on the military to prevent the Popular Front from taking office, as following Alessandri's purge, the military was weak and divided. Moreover, Ibáñez, without whom any military conspiracy would have failed, had supported the Popular Front candidate—albeit at the last minute. In any event, the Right did not trust the military as the policies implemented by the succession of short-lived military administrations in the late 1920s and early 1930s had a distinct antioligarchic orientation. The political position of the right-wing parties was also vulnerable. In the 1930s two new political movements emerged: the *Movimiento Nacional Socialista* (MNS), a fascist-inspired organization; and the *Falange Nacional*, a youth group with left-wing tendencies that had broken away from the Conservative Party (Deutsch 1999:145–146). Although neither group posed an immediate threat, their very existence had a moderating influence on the right-wing parties, and hence their decision to opt for the path of constitutionalism.

In any event, by accepting the verdict of the polls, the right-wing parties were risking little (Gómez 2004:177). They controlled the majority of seats in the congress and were implacable in their opposition to every initiative of the Aguirre administration. Their approval of the CORFO bill was indeed an exception to their obstructionist parliamentary strategy. Apart from paralyzing the congress, they encouraged and condoned military conspiracies against the government (Joxe 1970:78–80) and launched a vicious propaganda campaign depicting the Popular Front as an assortment of mental and physical degenerates, enriched bureaucrats, and Moscow-bought communists (Super 1975:82). They also attempted to distance the president from the Marxist parties by depicting him as a genuine democrat unable to govern because of the disruptive influence of communists and socialists.

In November 1940, the right-wing parties, claiming that the government was unable to guarantee free and fair elections, threatened to boycott the general elections due to take place the following March. The electoral boycott was a fundamental challenge to the constitutional order. The government was thus forced to make concessions that included a commitment to repress strikes in the countryside and to disband unions in the state sector. The government also agreed to hand over to the army control over law and order on the day of the election. After securing these concessions, the Right called off the boycott. The outcome of the general elections of 1941 explains why the Right was keen on the boycott. In these elections the Popular Front parties achieved a spectacular victory, gaining control of the majority of seats in both chambers of the congress. This victory, however, was of no use as by then, worn out by internal strife, the Popular Front had effectively collapsed. The death of President Aguirre later in 1941, after only half of his term completed, dashed any hope of reviving the Popular Front coalition. It was only after the demise of the Popular Front that the right-wing parties began actively to participate in broad coalition governments (Stevenson 1942:113–121).

The unease of the right-wing parties toward the new democratic regime was matched by a similar attitude among most of the leaders of the Socialist and Communist Parties. Some were uncomfortable with the idea of forming alliances with bourgeois parties, while others regarded the policies implemented by the coalition governments as not sufficiently radical. Despite these misgivings, they vigorously promoted the interests of their electoral constituencies and fought hard to expand the boundaries of the political system—as evidenced by the persistent attempts to secure the unionization of agricultural workers. Yet, these efforts were spoiled by their dogmatic policies toward the union movement. In this area, the overriding objective of the Socialist and Communist Parties was to eliminate each other's influence among organized workers so as to become the sole representative of the mining and incipient industrial proletariat. In pursuit of this objective, each party made full use of its occasional influence in government coalitions to undermine the other, thus weakening the labor movement as well as the political regime.

The Popular Front won the presidential elections in 1938, only two years after its establishment. Because of its meteoric rise to political prominence, its roots were shaky. The Radical Party's decision to form an alliance with the Marxist parties was based largely on short-term electoral calculation, as they had come to realize that in any future alliance with the Right they were destined to play a secondary role. The Radical Party's shift to the left, however, was never fully endorsed by party patriarchs, especially by the large landowners from the province of Concepción. The socialists, many of whom had been involved in military conspiracies after the fall of Ibáñez and had supported the short-lived military administrations of 1932, disliked the slow pace of the government's decision-making process. Besides, they never fully accepted the leadership of the Radical Party, as they believed that the coalition should have been led by Marmaduque Grove, a socialist who enjoyed enormous popular appeal. The enthusiasm of the communists for the coalition was qualified by the fact that the decision to enter into alliances with what they characterized as bourgeois parties had been prompted by a shift in the policy of the Third International. It had not been a decision of the rank and file. Their commitment to the success of the Popular Front was thus half-hearted, subordinated as it was to its unquestioned loyalty to the dictates from Moscow (Drake 1978:175–181).

The fragile foundations of the Popular Front coalition were further undermined by the intense competition between the Marxist parties to enhance their influence among organized workers. Until the early 1930s, the Communists Party's popularity among workers in mining and manufacturing was virtually unchallenged. The establishment of the Socialist Party in 1933 posed an unexpected threat to the communist hegemony among organized workers. This threat was compounded by the fact that the socialists had a much wider electoral appeal than the communists and they repudiated the latter's unquestioned loyalty to the international communist movement. Despite their rivalry, communists and socialists jointly sponsored the establishment of the CTCH. Initially, union leaders benefited from their close relationship with the Marxist parties, as it created political opportunities that only a few years earlier would not have been possible. Yet, the continuous bickering and competition between socialists and communists had devastating consequences for the union movement. The socialists resented the communists' decision not to accept cabinet posts in the Aguirre administration, interpreting it as an opportunistic move designed to give the communists the chance to strengthen their influence among working-class constituencies without assuming responsibility for the failings of the government. The communists, for their part, lost no opportunity to discredit the socialists, even when their criticism involved challenging key government policies. Thus, when the socialist minister for development went to Washington to seek financial assistance to compensate for the fall in copper and nitrate prices, the communists strongly criticized him, insinuating that the Socialist Party had sold out to imperialism (Faundez 1988:66). The animosity between the two parties grew to such an extent that in December 1940, the socialists withdrew from the Popular Front, though not from government. The socialists claimed that they were withdrawing from the coalition because it was heavily influenced by the Communist Party, a party that espoused policies contrary to the national interest (Stevenson 1942:109).

The feud between the Marxist parties was so intense that in 1946 the Socialist Party provoked a split within the CTCH in order to make itself more appealing to the government of the day and thus gain representation in the cabinet. Later on, in the same year, when the communists took up cabinet posts in the new González administration, they took their revenge and used their influence in the new administration to discredit the socialists and enhance their position within the union movement. The communists were unable to fulfill their objectives as shortly thereafter they were expelled from the cabinet and outlawed on the grounds that they constituted a menace to democracy and state security. Thus, at one time or another, both socialists and communists made use of their influence within the labor movement to further their short-term political objectives. In the process they weakened the labor movement and undermined their own position within the political system.

End of Coalition Politics

Between 1932 and 1952 there were important advances in the democratization process. The number of workers belonging to unions rose from 55,000 to a little over a 250,000 (Correa et al. 2001:78) and union leaders were able to exercise some influence on public policy, especially during the early days of the Aguirre administration (1938–41). Moreover, between 1940 and 1952, the share of labor in domestic income rose slightly from 42 percent to 45 percent, although those who benefited were mainly white-collar workers and workers in the mining industry (Mamalakis 1976:212). The rate of literacy increased from 56 percent to 75 percent and the percentage of the population registered to vote rose from just over 9 in 1932 to 18 in 1952. The party system, however, was weak and fragmented. The number of parties represented in the congress increased from 11 in 1934 to 19 in 1953. The fragmentation of the political parties, prompted by the dynamics of the system of coalition politics, reached such a level that, by the early 1950s, the Radical Party—which represented a respectable 22 percent of the vote—was unable to find partners for the presidential elections of 1952 (Urzúa 1986:51, 86). The problems of the political system were replicated on the economic front also.

By the early 1950s, although the manufacturing sector had expanded, the agricultural sector had not. Between 1932 and 1952, agricultural production in fact declined by 16 percent, while the index of industrial production between 1932 and 1952 increased by 126 percent and total production rose by 59 percent (ECLA 1949:264). The decline of agricultural production was compensated by an increase in imported foodstuffs, which, in turn, diverted scarce, foreign exchange from industrial development projects. These problems were made worse by the fact that, after the end of World War II, there was a sharp drop in the demand for copper, which intensified the pressure on the balance of payments. These factors unleashed an inflationary process that, by the end of the 1940s, had begun to run out of control. The rate of inflation increased from an annual average of 15 percent between 1940 and 1946, to 21 percent between 1947 and 1951. After 1952, inflation continued to increase, reaching record levels of 56 percent in 1953 and 84 percent in 1955 (Faundez 1988:55).

The main factor causing inflation was the inefficiency of the agricultural sector. The sharp fluctuations in earnings from copper exports after 1945 considerably worsened the situation. Unable to control the economy, President González (1946–52) began to increasingly resort to repression, with the result that during his administration the country was in a state of emergency for nearly half of his term of office. The main target of repression was the union movement in urban and mining areas, as well as agricultural workers seeking to form unions. Persistent reliance on emergency measures eroded the legitimacy of the regime and the credibility of the party system. Indeed, because presidents did not have stable backing in the congress, they were often forced to implement policies diametrically opposed to those on which they had been elected. Thus, President Aguirre, who was elected on a platform that promised political rights and better standards of living for the working class and the poor, ended up reaffirming a policy that denied basic political and trade union rights to agricultural workers. Likewise, President González, also elected on a left-wing platform and with the enthusiastic support of communists, soon abandoned his political program and put forward legislation that repressed the union movement, prolonged the exclusion of agricultural workers from the political system, and outlawed its main ally, the Communist Party (Blasier 1950:371–373). Given these circumstances, it is not surprising that, by the early 1950s, the Radical Party, hitherto the traditional leader of electoral coalitions, was unable to persuade any of the other major parties to form an alliance for the presidential elections to come. These circumstances provided an opportunity for the indefatigable General Ibáñez to make a successful bid for the presidency on a populist platform that promised a strong government that would forever rid the country of the scourge of politics.

Market Failure and Political Liberalization

The weakness and fragmentation of the political parties that brought coalition politics to an end also shattered the broad consensus on economic policy. Thus, during the 1950s two successive administrations sought to shift the economy toward the market. But, in the absence of a broad political consensus, these efforts encountered multiple obstacles. The tight incomes policy that accompanied market-based policies was strongly resisted by the parties of the left and by the union movement. Indeed, the struggle for higher wages contributed to strengthening of the union movement and galvanizing of the solidarity between blue- and white-collar workers. The shift toward the market failed also because it did not have firm support from the business community. While industrialists dreaded the consequences of an open commercial policy, landowners did not even contemplate the possibility of modernizing their activities and working under market discipline. The strong resistance to market-orientated policies was met partly by repression, but largely by measures of liberalization that included lifting restrictions on union activities and electoral reform. Under the shadow of an ailing economy political liberalization had the effect of radicalizing the electorate. Thus, by the early 1960s support for the right-wing parties had plummeted and the overwhelming majority of the electorate supported the center parties and left-wing parties that advocated radical change. Political change, however, was no longer achievable through the system of coalitions that had characterized party democracy.

Neutralizing Populism

By 1952, political and economic conditions had seriously deteriorated: social tension was high and inflation was rapidly eroding income gains. That the political system managed to avert a major crisis was, ironically, largely due to General Carlos Ibáñez. Relying on the same rhetoric that he used in the 1920s, he vowed to eliminate political corruption, sectarianism, and inefficiency, all evils that he attributed to the prevailing system of party democracy. His electoral campaign caught the public imagination, enabling him to win a decisive victory with 47 percent of the vote, and thus marking the end of the electoral hegemony enjoyed by the Radical Party since 1938. His administration was erratic, somewhat corrupt and, often, showed little concern for the principle of legality. Yet, it provided an outlet for the political ambitions of the military, thus helping to preempt military intervention. In this way, the Ibáñez administration greatly contributed, albeit inadvertently, to strengthening of the political system and to legitimization of the constitution.

During the 1940s, the military became restless as successive administrations resorted to emergency measures that placed public order in the hands of the armed forces. While reliance on the military provided a guarantee that presidents would not abuse their power, it also had the effect of reinforcing the view within the military that politicians could not be trusted to run the country. Thus, it is not surprising that, after Ibáñez's electoral victory, two political movements emerged from within the military: *Por un Mañana Auspicioso*, PUMA (For a Better Tomorrow) and *Línea Recta* (Straight Line). PUMA came into existence immediately after Ibáñez's victory. Its objective was to ensure that the congress ratified the General's victory. *Línea Recta* was established late in 1954 (Joxe 1970:80–81). Its objective was to ensure that the government did not depart from the nationalist principles on which it had been elected (Loveman and Lira 2000:154–155). *Línea Recta* and PUMA were not rivals. Their membership overlapped and consisted mainly of middle-ranking and senior military officers. These two organizations attracted remarkably little political attention despite the fact that under the constitution members of the armed forces were barred from engaging in any form of political deliberation. It was not until 1956 that serious questions were raised in the congress about the constitutional propriety of these organizations (Loveman and Lira 2000:178). The reticence of politicians to openly question the political activities of military officers reflects to some extent the weakness of the party system during the early years of the Ibáñez administration.

Yet, their reticence could also be attributed to the fact that Ibáñez used these organizations to underpin the constitutional legitimacy of his government, thus directly contributing to strengthening of the democratic process. Although there is little doubt that most members PUMA and *Línea Recta*, as well as many of Ibáñez's civilian supporters, would have preferred a military government, Ibáñez was unwilling to abandon the democratic road. His electoral victory was political vindication after his humiliation in 1931 when, after the collapse of his government, he was forced to flee the country. Moreover, when Ibáñez was elected he was 75 years old and unlikely to have any interest in overturning the constitution that he had so enthusiastically supported in 1925.

Ibáñez, however, took good care of the interests of the military. Indeed, during his administration military officers were appointed to key cabinet posts, including defense, interior, foreign affairs, economics, education, labor, and public works. Retired military officers were also appointed as ambassadors and to other public posts, such as the major of Santiago. These appointments were part of a calculated effort by Ibáñez to neutralize the political ferment within the armed forces (Fernández 1996:241–245, 253).

In Search of the Market

Ibáñez soon abandoned his populist stance. Chronic inflation and low levels of economic growth were the reasons why he diverted from his original objectives. His administration thus concentrated on fighting inflation by means of a market-oriented policy that sought to liberalize the economy and reduce excessive state intervention. After experimenting with a variety of economic measures, he put forward a comprehensive stabilization program that called for drastic cuts in public expenditure, substantial liberalization of foreign trade, major increases in the levels of taxation, and an overall reduction of state intervention in the economy. But his attempt to tackle inflation through economic liberalization was supported neither by the private sector nor by the unions (Ffrench-Davis 1973:29–35). Landowners resisted attempts to impose realistic levels of taxation on agricultural enterprises, while industrialists deeply resented the withdrawal of state subsidies. Unions also strongly resisted Ibáñez's stabilization program, as it restricted employment opportunities and increased direct and indirect taxes (Sierra 1969:61–71).

Popular resistance against market-based policies prompted a brief strategic alliance in the congress between the Marxist parties and the

Christian Democratic Party (CDP). This alliance led to the repeal of the 1948 State Security Act, thus lifting the ban on the Communist Party and easing state control over union activities. It also brought about a major electoral reform that made vote buying more difficult. These changes had the effect of breaking the landowners' stronghold in rural areas, thus enabling the CDP and the Marxist parties to mobilize voters in the countryside. The cumulative effect of these changes brought about a sharp increase in electoral registrations, rising from 18 percent in 1952 to 21 percent in 1958 and 35 percent in 1964 (Borón 1971b:47, 51). Political liberalization did not, however, prevent efforts to stabilize and liberalize the economy. They continued under Jorge Alessandri's administration (1958–64). Alessandri, son of Arturo, and prominent businessman, also ran on an antiparty platform. During the first half of his administration, he excluded political parties from any involvement in the appointment of his cabinet. Alessandri did not, however, seek to eliminate the party system. After all, although he ran as an independent, he was the candidate of the right-wing parties, and both he and members of his family had close links with the Liberal Party. According to Alessandri, the economic problems affecting the country had their origin in the misconceived interventionist policies of the 1940s. Accordingly, his objective was not to eliminate politics or politicians, but to reorient the state so that it could play a positive role in the economy. His aim was to ensure that state intervention would further market relations rather than undermine them. He wanted politicians to take seriously the constraints imposed by the market economy on the policy process. That is why he refused to allow political parties any involvement in the appointment of his cabinet, insisting, instead, that his cabinet would be made up of technically qualified individuals, rather than people whose sole qualification was their membership in a political party. The Conservative and Liberal Parties accepted this departure from practice with some reluctance. In any event, all the ministers appointed by Alessandri were prominent professionals or leading business managers with close links to one or the other right-wing parties.

Alessandri's technocratic approach to governance proved unsustainable. By mid-term, as his market-oriented reforms began to flounder, he was forced to seek support from the Radical Party in exchange for cabinet posts; thus he momentarily revived the style of coalition politics that had prevailed in the 1940s. His economic policy sought to release the market from excessive state intervention and to keep inflation under control. Accordingly, he introduced a strict incomes policy and after slightly increasing public investment to reactivate the economy, he sharply reduced tariff barriers, introduced incentives to promote exports, and enacted a new foreign investment code. His expectation was that trade liberalization would improve the competitiveness of domestic firms and would stimulate investment. He also expected foreign investment and foreign loans to further stimulate the economy. His expectations, however, did not materialize: imports grew faster than expected and foreign investors did not respond to the new liberal regime. Moreover, as inflation once again ran out of control, he had to abandon his strict incomes policy. Thus, by the end of his administration the rate of inflation stood at 45 percent, that is, 12 percent higher than when he took office in 1958; foreign direct investment did not significantly increase, yet foreign debt trebled; and, contrary to his expectations, the share of the state in public investment increased (Ffrench-Davis 1973:48–50; Stallings 1978:88).

Discredit of the Market

The attempt to shift the economy toward the market was unsuccessful. During the 1950s, GDP per capita grew at an annual average of 1 percent, that is half of the average rate of the 1940s. Moreover, during the second half of the decade industrial production registered negative growth rates, while the agricultural sector was still unable to satisfy the demand for foodstuffs. Export revenue also registered disappointing levels of growth, and expectations of massive new investment in mining were not fulfilled. In addition, while inflation was kept within manageable levels, its underlying causes were not eradicated. The failure of these policies discredited the market and had a major impact in shaping political options.

One of the shortcomings of the market-based policies implemented in the 1950s was that they excluded the agricultural sector. Indeed, it is remarkable that Alessandri's administration did nothing to liberalize the agricultural sector despite its commitment to the market. Thus, it is not surprising that agricultural production continued its steady decline while the import bill for foodstuffs consistently rose. In 1956 food imports were 9 percent of total imports, by 1962 their share on the import bill had risen to 22 percent (Mamalakis 1976:131).

Alessandri's neglect of agriculture stemmed largely from the fact that large landowners were unwilling to exchange state protection for the uncertainty of market forces. In the early 1950s, landowners had fiercely resisted Ibáñez's attempt to introduce market discipline. Therefore, not surprisingly, Alessandri did not wish to antagonize them. During the second half of his administration, and in response to pressure from the Alliance for Progress, a U.S.-sponsored foreign-aid program, he timidly began to take steps toward addressing some of the problems of the agricultural sector. One of the most pressing problems was land concentration, which ranked as one of the highest in the world. In 1955, 4 percent of landholders owned 81 percent of all farmland, while a large number of smallholders (*minifundistas*) barely scraped a living on 2 percent of irrigated land (Thiesenhusen 1966:10). The scope of Alessandri's land reform was, however, limited. It envisaged the expropriation of agricultural properties that had either been abandoned or were so poorly exploited that they could be deemed abandoned. Yet, despite its limited scope, landowners strongly opposed Alessandri's land reform. The powerful *Sociedad Nacional de Agricultura* (SNA) objected to the bill, especially to the clause that allowed for deferred compensation in the event of expropriation. The *Consorcio Agrícola del Sur* (CAS), another influential association of landowners, also objected to the deferred compensation clause, claiming that it was a first step toward the abolition of property rights (Kaufman 1972:64–66).

Alessandri's land reform was approved by the congress, but only after a bitter debate that exposed serious differences within the private sector and created considerable tension between the right-wing parties and the business community. The Conservative and Liberal Parties were aware that, unless there was some change in the countryside, they would become politically irrelevant (Kaufmann 1972:60–61). They supported Alessandri's bill as a necessary evil. Landowners were naturally disappointed, and many felt that this was an unacceptable betrayal by their right-wing allies. But landowners also had a grudge against the associations representing industrialists as the latter had refused to join them in their campaign against the agrarian reform bill. They blamed Alessandri for this lack of solidarity as he had at one time been president of a leading association of industrialists, the *Confederación de la Producción y del Comercio*. Thus, by the end of the Alessandri administration, relations between the business community and right-wing political parties reached an all time low (Pereira 1994:278–280). The Alessandri administration thus succeeded in discrediting the market and seriously denting the political base of the right-wing parties.

Labor and the Political Process

The role of organized labor in the political process is generally regarded as one of the most distinctive features of the period of party democracy. Indeed, many observers regard the incorporation of organized workers into the political system as one of the main factors that contributed to the consolidation of democracy after 1932 (Rueschemeyer et al. 1992:184–185). While the prominence of the union movement during this process is undeniable, their incorporation into the political process was only partial. Unions were both courted and severely repressed. In 1938 they were part of government; ten years later repressive legislation imposed severe restrictions on workers' freedom of association. But the union movement was resilient, as evidenced by the fact that in the 1950s it became once again an important actor in the political process. This section examines the contradictory roles of the union movement during the years when party democracy prevailed.

Denial of Rights to Agricultural Workers

Advances in the process of democratization during this period were largely offset by the persistent refusal to extend rights to agricultural workers. This refusal was largely a consequence of the inordinate power and influence of the landed oligarchy. The historical record shows that large landowners, supported by the Conservative and Liberal Parties, strongly opposed extending constitutional and legal rights to agricultural workers. But landowners and right-wing parties were not alone in the stance they took. Indeed this policy had the support, albeit grudging, of the coalition governments in which the Radical Party and the Marxist parties were partners. Thus, the exclusion and repression of agricultural workers cannot be easily divorced from the wider process that led to the consolidation of democracy. The following paragraphs offer a brief overview of the various stratagems used to deny rights to agricultural workers.

The first attempt to organize rural workers took place in the early 1920s under the leadership of FOCH, the powerful confederation of manufacturing and mining workers. It found a receptive audience, particularly among rural workers in parts of the Central Valley close to mining sites (Affonso et al. 1970:1:17). Alarmed by these developments the SNA requested Arturo Alessandri, in May 1921, to take measures to stop FOCH's activities. Alessandri's response was ambiguous. It reaffirmed his administration's commitment to law and order in the countryside, but reminded landowners of the need to improve social and economic conditions of rural workers (Wright 1982:149). The landowners, who feared that FOCH activities in the countryside would create a powerful alliance between urban and rural workers, did not heed the president's plea. Instead, taking the law into their own hands, they used force against peasants who sought to form unions. Despite this, the number of agricultural workers belonging to unions reached 5,000 in 1925. By the late 1920s, however, military intervention and political repression brought this phase of agricultural unionization to an end (Wright 1982:149).

The unionization of agricultural workers acquired new impetus in the 1930s, during Arturo Alessandri's second administration. In accordance with the provisions of the just then enacted Labor Code, agricultural workers began to register new unions. The Ministry of Labor, complying with the provisions of the Code, registered these unions. Although the number of unions was small, the registration process was sufficiently widespread to prompt serious concern among landowners. Once again, the SNA requested the government to immediately stop the registration process, claiming it was illegal. The government's legal advisors disagreed as, in their view, the Labor Code authorized the unionization of all workers, including agricultural workers, in enterprises employing more than 25 persons (Affonso 1972:45). The president, however, disregarding the views of his minister and legal advisors, instructed the Ministry of Labor to suspend union registrations. As unions could not be legally established without government intervention, the president's order effectively denied the right of unionization to more than one-third of the country's labor force.

This misguided policy was reaffirmed and further developed by Presidents Aguirre (1938–41), Ríos (1942–46), and González (1946–52). On the surface, it seems surprising that Aguirre should have given in to the landowners' demands. After all, the Popular Front coalition had been elected on a platform that envisaged improving conditions in the agricultural sector. Yet, Aguirre's policy is not surprising, as the prevailing governance pact protected the interests of landowners. The issue of the unionization of agricultural workers did not, however, disappear from the political agenda. It was revived in 1946 when the Communist Party, as a member of the coalition that had supported the González administration, spearheaded a new drive to organize agricultural workers. The president, however, once again gave in to the landowners, brought the process to an end, and shortly thereafter expelled the communists from government (Carrière 1981:41–164). In 1947, he introduced legislation to regulate the unionization of agricultural workers. This new law, presented as a device to promote unionization, had the opposite effect. It imposed strict conditions on the establishment and operation of unions. Agricultural unions could be established only in enterprises employing more than 20 workers. Union members had to be over 18 years of age, in employment at the relevant enterprise for more than 1 year, and at least 10 of the would-be members had to be literate. The requirement that unions could be established only in estates employing more than 20 workers effectively excluded more than 85 percent of agricultural workers. Moreover, the literacy requirement was also a serious obstacle to unionization, as illiteracy in rural areas was about 35 percent. The law also included provisions that prohibited strikes and required compulsory arbitration. Given the features of this law, it is not surprising that, during its 17 years in force, only 24 agricultural unions were established, of which less than half were able to carry out their function (Affonso 1972:53–55). Discrimination against agricultural workers continued for 20 years more, until 1967, when the law finally acknowledged that, under the constitution, they had the same rights as workers in other sectors of the economy.

Overcoming Labor Regulation

Workers in the manufacturing and mining industries and in the public sector fared better than agricultural workers. Nonetheless, they had to contend with labor regulation that had been especially designed to discourage the exercise of union rights. As explained in the preceding chapter, the rules on unions, collective bargaining, and strikes suggest that the main objective of the Labor Code was to contain and fragment the labor movement. A special concern of labor legislation was to ensure that unions concentrated solely on representing the interests of their members and did not become involved in politics. In practice, the consequences of labor law were mixed: while on the one hand, the law undoubtedly contributed to shaping union structures and practices, on the other, it was unable to prevent the emergence of a highly politicized union movement.

The relatively low levels of unionization during this period are partly attributable to the restrictive provisions of the Labor Code. Indeed, until the early 1960s, the rate of unionization stood at only 10 percent of the workforce. It was only between 1965 and 1973 that the rate of unionization sharply increased, first to 20 percent in 1970 and then to 30 percent in 1973 (Sader 1973:37). The Code required a minimum of 25 workers for the establishment of plant unions and prohibited the creation of unions across enterprises or in the public sector. Despite these restrictive provisions, workers who were not formally allowed to form unions did establish organizations, which, though legally not unions, performed the same functions and were acknowledged as genuine representatives of their members' interests. Such was the case of the association of white-collar municipal workers, the association of blue-collar municipal workers, the association of central government employees, and the association of public sector workers (U.S. Department of Labor 1969:33). Likewise, the Code's provisions prohibiting the establishment of labor federations and confederations were also ignored. National labor confederations were some of the oldest institutions of the labor movement. The first national federation of unions, the FOCH, was established in 1909, long before the law even acknowledged the existence of unions. In 1936 another labor confederation was established, the CTCH, and finally in 1953, yet another confederation, the *Central Unica de Trabajadores* (CUT), emerged. All these national confederations played a major role in national politics, although, under the terms of the Code, they were illegal. The CTCH was a member of the Popular Front coalition. The CUT, for its part, acquired enormous political influence as it represented about 75 percent of unionized workers (U.S. Department of Labor 1969:33). It should be noted that many of the unions affiliated to the CUT were also illegal, as was the case of the association of central government employees and the association of public sector workers. The Code's elaborate provisions on strikes also proved ineffective as they were so complex and formalistic that, in practice, they were largely ignored. Indeed, as more than 50 percent of strikes were illegal, the distinction between legal and illegal strikes became meaningless (Ietswaart 1978:292–293; Loveman 1979:266).

The Labor Code's objective of depoliticizing the union movement was further undermined by the interplay between the limited the scope of its provisions on collective bargaining and the governments' attempts to take tough measures to control inflation. Indeed, as unions at the local level virtually had no bargaining power or capacity to press for wage increases, they naturally sought the assistance of other unions and political parties. Thus, the limited scope of the collective bargaining system operating within a highly inflationary context had the effect of instantly transforming local demands into national struggles, for it was at the national level that union leaders could find solution to their demands for higher wages (Angell 1972:36; Barrera 1979:40; Morris 1966:18–19). The politicization of wage demands served to reinforce the political prominence of the CUT during the late 1950s and throughout the 1960s.

Unions and Political Parties

While some of the provisions of the Labor Code had the unintended effect of politicizing the union movement, the political prominence of unions during the late 1930s and early 1940s was largely due to their close links with the Marxist parties. These links date back to 1917, when the Communist Party, known at the time as the Socialist Workers' Party (*Partido Obrero Socialista*), took over the leadership of the FOCH. Shortly thereafter, the FOCH issued a manifesto calling for the abolition of capitalism (Angell 1972:59). During the first Ibáñez administration (1926–31), the FOCH was severely repressed as the government sought to break the ties between the unions and political activists, especially Marxists. By 1931, when the Ibáñez administration collapsed, FOCH membership had plummeted from nearly 80,000 in the mid-1920s, to a few thousand members (Valenzuela 1979:567).

In the early 1930s, the reconstitution of the labor movement began in earnest, and, by 1936, the Socialist and Communist Parties joined forces to support the establishment of the CTCH, which became a member of the Popular Front coalition, and, for all practical purposes, was an extension of the Marxist parties. Thus, when the Popular Front coalition won the elections of 1938, communists and socialists could convincingly claim that working-class support for the new government was largely due to their tight control over the CTCH. The close relationship between the CTCH and the Marxist parties gave their leaders some influence on policy decisions, especially during the early days of the Aguirre administration (1938–41). Yet, on balance, this relationship had disastrous consequences for the labor movement. Although unionization in the 1940s amounted to only 10 percent of the workforce, the CTCH represented the vast majority of organized workers. Its political influence was thus crucial, especially because it represented the powerful unions in the mining and manufacturing sectors. This influence was magnified, as at the time, the number of unionized workers was high in relation to the size of the electorate. In the 1940s, while the number of registered voters was roughly half a million, total union membership was 250,000. Thus, through their control of the CTCH, the Marxist parties had a solid electoral base that made them attractive partners in government coalitions. This fact was candidly acknowledged by President González (1946–52), not long before he launched a major repression against the union movement (Urzúa 1968:151). On balance, however, the close relationship between the CTCH and the Marxist parties was negative. Bitter competition between communists and socialists over the leadership of the labor movement, as well as over their respective roles in coalition governments, contaminated the union movement. In 1946, this rivalry brought about the division of the CTCH into two confederations, one controlled by the communists and the other by the socialists

(Drake 1978:279–281). Thus, only ten years after the establishment of the CTCH, the unity of the labor movement was shattered, leaving workers with no effective organ to voice their interests.

The labor movement soon recovered from the debacle of the late 1940s. After patient work, done largely by white-collar workers, the labor movement came together in 1953 under the umbrella of a new confederation, the CUT. Leaders of the CUT had been at the fore-front of workers' struggles at a time when internal divisions paralyzed the Socialist Party and the Communist Party was severely restricted by the legal ban. The undisputed union leader at the time was Clotario Blest, a devout Catholic and a fiercely independent white-collar worker. Having learned a bitter lesson from the 1940s upheaval, Blest was determined that unions should not be used to further the electoral ambitions of any political party. Initially, his determination to keep political parties at arm's length proved successful. Eventually, how-ever, the Communist and Socialist Parties managed to remove Blest from office and thus, once again, the interests of the union movement were subordinated to the interests of the political parties.

Ironically, when the communists and socialists reasserted control over the movement their objective was to curb the radicalism of the CUT. Indeed, after narrowly losing out on winning the presidency in 1958, the Marxist parties became aware that CUT radicalism would undermine their bid for the presidency in 1964. Yet, for the Marxist parties getting rid of Blest was easy, they soon discovered they were no longer the only political force among organized workers. In the past, the Radical Party had gladly played the role of the center party with-out attempting to challenge the influence of Marxist parties among workers in mining and manufacturing. In the early 1960s, however, they faced the challenge of the CDP, a party determined to change the mould of politics and to create its own base among organized workers and the urban poor. The challenge posed by the CDP disconcerted the Marxist parties and prompted an interesting and unusual public debate between the leadership of the Socialist and Communist Parties (Halperin 1965:144–158). The communists were keen to include the CDP into a broad political alliance for social and economic reform. The socialists were strongly opposed to any form of alliance with the CDP on the ground that it was a bourgeois party firmly on the side of capitalism and, as such, uninterested in pursuing meaningful social and economic change. Underlying their opposition was their awareness that an alliance would be led by the CDP and that they would be rele-gated to a subordinate position. But beyond electoral calculations, the Marxist parties were threatened by the CDP because of its enormous popular appeal and its determination to undermine their influence within the labor movement.

End of Party Democracy

Consequences of Electoral Mobilization

Party democracy brought about a large expansion of the electorate. From 1932 to 1964, the electorate expanded from 10 percent of the population (half a million people) to 35 percent (just under three million) (Borón 1971b:47, 51). A major factor accounting for this increase was the extension of the vote to women. The liberals of the nineteenth century had completely neglected the political rights of women. Worse, in 1884, as liberals sought guarantees to ensure the secrecy of the vote, they endorsed a law explicitly excluding women from voting. This is the situation that prevailed until 1935, when women were given the vote, but only in municipal elections. It was not until 1949 that the legislature finally extended full voting rights to women (Borón 1971a:409).

The belated recognition of political equality places the achievements of the period of party democracy in perspective and also contradicts the view that the period of coalition governments constituted the heyday of democracy. The late extension of political rights to women is revealing of cultural mores as the provisions of the 1925 constitution on the right to vote were gender-neutral. Given the political influence acquired by unions between 1938 and 1949, the exclusion of women during this period is astonishing as, throughout the time that working-class organizations were struggling to establish a political identity, women had been actively involved in the emerging union movement. By 1912, one-third of factory workers in Santiago were women. They actively participated in strike action and belonged to unions affiliated to the FOCH (Hutchinson 2001:5, 47, 67, 74–76; Lavrin 1989). It thus seems that while male-dominated unions were willing to support women's struggles at the union level, they had no interest in helping them secure the extension of the franchise. At the wider political level the Marxist parties also neglected women's rights (Rosenblatt 2001). Indeed, as the political strength of the Marxist parties was largely determined by their influence within the union movement, they neglected electoral mobilization altogether. In fact, during the time that the Marxist parties were active in government coalitions, the size of the electorate declined from 10 percent of the population in 1938 to 9 percent in 1949 (Borón 1971b:51). The expansion of the electorate began only after the extension of the franchise to women in 1949 and acquired new impetus after the electoral reforms of 1957.

Electoral registration of women proceeded slowly. The proportion of eligible women that actually registered to vote rose slowly during the 1950s, from 27 percent in 1952, to only 42 percent in 1961. It was only in 1964 when mobilization intensified, that 77 percent of women eligible to vote registered and 74 percent of those who were registered exercised their rights (Borón 1971a:429). The main party promoting the registration of women was the CDP. The Marxist parties were slow to respond, as they feared that women would support the traditional parties. Their fears were not groundless. In 1952, most women supported the populist alternative offered by Carlos Ibáñez. In 1958 and then again in 1964, the majority of women voted in favor of Alessandri and Eduardo Frei, respectively. It was only after 1964, that the Marxist parties managed to get a respectable share of women's vote.

A Divided Majority

The main beneficiaries of the expansion of the electorate were the CDP and the two Marxist parties. Alessandri's electoral victory in 1958 in fact marked the electoral decline of the right-wing parties By the late 1950s, the right-wing parties represented less than one-third of the electorate, while, on the eve of the 1964 presidential elections, the combined electoral strength of the CDP and Marxist parties was easily more than half of the electorate. The massive swing to the left raised fears among right-wing parties that Salvador Allende, the perennial Marxist candidate, would win the presidency. To avert this possibility, they attempted to form an electoral alliance with the ailing Radical Party, which had moved to the right after being displaced from the center by the CDP. Yet, the continuous electoral growth of the Marxist left, particularly in rural areas, caused such panic among Conservatives and Liberals that they abruptly terminated their alliance with the Radical Party, and sought instead an alliance with the CDP. Even though Eduardo Frei, the CDP candidate, unequivocally rejected the offer, the right–wing parties ordered their members to unconditionally support him. Thus, the fear of Marxism forced the right-wing parties to take a humiliating decision that would have been unthinkable in the early days of party democracy.

The right-wing parties' decision to unconditionally support the CDP proved disastrous. As predicted by Francisco Bulnes, a prominent Conservative Party member who had opposed the decision, the right-wing parties lost the loyalty of their traditional supporters (Pereira 1994:282). Indeed, in the congressional elections of 1965, the electoral support of the Conservative and Liberal Parties was reduced to 5 percent and 8 percent, respectively, thus virtually wiping out their representation in the congress. These bleak electoral prospects led to the dissolution of these parties and to the creation of a new party, the National Party, which included former right-wing supporters and an assortment of Far Right nationalist groups that in the past had supported Ibáñez.

As the electoral strength of the Right declined, support for the CDP and the Communist and the Socialist Parties increased sharply. This trend suggests that there might emerge a reform-minded coalition of parties that would finally tackle the persistent economic problems that previous administrations had failed to resolve. This expectation was not altogether unreasonable, as the two Marxist parties and the CDP drew inspiration for their economic policies from the same source: the United Nations Economic Commission for Latin America and the Caribbean. They both agreed that purely market-based economic policies would not resolve the country's economic problems. They also agreed that the persistent inflationary process was caused by a structural imbalance within the economy. Accordingly, they called for the modernization of the agricultural sector through an agrarian reform that would significantly restructure property relations in the countryside and at the same time would recognize the political and social rights of agricultural workers. They also believed that the state should have a greater involvement in the production and marketing of copper in order to secure a fairer and more stable share of revenue from copper exports. Their expectation was that the reform of the agricultural sector would generate sufficient financial resources to revive the economy. Both Marxist parties and the CDP also called for a substantial redistribution of income to expand the domestic market and to bring about greater social justice. Yet, despite the policy convergence, relations between the Marxist parties and the CDP seriously deteriorated, and by the early 1960s they were involved in a persistent feud. In addition to competition for organized workers, two other factors conspired to divide them. One was the hostility of the Catholic Church toward Marxism. As it regarded Marxism as an atheist ideology, it was difficult, if not impossible, for Catholic parties to form alliances with Marxist parties, and even to vote for a Marxist candidate. Indeed, it was only in the late 1960s, when a group of left-wing parliamentarians resigned from the CDP, that Catholics began to feel free from political alliances with Marxists (Smith 1982:126–178).

The other, and more lasting, reason that kept the progressive parties divided was the covert intervention by the United States in the electoral process. At the time, the United States' main policy objective in the region was to isolate Castro's Cuba. Hence, the possibility that a Marxist should win the presidential elections in Chile was a source of serious concern. Therefore, Washington had a strong interest in adding fuel to the fire of of dispute between the CDP and the Marxist parties. Thus, during the 1964 presidential elections, the United States covertly financed a campaign in the local media, depicting Salvador Allende as undemocratic and as a puppet of the Soviet Union (Hersh 1982). Although Eduardo Frei, the CDP candidate denied having had any involvement in this campaign, he benefited from it, as it enabled him to win the election by a comfortable margin. Not surprisingly, when Frei took office in 1964 relations between the CDP and the Marxist parties became bitter and were to deteriorate even further over the subsequent nine years.

Conclusion

Consensus on economic policy in the late 1930s made possible the consolidation of party democracy. Although initially neither the right- nor the left-wing parties were fervent democrats, by the early 1960s, the authority and legitimacy of the constitution was beyond dispute. But the consensus on economic policy had serious limitations. It did not address the inefficient and socially backward agricultural sector and it restricted workers in the exercise of their rights. Consequently, the political system remained static from 1932 to 1952. Moreover, while the consensus on economic policy was successful in securing political stability, it was not so in promoting economic growth or even in containing inflation. By the early 1950s, party democracy was in disarray. It was rescued, albeit unintentionally, by Carlos Ibáñez, who, capitalizing on widespread popular discontent, managed to keep the constitutional system alive. The economic crisis diverted Ibáñez from his populist objectives and paved the way for two successive attempts to implement market-based economic policies. These policies failed, as they were resisted by the unions, center and left-wing parties, and even by prominent members of the private sector. Because attempts to implement these policies were accompanied by the progressive liberalization of a political system that had significantly expanded the electorate and lifted restrictions on trade union activities, a process of political radicalization began to take place. It crushed the electoral support of the right-wing parties and transformed the CDP and the

Marxist parties into dominant players within the party system. Thus, by the early 1960s the party system had undergone a major transformation. Political parties were focused in their objectives, and their ideologies were coherent. But they had also become more rigid and unwilling to form broad electoral coalitions. The union movement, for its part, was united, but the political parties had again asserted control over their leadership, and its independence was under threat. Business associations, which in the early days of the Popular Front had embraced the consensus on economic policy, were rapidly losing faith in the ability of the party system to represent their interests. Moreover, they were divided as the modest agrarian reform law enacted during the final days of the Alessandri administration had exposed serious divisions within the private sector. It was thus that, by 1964, party democracy gave way to radical democracy.

Chapter 5

Governance and Accountability

Introduction

Governance had some peculiar features under party democracy. The framers of the constitution intended to establish a strong presidential regime. In practice, however, the regime that emerged was a hybrid between presidentialism and parliamentarism, in which the political parties had a say in the making and unmaking of cabinets. Yet, although the autonomy of the president was significantly curtailed, there was, at the same time, a dramatic expansion of the regulatory powers of the executive in all areas of public policy, especially in matters concerning economic regulation. The expansion of the powers of the executive, however, was not done exclusively by the president. It was largely the outcome of concerted action by the president and the congress. Moreover, this process was carried out with little or no concern for the constitution or legal procedures, thus belying the general perception that legality was one of the main attributes of governance under party democracy.

The objective of this chapter is to unravel the maze of these seemingly contradictory features. The first section explains how the political parties tamed presidentialism and why, despite the enormous expansion of executive power, leading politicians believed that the office of the president needed further strengthening. The second section examines the process that led to the expansion of executive powers in the areas of price controls and state security. The final section focuses on the legality review procedure administered by the Office of the Comptroller General (*Contraloría*) and explains how it came to be regarded as an effective restraint on the exercise of executive power.

Taming Presidentialism

Reviving Parliamentarism

The main objective of the drafters of the 1925 constitution was to establish a strong presidential regime, based on the 1833 constitution. Accordingly, executive power was vested in the president, who was the head of government and chief administrative authority. The president was elected for a six-year period by direct popular election and he or she could not stand for reelection. Cabinet members were appointed by the president and were directly accountable to him. They could not be removed by the congress on political grounds. Members of the congress were not allowed to hold cabinet posts, and this emphasized their independence from the executive. The regime established by the constitution was thus unambiguously presidential. In practice, however, the party system transformed it into a hybrid that had many features of the old parliamentary republic.

Political parties during this period had a say in the composition and stability of cabinets. Members of political parties could not be appointed to the cabinet without the agreement of their party. Likewise, they could remain in office only as long as their parties supported the government. An early acknowledgment that presidents could not afford to ignore the views of the parties in the congress came from none other than President Arturo Alessandri, who, in the 1920s, had been a leading proponent of presidentialism. Addressing the congress in 1936, he admitted that, although the constitution gave him exclusive power to choose his cabinet without intervention by the congress, his administration had always sought to ensure that those appointed to the cabinet were acceptable to the parties controlling the majority of seats in the congress "as if we still lived under a parliamentary regime" (Donoso 1976:336). Alessandri's approach was adopted and further developed by the Aguirre, Ríos, and Gonzalez administrations. Initially, President Aguirre tried to assert his constitutional prerogative to appoint and remove ministers, but he did not have the support from his own party. Thus, in the end, after the Radical Party instructed its members to withdraw from the cabinet, President Aguirre had no choice but to accept their resignations. President Ríos, who was more concerned with the survival of his administration than with the integrity of the presidential regime, actively sought the support of political parties in exchange for cabinet posts. His views on the matter are clearly expressed in his statement to the congress: "I hope for and expect the support of all political parties and I am willing in exchange to acknowledge such support with posts in the cabinet" (Ríos 1943:iv).

President González followed a similar policy. Indeed as he had only obtained plurality of the vote and it fell upon the congress to choose between him and the runner-up, he was forced to do a deal with the Liberal Party. In exchange for their support in the congress, the Liberals were given three cabinet posts (Loveman 1976:124).

The intense participation of political parties in the making and unmaking of cabinets undoubtedly contributed to the invigoration of the system of coalition politics. However, it also brought about permanent cabinet instability that significantly weakened the role of the president within the political system (Abbott 1951:450–451). Between 1942 and 1952, cabinets lasted an average of six months. The Aguirre administration (1938–41) had 44 ministers, the Ríos administration (1942–45) had 84, the González administration (1946–52) had 73, and the Ibáñez administration (1952–58) had 75 (Valenzuela 1994:128). The mindless tussle for cabinet posts also brought about a dangerous fragmentation of the parties. The prize of a seat in the cabinet encouraged dissident factions in every major party to set up miniscule parties. Factionalism was encouraged and promoted by the president of the day, who generally rewarded leaders of small factions with cabinet posts. However, their period in office was invariably brief, as coalitions were shaky and splinter groups in other parties were ready to replace the incumbents. Thus, cabinet instability and the fragmentation of the party system seemed to go hand in hand.

Demanding a Stronger President

As the party democracy period drew to a close, the perception of leading politicians was that the executive was weak and that if improvements in the quality of governance were to be made, a fundamental redesign of the office of the presidency was required. This perception is surprising, given that in the 1940s—as explained in the section that follows—an enormous concentration of power on the executive had been taking place. It seems, however, that what lent credence to this perception were the disappointing results of the economic policies implemented in the 1950s and the surge of popular mobilization in the early 1960s. Thus, reflecting the view that not all was well with governance, Jorge Alessandri, just before leaving office, submitted to the congress a constitutional amendment designed to strengthen the powers of the president (Alessandri 1964). Although the amendment stood no chance of approval and was, in fact, not approved, it provided Alessandri with the opportunity to formally express his opinion about the weaknesses of the political system. This amendment merits attention, not only because it contains Alessandri's views, but also because his views were shared by Eduardo Frei, his successor. Indeed, shortly after taking office in 1964, Frei proposed a constitutional amendment—which was also later rejected—that in many respects was similar to Alessandri's proposal (Frei 1964).

The constitutional amendments proposed by the two presidents were in agreement on the fundamental point that it was necessary to strengthen the powers of the president in order to revitalize the political system. According to Alessandri, the office of the presidency had to be strengthened because only presidents were capable of safeguarding the interests of the nation as they had a proper perspective on the common good of the nation. The congress, according to Alessandri, lacked such perspective because petty regional interests dominated it. Alessandri also believed that it was indispensable to strengthen the powers of the president in order to contain and channel the growing demands for social and economic change (Alessandri 1964:1158). Frei, who in 1964 was about to launch a massive program of social and economic reforms, shared Alessandri's view that it was necessary to strengthen presidential powers. However, his objective was different. He regarded a strong presidency as indispensable, not to contain, but effectively to respond to demands for social and economic change. Indeed, what Frei sought was a mechanism that would provide incoming administrations with broad powers to implement their political programs, thus circumventing delay and obstruction by the congress (Frei 1964:280). Thus, Alessandri and Frei agreed, albeit for different reasons, on the need to shift the balance of power in favor of the president.

The argument in favor of strengthening the presidency was based on the view that the congress consistently undermined the president. This view, however, is surprising, as throughout the 1940s congress had seldom refused to expand the powers of the executive. Even in the 1950s, after the demise of the system of coalition governments led by the Radical party, the congress had continued to behave sensibly toward the executive. Indeed, despite his rebuff of political parties, Alessandri successfully secured congressional approval for his major legislative initiatives (Hughes 1971:62–64). Moreover, on at least six occasions the congress approved laws delegating broad legislative powers on matters ranging from the restructuring of the civil service, to the establishment of a new foreign investment regime, tax reform, and the development of a comprehensive legal framework for a new housing policy (Evans 1970a:144). Frei also secured congressional approval for the most important components of his program, even though his party never had an overall majority in the congress (Agor 1971:137).

An area where the congress did in fact disrupt government plans was public expenditure. Here, members of the congress had considerable scope to propose legislation that could derail public expenditure programs and undermine policies designed to contain inflation. Thus, not surprisingly, the rules governing public finance and expenditure were a continuous source of dispute between the executive and the congress. Under the 1833 Constitution, the congress had often created disruption to government policy by delaying the approval of the annual budget. Indeed, President Balmaceda's opponents had successfully used this tactic in the 1890s. The 1925 Constitution introduced a provision to remedy this problem. It provided that in the event of delays in the approval of the budget, the current budget would automatically extend for one more year. The constitution, however, did not set clear rules regarding who was entitled to initiate legislation authorizing public expenditure. As a consequence, members of the congress, through parliamentary motions, incessantly introduced legislation to increase public expenditure, thus disrupting government control over public finance. In 1943, a constitutional amendment attempted to resolve this problem. It provided that only the president could initiate legislation to establish new posts or to increase salaries in the public sector. The 1943 amendment, however, did not clearly define the responsibilities between the president and the congress. While the amendment did not allow members of the congress to introduce bills raising salaries in the public sector, it did not prevent them from introducing bills calling for pay increases in the private sector. Thus, members of the congress regularly introduced legislation providing for mandatory pay increases for workers in the private sector at rates generally higher than those set by the government for public sector workers. This practice undermined the government's efforts to control inflation, as it encouraged public sector workers to demand further pay increases (Alessandri 1964:1161). Moreover, as members of the congress were also allowed to introduce bills on matters concerning social security, there developed a chaotic social security system with a variety of special regimes for selected groups of workers (Borzutzky 2002:45–69). This problem was not resolved until 1970 when congress approved a constitutional amendment that gave the president exclusive legislative initiative on matters concerning public expenditure (Evans 1973:33–170). At the time, this amendment was strongly criticized on the ground that it was establishing a presidential dictatorship.[1] This criticism, however, was misplaced for this amendment merely gave effect to the principle that the executive, whether in a parliamentary or in a presidential regime, should have control, as well as responsibility, for the management of public finance.

It is undeniable that despite the enormous concentration of power on the executive, successive presidents found it increasingly difficult to implement their programs. Yet, contrary to the assessment of both Alessandri and Frei, these difficulties did not stem mainly from congressional obstruction. In the 1940s, when the electorate was small, presidents had a good working relation with the congress, although not necessarily with their individual parties. Yet, as explained in chapter 4, even during the 1940s presidents did not have full control over the political agenda because of the constraints imposed on them by the limits of the import substitution policy. Nevertheless, during the 1940s, the congress and the president shared common objectives: maintaining economic and political stability. That is why presidents could always find parties in the congress that would endorse their legislative proposals. Parties, though, on the whole, faithful to their ideologies, enjoyed considerable flexibility, as their constituencies were small and relatively stable. In the late 1950s and early 1960s, however, as electoral participation expanded to include nearly all the adult population and organized labor became more militant, the political dynamics changed. Political parties lost their flexibility as they could not easily postpone or abandon the aspirations of their constituencies or the promises made in their electoral manifestos. As parties began more seriously to promote the interests of their constituencies, their opposition to government policies became more forceful, which brought about an increase in political mobilization. Although Alessandri and Frei managed to secure approval of their legislative programs, the difficulties they faced in their implementation was not due to the formal powers of the congress, but to fundamental changes in political behavior. Tinkering with the constitution would not have resolved this issue.

Expansion of Executive Powers

The transformation of the presidential regime into a hybrid between presidentialism and parliamentarism enabled presidents to establish good working relations with the congress. So stable were the relations that during this period the congress rarely refused to delegate powers to the executive. The powers granted to the executive by the congress were often exorbitant, sometimes unconstitutional, and generally not subject to any form of judicial control. Moreover, in addition to seeking delegated power from the congress, the executive frequently further extended these powers through executive decrees or regulations. This section examines how the expansion of executive power came about in two key areas of policy: price controls and state security.

Price Controls

The economic crisis of the late 1920s and early 1930s brought about the establishment of several mechanisms to regulate the economy. Prominent among these was a system of price controls that soon developed into a comprehensive instrument of economic regulation. It gave government officials extensive powers, including the power to requisition goods and production facilities, to set production targets, and even to expropriate these enterprises if targets were not met.

The price of food became a major political issue in the early years of the twentieth century, as the process of urbanization accelerated. Between 1875 and 1895, the market for commercial agriculture doubled, and it doubled again in 1920 (Wright 1982:100). The Great Depression complicated matters, as the collapse of nitrate revenue seriously disrupted the supply of foodstuffs and other basic consumer goods. Thus, by the early 1930s various administrations began experimenting with mechanisms to control the price of basic consumer goods. The mechanism that proved most durable was Decree Law 520 of 1932 (DL 520). DL 520 established the Prices and Subsistence Agency (PSA), which was given broad powers to regulate the production, distribution, transport, as well as import and export of any basic consumer good. The PSA could fix prices for basic consumer goods and set output targets for enterprises producing these goods. It could also restrict the number of distribution outlets and impose import and export restrictions on essential consumer goods (Talesnik 1940:73; Von Brunn 1972:68–73). DL 520 also gave the PSA broad enforcement powers. It could, without prior judicial authorization, request the assistance of the police to enforce any of its decisions (Talesnik 1940:71–72). In the event of noncompliance, the PSA could either levy fines or requisition basic consumer goods and sell them directly to the public. It could also order the expropriation of enterprises that did not meet production targets set by the PSA. The activities of the PSA were not subject to any form of judicial control, with the exception of fines and sanctions that involved imprisonment. The only control exercised over the PSA was the legality review administered by the comptroller general, which, at the time, was mostly ineffective.

Given the exorbitant powers of the PSA, it is not surprising that upon the restoration of democracy in 1932, the business community raised questions about the constitutionality of DL 520, which was one of nearly 700 decrees enacted by one of the four de facto administrations that ruled the country between June and September 1932. Under the terms of the constitution, Decree Laws were invalid, as they had not been approved by the congress. But the possibility of challenging the constitutionality of DL 520 was preempted when, in the same year, the Supreme Court held that Decree Laws enacted by de facto administrations could not be challenged solely on the ground that they had not been enacted in accordance with the procedures prescribed by the constitution (Aylwin 1952:210; Silva Bascuñán 1963:3:440). After this decision, the business community turned to President Alessandri and requested him to repeal the Decree (Talesnik 1940:72). The president responded promptly, appointing a committee of prominent lawyers to examine these allegations. The committee's view was that DL 520 was unconstitutional. Yet, the president did not repeal it. Instead, over the years, DL 520 was the object of several amendments and it not only validated, but also significantly expanded the scope of the powers of the executive and transformed the original price control mechanism into a comprehensive system of economic regulation (Talesnik 1940:72, 98).

Having failed to secure the repeal of DL 520, business associations turned their attention to its implementation. Their concern stemmed from the tendency of the executive to continuously stretch the powers of the PSA beyond the limits set by DL 520 (Aramayo 1964:113–114). These concerns came to a head in 1945 when the PSA issued a decree requiring business enterprises to make contributions to fund clothing and foodstuffs for the poor (Soto 1972a:63). Several business associations made strong representations to the government about the legality of this decree. Realizing the legitimacy of the grievances of the business community, the government appointed an interdepartmental committee to defuse the situation. The committee was to draft regulations that were meant to clearly define the jurisdiction of the PSA.

The new regulations, however, gave rise to even greater controversy, as instead of clarifying the PSA's jurisdiction they expanded it. While under DL 520, the PSA could requisition essential consumer goods when they were not sold at the price fixed by the government, the new regulations dramatically expanded the scope of these powers. The regulations authorized the PSA to take over the administration of enterprises involved in the production or commercialization of any basic consumer good if it deemed that this measure was necessary to ensure adequate and prompt distribution of such goods (Aramayo 1964:108; Makluf 1973:160–161). The new regulations outraged the business community and prompted the leading business associations to demand their immediate withdrawal. (Soto 1972a:65–68). The under-secretary for economics, who had chaired the committee that drafted the regulations, conceded that the regulations did stretch the powers of the PSA beyond the limits set by DL 520 and promised that they would be amended. As the regulations were not amended, a group of parliamentarians sought to impeach the minister of economics for abuse of power (Soto 1972a:69–70). The motion of impeachment, however, failed, as it did not secure enough votes in the congress (Aramayo 1964:115). In 1945, however, the congress impeached the comptroller general on several grounds, one of which was that he had failed to object to the legality of these regulations. Yet, a few years later, the congress enacted legislation that retrospectively validated both DL 520 and the controversial regulations (Soto 1972a:183). During the next two decades, successive governments made ample use of the price control mechanism. They also occasionally used the broad requisition powers (Santa María and Alessandri 1944). After 1945, however, as I explain in the section that follows, the comptroller general imposed some restraints on the exercise of these powers (Santa María 1972:25).

State Security

The expansion of executive powers in the area of price controls went hand in hand with the expansion of powers in state security. This process was carried out with little concern for basic rights guaranteed by the constitution. Under the constitution, the use of emergency powers was vested primarily in the congress. Only in exceptional circumstances was the president authorized to use these powers without the consent of the congress. The powers of the congress and the president in this area were briefly as follows: the restriction or suspension of certain constitutional rights could only take place with the approval of the congress through special emergency laws (*leyes de facultades especiales*). These laws could be enacted only in exceptional circumstances to safeguard the security of the state. In the event of serious domestic unrest, the congress was also empowered to declare one or more areas of the country in a state of siege. The president, for his part, also had the power to declare a state of siege in case of domestic unrest, but he or she could do so only when congress was not in session. In addition, the president could declare a state of siege in the event of external aggression and a state of public alert (*estado de asamblea*) in case of war (Mera et al. 1978).

The powers of the president under a state of siege were strictly regulated by the constitution: he or she could transfer persons from one district to another and could detain them in their homes or in locations other than prisons. Special emergency laws, on the other hand, could have a wider scope. These laws could suspend the right of assembly and restrict personal liberty and freedom of the press, but could only remain in force for a maximum of six months. The constitution also provided that emergency measures could not undermine the jurisdiction and authority of ordinary courts or restrict the right of habeas corpus. These constitutional safeguards, however, were largely ineffective.

After the restoration of democracy, governments made extensive use of emergency powers. Between 1932 and 1957, the congress approved ten emergency laws and presidents declared a state of siege on at least ten occasions (Caffarena 1957:22). Most of these special emergency laws were in force for the maximum allowable time of six months, so altogether, they had the effect of suspending or restricting basic constitutional rights for nearly five years (Silva Bascuñán 1963:2:363). The first emergency law of this period, approved in 1933, became the model on which subsequent emergency laws were based (Estévez 1949:396). It contained broad provisions restricting personal freedom beyond the limits allowed by the constitution. It gave administrative authorities the power to order house searches and to place individuals under surveillance and house arrest without intervention by the courts (Caffarena 1957:122). In 1937, a newly enacted State Security Act introduced additional restrictions on civil and political rights. Although this act was only meant to target subversive activities within the military, its tentacles extended beyond its original objective. As well as severely punishing anyone who incited the armed forces to disobey orders or encouraged others to disturb public order, the act gave broad powers to the president to order the dissolution of any organization which, in his view, aimed to disrupt social order or used flags or emblems of a revolutionary nature. The State Security Act of 1937 was a prelude to the much tougher law, the State Security Act of 1948. This Act banned the Communist Party and relegated its leaders to remote parts of the country. Party members were disenfranchised and banned from employment in the public sector (Estévez 1949:408–445). The anticommunist focus of the 1948 Act was warmly welcomed in Washington, as it was consistent with the emerging cold war ideology. Indeed, there is evidence to suggest that the adoption of the 1948 State Security Act was forced upon the government as a condition for Chile to become eligible for American foreign aid (Faundez 1988:74–75).

The 1948 Act was as much against organized workers as it was against communism. Indeed, it is arguable that the anticommunist provisions of the act made its antiunion provisions acceptable to moderate members of the congress. The act curtailed the right to strike. Under the Labor Code the president had sweeping powers to break strikes and broad powers to issue decrees known as back-to-work decrees (*decretos de reanudación de faenas*), whenever a strike posed a threat to public health or to the economy. Once these decrees were issued, workers had to immediately report to work while the dispute was submitted to compulsory arbitration. The State Security Act of 1948 further expanded the power of the executive to break strikes. It gave the president the power to issue back-to-work decrees in the event of strikes in the public sector or in industries deemed to be vital for the economy. Moreover, and consistent with the trend of excluding the judiciary, labor law decisions taken by the executive under the act were not subject to review either by labor courts or by any other court (Cabrera 1971:246–247). The antiunion provisions of the 1948 Act were strictly enforced and they had a more lasting effect on the legal system than its anticommunist provisions.

The expansion of powers in the area of state security also brought about the development of new legal concepts. One of these was the introduction in 1942 of the so-called emergency zones by law No. 7,200. The enactment of this law was prompted by a decision by the Third Inter-American Conference of Foreign Ministers following Japan's attack on Pearl Harbor. This decision called for hemispheric solidarity and cooperation to combat Axis political influence in the region. Under this law, the president could declare emergency zones in case of external aggression, foreign invasion, or sabotage against national security. This law was plainly unconstitutional, as it gave the president exclusive power to determine the existence of an emergency and to take measures to deal with such an emergency without any involvement by the congress. During the parliamentary debate, the government acknowledged that the bill was inconsistent with the constitution, but claimed that its enactment was necessary because of the international situation. It also argued that it was unlikely that, in practice, this law would affect individual liberties and political freedoms because it addressed mainly military matters of an operational nature. In any event, according to the government, these restrictions were temporary, as the new law would remain in force only for six months (Caffarena 1957:138).

As it turned out, however, the concept of emergency zones soon acquired a life of its own and became the instrument for repressing and containing labor and other forms of political mobilization. As ever, the act significantly expanded the notion of emergency zones. Under its regulations, military officers in charge of emergency zones were given broad powers not only on military matters of an operational nature, but also on civil matters. The military commander had the power to control the movement of persons and goods to and from the zone, and his decisions were binding on all persons found within it. The powers given to military officers were unconstitutional and they contravened the government's assurance that the new law was meant to address only military matters of an operational nature (Schweitzer 1972:144).

The transformation of the six-month emergency zone provision into a permanent policy instrument was a complex process that involved several cross-references from one law to another and one regulation to another. The emergency legislation adopted after 1942 (Laws No. 8,837, 1947 and No. 8,940, 1948) retained the concept of emergency zones and sought to validate it by invoking as precedent Law No. 7,200 and its regulations, although neither this law nor its regulations were in force. In any event, this process of lateral validation was flawed, as both the law and the regulations invoked were manifestly unconstitutional. Moreover, the emergency legislation enacted after 1942 extended the application of emergency zones to matters of internal security (Mera et al. 1978:43). The evolution of the emergency zones mechanism entered a new phase in 1948 when law No. 8,960 gave the president the power to suspend the implementation of emergency zones decrees 15 days before any congressional election (Estévez 1949:445). The bizarre notion that an emergency could be suspended and reactivated suggests that emergency powers were used as an ordinary instrument of governance rather than as a device to deal with genuine national emergencies (Caffarena 1957:137).

The expansion of the emergency zone mechanism continued well into the 1950s. In 1958, a new State Security Act (Law No. 12,927, Section 31) revived the notion of emergency zones under the name of "state of emergency." Under the act, the president could only declare a state of emergency in order to protect the external security of the state. Not surprisingly, this restriction did not last long. Only two years after its approval, the congress amended it to authorize the president to declare a state of emergency in case of a public calamity. Although the objective of the amendment was to enable the government to deal with the consequences of a major earthquake, this new provision was regularly used to maintain public order. The notion of public calamity was also interpreted broadly to include any threat to economic and political stability (Mera et al. 1978:54). The state of emergency powers thus became a powerful instrument to contain popular discontent, to break strikes, and to respond to any breakdown of law and order (Schweitzer 1972:164).

Restraining the Executive—the *Contraloría*

As noted above, the expansion of powers of the executive was carried out with little or no concern for constitutional or legal procedures. While the congress was willing to adopt state security legislation that was clearly unconstitutional, the executive behaved as if its regulatory powers were equal in status to ordinary legislation and thus interpreted them expansively to further increase its powers. Moreover, because the main objective of the expansion of powers was to enable the executive to handle economic and political emergencies, courts were consistently sidelined. While in the area of economic regulation, judicial review of administrative action was invariably ruled out, in the area of state security the role of the courts was kept to the minimum. The exclusion of courts from involvement in these areas of public policy reinforced the view among the political elite that executive action was unassailable and infallible. This process weakened the judiciary and had a lasting impact on the relationship between the political process and the legal system. I explore this issue in the chapter 6. In this section, I examine the role of the legality review procedure administered by Contraloría that was often regarded as an adequate substitute for judicial review.

The Legality Review Procedure: Background

The Contraloría was established in 1927 as part of a package of measures recommended by Edwin W. Kemmerer, a professor of economics from Princeton University hired by the government to advise on monetary, fiscal, and banking reform. The Contraloría's main objective, as envisaged by Kemmerer, was to support the enforcement of the new legislation on public finance. Its main tasks were to draw up public accounts and to monitor public expenditure (Drake 1989:103). The government accepted Kemmerer's proposals for the Contraloría, but introduced one important change. It gave the Contraloría authority to rule on the constitutionality and legality of government decrees. In this respect, the Chilean Contraloría is different from similar agencies established during this period, also upon the recommendation of Professor Kemmerer, in other Latin America countries such as Colombia, Perú, Bolivia, and México (Drake 1989:104). The Contraloría was set up as an autonomous agency. The president with the consent of the senate appointed its chief officer, the comptroller general. In 1943, a constitutional amendment reinforced the independence of the Contraloría. It elevated it to the rank of a constitutional organ and gave the comptroller general the same security of tenure as enjoyed by members of the Supreme Court. Only the congress, through impeachment proceedings, could remove the comptroller general from office (Silva Cimma 1969:367–383). Between February 1932 and January 1967, there were five comptroller generals. The first three served six years each and the last two—who had close links with the Radical Party—served seven and eight years, respectively (see appendix D).

The objective of the legality review procedure was to ensure the consistency of government decrees, regulations, and other administrative acts with the terms set by the constitution and the law (Silva Cimma 1968:284). This procedure had several unusual features. First, unlike judicial review of administrative action, which takes place after administrative decisions are taken, the legality review procedure takes place before. Second, the agency in charge of carrying out the review was part of the central system of public administration, but independent from the government. Third, although the legality rulings of the Contraloría were not strictly binding, governments willingly complied. Despite these unusual features, over the years, this review mechanism became enormously important and played a critical role in shaping administrative practice.

The Contraloría was required to review all government decrees (*decretos supremos*) and regulations as well as other government orders and instructions within a fixed term of 30 days. The Contraloría could either approve or reject the decree in question. Only decrees approved by the Contraloría could take effect. In cases where the Contraloría objected to the legality of a particular decree, the decree in question was returned to the issuing agency with reasons for the decision. The issuing agency had three alternatives: first, it could accept the Contraloría's views and make the required changes; second, it could respond to the Contraloría's objections by offering further arguments or by supplying further information on the specific matter at issue; and third, it could override the decision of the Contraloría by means of a special presidential decree (hereafter, *decreto de insistencia*). The decision to issue this type of decree was not taken lightly: *decretos de insistencia* had to be countersigned by all the members of the cabinet, and the Contraloría was required to forward it to the chamber of deputies. This referral provided the opposition with the opportunity to further scrutinize the government's decision.

The number of decrees subject to the legality review procedure was enormous, reaching approximately 200,000 per year in the 1960s.[2] To avoid overloading the Contraloría and to prevent excessive delay, the comptroller-general was allowed to exempt certain categories of decrees from the legality review procedure. The decrees so exempted amounted to approximately one-third of the total decrees issued each year. Moreover, in some areas of public policy—such as price and exchange controls—government decrees were allowed to take effect before the Contraloría ruled on their legality. Despite these measures, the legality review procedure imposed a heavy workload on the Contraloría. It also slowed down the administrative process, although complaints about bureaucratic delays did not single out the legality review as the main problem.

The legality review procedure was introduced in 1927 (Silva Cimma 1969:367–383). During its first 20 years, the Contraloría was largely ineffective, as it rarely challenged the legality of government decrees and, when it did, its rulings were either overruled or ignored. However, as the system of party democracy consolidated, the authority of the Contraloría within the political system increased and so did the efficacy of the legality review procedure. Two events account for these changes. First, in 1943 the Contraloría was elevated to the status of a constitutional organ and second, in 1945, the congress impeached the comptroller general for failing to adequately scrutinize the legality of government decrees. Taking notice of these events, the Contraloría significantly expanded the scope of its review powers. At the same time, government compliance with the legality rulings of the Contraloría dramatically improved.

There was, however, considerable confusion regarding the nature and limits of the legality review procedure. Initially, the Contraloría characterized its review powers as a formal jurisdictional check that was not concerned with the policy underlying the decrees under review. This characterization seemed appropriate, as the Contraloría had to distinguish its role from the policymaking role of the administration. After 1945, however, although the Contraloría significantly expanded the scope of its review powers, it did not attempt to develop an alternative conceptual framework. Although the expansion in the scope of legality review did not affect all areas of administrative practice in the same way and the legality review was not applied consistently, it gave the Contraloría enormous power to shape the form and content of administrative action. Interestingly, however, these developments went largely unnoticed as both lawyers and politicians continued to regard the legality review procedure as a formal jurisdictional check and showed no interest in examining the Contraloría's practice. It was not until 1970, during the short-lived Allende administration, that observers finally realized that this obscure mechanism gave the Contraloría an inordinate amount of power (Soto 1977). This section explains how this improbable mechanism of control came to play such an important role and examines the factors that account for its success during the party democracy period.

A Narrow Approach: 1927–45

During its early years, the Contraloría displayed extreme deference toward the executive branch and, consequently, its approach to the legality review procedure was narrow. The Contraloría sought to ensure that the statute invoked as the basis for the decree was in force; that it granted the powers that the official issuing the decree purported to exercise; and that the official was acting within the time limits prescribed by the statute. Under this approach, the Contraloría did not inquire into the merits or the timing of the decision. In local legal parlance, the legality review was not concerned either with the "convenience" (*conveniencia*) or "timing" (*oportunidad*) of government decisions (Humeres 1971:209–211; Silva Cimma 1968:362).

This narrow approach to the legality review procedure is, on the surface, appealing. The following example illustrates this point. As noted in the preceding section, the Labor Code (Article 626) authorized the minister of labor to break strikes and order workers to return to work whenever, in his view, the strike "posed a threat to public health or general economic welfare." Under these decrees—known as back-to-work decrees (*decretos de reanudación de faenas*)—the government took over the administration of the relevant enterprise until the conflict was resolved. In order to safeguard the interests of the parties to the conflict and to secure the prompt resolution of the underlying conflict, the minister was also required to set in motion a conciliation procedure. Back-to-work decrees were thus conceived of as exceptional measures that temporarily suspended the right to strike. An interesting question raised by these decrees was whether the review powers of the Contraloría extended to the government's judgment as to whether or not the strike "posed a threat to public health or general economic welfare." Until 1945 the Contraloría took the view that the assessment as to whether the strike posed a threat to public health or economic welfare fell exclusively within the jurisdiction of the executive, as this was a matter that concerned the "convenience or opportunity" of the decree.[3]

The Contraloría applied the same approach to the review of decrees in the area of price controls. The government had established a rent control scheme and had invoked as the basis for its authority a statute that gave the president the power to fix prices for essential commodities in the "general interest." This decree was arguably illegal as it was doubtful whether the enabling statute allowed the government to extend the system of price controls to the area of housing. The Contraloría, however, did not object to the legality of this decree because, in its view, only the government had the power to decide whether the extension of the price control scheme in the way proposed by the government was in the general interest.[4]

Comptroller General's Impeachment

Despite the Contraloría's extreme deference, the executive did not take the legality review seriously. Indeed, in order to circumvent it, the executive adopted the practice of issuing *decretos de insistencia* before forwarding the decree to the Contraloría. This anticipatory breach of legality—known locally as *decretos nonatos*—made the legality review redundant. Notwithstanding their manifest illegality, the number of *decretos nonatos* enacted between 1932 and 1942 was staggering: 116 between 1932 and 1937 (Alessandri administration); 65 between 1938 and 1941 (Aguirre administration); and 24 in 1942, the first year of the Ríos administration (Macías 1946:55).

During this period, the Contraloría also became involved in a series of disputes with the executive, all of them concerning public expenditure. In the mid-1930s, as the country faced serious economic problems, governments often exceeded the expenditure limits set by the annual budget. The Contraloría regularly objected to this practice, but was consistently overruled by the executive. Extensive use of *decretos de insistencia* enabled successive administrations to spend without any regard for the limits set in the budget. This situation prompted the congress in 1943 to adopt a constitutional amendment that expressly enjoined the government from overriding the Contraloría on matters relating to public expenditure. The amendment, however, allowed the government to spend up to 2 percent in excess of the amount provided for in the annual budget, but only in the event of national emergencies or natural disasters. As already noted, the 1943 amendment also elevated the Contraloría to the status of a constitutional organ and strengthened its independence from the executive.

The first indication that the congress was serious about strengthening the independence of the Contraloría and about ensuring the efficacy of the legality review procedure came in 1945, only two years after the approval of the constitutional amendment, when it impeached Agustín Vigorena, the serving comptroller general. Ironically, Vigorena—a distinguished lawyer and sometime dean of the University of Chile Law School—became the first victim of the constitutional amendment, although he had been one of its most enthusiastic supporters.[5]

Proponents of the impeachment claimed that the comptroller general had failed to fulfill his duty to control the legality of government decrees. In connection with so-called back-to-work decrees, they claimed that the comptroller general had merely rubber-stamped them because he had not required the government to produce evidence that the strikes in question did in fact endanger public health and general welfare. A similar allegation was made in connection with a decree that established a rent control system. In this case, the proponents of the impeachment claimed that the Contraloría should have ascertained whether the action by the government was "in the general interest," as required by the enabling legislation. In his defense, the comptroller general argued that the decision as to whether the "general interest" required the enactment of back-to-work decrees fell exclusively within the jurisdiction of the administration.[6] The government, according to the comptroller general, was the sole judge as to whether the general interest required issuing a back-to-work decree. On this question, the government had absolute discretion and, accordingly, the Contraloría could not substitute its view of the general interest for that of the government.[7] The comptroller general made a similar argument in response to the allegation that he should have been stricter in the scrutiny of the decree that established the rent control scheme. According to the proponents of the impeachment, the rent control scheme constituted unlawful expropriation because it exceeded the powers delegated by the enabling statute. In his defense, the comptroller general argued that the Contraloría could not question the government's interpretation because the enabling statute had given the president the power to fix prices for essential commodities whenever this course of action was required by the "general interest." As a consequence, claimed the comptroller general, it was for the president and not for the Contraloría to judge whether a particular measure was required.[8]

The impeachment of the comptroller general posed a fundamental challenge to the way presidents had interpreted the scope of their regulatory powers. Its message to the executive was unambiguous: congress, though willing to delegate broad powers to the executive, was determined to ensure that presidents would not abuse these powers. Its message to the Contraloría was also clear: it called for a more comprehensive scrutiny of the legality of government decrees. Not surprisingly, the impeachment brought about a sharp reaction from President Juan Antonio Ríos (1941–45), who described it as unconstitutional and hinted that he would not accept its outcome.[9] Leading figures in the senate strongly objected to the president's response, describing it as irresponsible and a threat to the constitutional order.[10] In the end, however, the president—who at the time was terminally ill—gave in and accepted the decision of the congress.

Legality Review Transformed

The impeachment of the comptroller general was a turning point, marking a shift in the Contraloría's interpretation of its legality review powers. It transformed the legality review from a rubber-stamping device that governments either took for granted or could safely ignore, into a procedure that both the executive and the congress had to take seriously. The transformation of the legality review procedure was, however, gradual. The two administrations after Ríos, the González (1946–52) and Ibáñez (1952–58) administrations, though by no means scrupulous in the exercise of their regulatory powers, abandoned the practice of issuing *decretos nonatos* to circumvent the legality review procedure (Gil 1966:96). By the mid-1950s, compliance with legality review rulings increased and governments were reluctant to resort to *decretos de insistencia* to overrule rulings of the Contraloría. Indeed, as Silva Cimma reports, from 1956 to 1959, the executive did not issue a single *decreto de insistencia* (Silva Cimma 1968:368). The reluctance of the executive to overrule the Contraloría continued well into the 1960s. Between 1964 and 1969, the Contraloría reviewed, on average, approximately 200,000 decrees per year and raised objections to the legality of about 10 percent of them. The overwhelming majority of these decrees were amended by the government and subsequently approved by the Contraloría. During this period, the number of *decretos de insistencia* issued each year was rarely more than ten.[11]

After the impeachment, the Contraloría expanded the scope of the legality review procedure also to include, in certain cases, a review of the facts invoked by the executive as the basis for its administrative decisions. However, this process was somewhat erratic, as in some areas of administrative practice, the Contraloría applied strict criteria, while in other areas was more lax. In the two policy areas singled out in the impeachment proceedings—labor law and economic regulation—evidence suggests that, after 1945, the functioning of the Contraloría underwent a major shift, as evidenced by the review of back-to-work decrees. As will be recalled, in his defense before the congress the comptroller general had argued that the review powers of the Contraloría did not extend to the minister's interpretation as to whether a particular strike endangered the health or welfare of the nation. After 1945, however, the Contraloría extended the scope of the review to include this component of back to work decrees (Oneto 1971:143; Yávar 1972:94). The Contraloría applied this broad interpretation of its review powers even to the review of back-to-work decrees issued under Article 38 of the State Security Act of 1958. This act gave the president sweeping powers to break strikes in the event of stoppages of industries or enterprises of fundamental economic importance. According to the Contraloría, its review powers extended to the president's identification of the enterprises that fell within the broad criteria set by the act. Applying this approach, the Contraloría ruled that the president could not invoke Article 38 to end strikes in the agricultural sector since production units in this sector were not commercial or industrial enterprises.[12] It also ruled that the government could not invoke Article 38 to bring to an end a strike affecting a large chain of privately owned shoe-shops (Oneto 1971:148). In all these cases, the decisions were based on the Contraloría's interpretation of broad, open-ended legal standards that, before 1945, were beyond the limits of the legality review procedure.

The Contraloría's approach to the interpretation of the powers of the executive in the area of economic regulation also changed. In 1962, the Contraloría prevented the Alessandri administration from relying on its requisition powers to secure the enforcement of price controls. The law authorized the requisition of essential consumer goods when, as a consequence of market disruptions, they failed to reach consumers. Under the statute, wheat and flour were classified as essential consumer goods and were thus subject to price controls. The government, in 1962, set an official price for wheat, but millers refused to process the wheat because, in their view, the official price for flour was too low. The government responded by ordering the requisition of all the wheat in possession of the mills. The Contraloría, however, objected to the legality of this order on two grounds: first, that the wheat already purchased by and in possession of the millers was no longer considered essential consumer goods within the scope of the requisition statute; and second, that the government had failed to provide evidence that marketing and distribution channels for wheat had been disrupted (Soto 1973:253–255).

While the cases mentioned above show that the Contraloría had shifted its approach, some cases point in the opposite direction. In 1952, the Contraloría refused to challenge the government's interpretation of a provision in the constitution that authorized public expenditure beyond a certain level when there arises "a situation that cannot be postponed" (*necesidad impostergable*). According to the *Contraloría*, only the president was allowed to interpret the meaning of this phrase because only he could determine the convenience and timing of government decisions (Fiamma 1977:194). Likewise, where the law authorized the president to take emergency measures in the event of a public calamity, the Contraloría often acknowledged that this was a matter that fell exclusively within power of the executive and, consequently, was not within the scope of the legality review (Silva Cimma 1968:284). This somewhat erratic practice explains why the Contraloría was unable to develop a coherent conceptual framework of its review powers. Indeed, although after 1945 the Contraloría significantly expanded the scope of the legality of the Contraloría procedure, it continued to characterize it as a jurisdictional check that had no bearing on the underlying policy. Thus, in 1968 it described it as a logical exercise (*juicio lógico*) that involved a judgment about the consistency between the letter of the law and the text of the proposed decree.[13] Although the Contraloría also acknowledged that its review powers extended to government's findings of facts, it did not provide any indication regarding the standard of review. That is, it did not indicate whether it would carry out an independent review of the findings of fact (de novo review), or whether it would apply a less demanding standard, such as the reasonableness standard. In general, however, after 1945 the Contraloría moved consistently toward an expansive interpretation of its legality review powers.

Explaining Compliance

The conceptual weakness identified above did not, however, affect the efficacy of the legality review procedure. In routine administrative decisions, the Contraloría did not need to apply a test of legality beyond a purely formal check: that is, a jurisdictional check that sought to ascertain whether the statute invoked as basis for the decree was in force; whether it vested the administrative agency with the powers it purported to exercise; and whether the agency or official was acting within the time limits fixed by the statute. The shaky conceptual foundations of the legality review procedure became obvious in decisions involving complex and controversial forms of state intervention, such as price controls, requisitions, and labor regulation. In these areas, the Contraloría often applied an expansive approach that significantly encroached on the government's capacity to respond to real or perceived public policy concerns. Yet, this expansive approach did not undermine the efficacy of the legality review either, as evidenced by the willingness of the executive to comply with the legality rulings of the Contraloría and by the absence of any major conflict with the executive. Two factors, both political, explain the surprisingly high level of compliance: first, governments did not, on the whole, abuse their power because they could always count on the congress to provide them with new regulatory powers; and second, governments took the legality review seriously because after the impeachment they came to regard the Contraloría as a proxy for the congress.

As explained in the preceding section, throughout the 1940s the congress acquiesced to a dramatic expansion of regulatory powers in key areas of public policy such as economic regulation and state security. As a consequence, the government had vast regulatory powers and did not need to abuse them. Indeed, during this period the executive only rarely used its draconian regulatory powers, such as the power to requisition essential consumer goods or to take over the administration of enterprises that failed to comply with government regulations (Santa María and Alessandri 1944). During the 1950s, as the fight against inflation occupied center stage, congress continued to delegate extensive regulatory powers for the implementation of comprehensive stabilization policies. Thus, the knowledge that the congress was there as a last resort to seek wider regulatory powers made it easier for the executive to accept the legality rulings of the *Contraloría*. The legislative evolution of back-to-work decrees illustrates this point. As will be recalled, after 1945 the *Contraloría's* interpretation of the provision in the Labor Code regulating back-to-work decrees imposed restraints on the executive. Yet, these restraints were circumvented, as several new laws approved by the congress gave the government increasingly wider powers to issue back-to-work decrees. Thus, apart from the provision in the Labor Code of 1931, there were three other laws that gave broad powers to the government to issue back-to-work decrees: the State Security Act of 1958, Salary Readjustment Law of 1966, and the Agrarian Reform Law of 1967

(Oneto 1971:178–179; Von Brunn 1972:65–66). These new laws did not repeal the original provision of the Labor Code, but they complemented it so that if the government wanted to end a strike, it was almost certain that its decision would be consistent with one or other of the four provisions that regulated back-to-work decrees.

The efficacy and success of the legality review thus depended largely on the moderation of the policies of the executive and on the willingness of the congress to expand the powers of the executive. These circumstances explain why governments only rarely resorted to *decretos de insistencia* to overrule the views of the *Contraloría*. *Decretos de insistencia* generally prompted a debate in the congress that called into question the government's integrity and its commitment to the principle of legality. As governments were keen to avoid such negative publicity, they generally avoided resorting to them. However, as the system of party democracy began to wither and relations between the congress and the executive became acrimonious, the efficacy of the legality review procedure also declined. Indeed, by the early 1960s, as governments began to implement policies that required more extensive state intervention, the executive found it more difficult to get legislation approved by the congress. At the same time, governments began to increasingly resort to their regulatory powers to implement their programs of economic and social reform. This process culminated in the 1970s when, as chapter 9 explains, the confrontation between the executive and the Contraloría exposed the fragile foundations of the legality review procedure.

The legality review procedure, despite its peculiar features and conceptual shortcomings, made an important contribution to governance. It kept the executive within the bounds of its delegated powers, and it inculcated in the executive the habit of giving reasons for its decisions. It also reinforced transparency in decision making as the exchanges between the government and the Contraloría were published, and therefore both the congress, and the public, had a reliable source to monitor government action.

The legality review procedure was successful, but only insofar as congress and the executive shared a common outlook. Because during the second half of party democracy such common outlook did exist, the legality review procedure fulfilled the crucial function of underpinning the congress in its role of making the government accountable. After 1964, however, as governments began implementing controversial structural reforms and major disagreements emerged between the congress and the executive, the legality review procedure as a device to restrain the executive became increasingly ineffective.

Conclusion

The taming of presidentialism brought about a hybrid political regime with many of the features of the old parliamentary regime. Under the new presidential regime, political parties exercised decisive influence in determining the composition of cabinets. In this respect, the regime that emerged after 1932 did not meet the expectations of the drafters of the constitution. Yet, this hybrid regime did not prevent the emergence of a strong executive. Indeed, during this period the powers of the executive underwent considerable expansion, as the party system was unwavering in its support of the executive's search for economic and political stability. The process that led to the concentration of power in the executive revealed a ruthless style of governance, reminiscent of that employed by the ruling elite in the nineteenth century. Governance was carried out with little regard for constitutional and legal procedures. As presidents appeared to have no misgivings about expanding their influence through self-propelled regulatory powers, congress was always willing to grant new powers or to retrospectively validate the president's constitutional delinquencies. As party democracy began to give way to radical democracy, this comfortable arrangement between presidents and the congress came to an end, thus prompting some leading politicians to demand a further strengthening of the office of the president. However, the rapidly diminishing capacity of the political system to resolve the pressing economic problems stemmed from the changing political context rather than from the presidency's weakness.

A remarkable feature of this period was that, despite the ruthless style of governance, the legality review procedure administered by the Contraloría greatly contributed to the restraining of the executive. The legality review procedure also served to consolidate the practice that executive agencies should give reasons for their decisions. The long-standing reputation of the political system as one that closely observed the principle of legality is due largely to the success of the legality review procedure. In many respects this reputation was well deserved, despite the fact the conceptual foundations of the legality review procedure were weak and the *Contraloría's* practice of it often erratic. Indeed, in some areas of public policy, the legality review procedure only superficially concealed a long-standing ruthless style of governance. For these reasons, the legality review procedure could not fill the void created by the absence of an adequate system of judicial review of administrative action.

Chapter 6

The Supreme Court

Introduction

As noted in chapter 5, the party democracy period witnessed an enormous concentration of power in the executive, which gave presidents extensive discretionary powers. Accordingly, courts were consistently and explicitly denied a role in controlling the legality of executive action. In the absence of effective judicial review, the president and the congress came to regard legislation and administrative decisions as politically infallible and legally unassailable. However, the exclusion of the judiciary from key areas of public policy was not brought about only by collusion between presidents and the congress. It was partly self-imposed, as the Supreme Court, almost invariably, was willing to defer to the political branches of the state.

Given these circumstances, the decision of the Supreme Court to keep a low political profile is not surprising. Yet, despite this, the Court did play an important role in the development of the political and legal systems. As head of the judiciary, it kept a tight rein on lower courts, thus contributing to the safeguarding of the independence and integrity of the judicature. It also zealously defended the constitutional prerogative of courts as the only organs vested with "judicial power" and, thus, consistently undermined attempts by the political branches of the state to establish independent administrative tribunals. Despite its reputation for passivity, the Court also displayed a surprising capacity for judicial activism as it attempted to fashion legal remedies for individuals aggrieved by government decisions. However, the Court's contribution to the development of the political and legal systems had important limitations. Its efforts to preserve its monopoly over judicial power alienated the political organs of the state, while failing to resolve the issue of administrative justice. Its measures to enforce discipline within the ranks of the judiciary were not carried out with due respect for the autonomy of lower court judges and made a travesty of its powers under the constitution. Moreover, the Court's attempts to restrain the executive were clumsy and inconsistent and, consequently, did little to enhance the confidence of politicians in the judiciary. But perhaps the main failing of the Court was that its challenging of government action was purely negative. Indeed, on the rare occasions that the Court challenged the government, it did so by mechanically invoking the sanctity of property and contract. As a consequence, instead of contributing to develop a consensus on the scope and limits of state action, it merely relied on private law principles to oppose administrative action. Thus, not surprisingly, this approach to legal reasoning reaffirmed the widely held view among politicians that neither the Supreme Court nor the rest of the judiciary could be trusted with delicate issues of public policy.

This chapter explains and assesses the role played by the Supreme Court during the party democracy period. It is divided into four sections. The first offers background on the Court and explains, in general terms, the Court's approach to legal reasoning. The second section examines the role of the Court as guardian of the constitution. The third section discusses the role of the Court as custodian of judicial power. The fourth section examines how the Court responded to the absence of judicial review of administrative action.

Background

History

The Supreme Court was established in 1824, but the structure of the judiciary, as it stood during the party democracy period, dates back to the second half of the nineteenth century. Some observers regard the old lineage of the court system as a reason that explains the country's attachment to constitutionalism and legality (Bravo 1976:108; Estévez 1949:322–323; Illanes 1966:272; Radtke 1964:94–96; Roldán 1913:483–484). Although throughout most of its history the Court tried to keep a low profile, it was not always sheltered from political controversy. As noted in chapter 2, in 1868 there was an attempt to impeach four members of the Supreme Court. It was prompted by allegations made against Manuel Montt, president of the Court and former president of the republic. The chamber of deputies approved the impeachment, but the senate rejected it. After the Civil War there was another attempt, which was abandoned after the congress approved a general amnesty law.[1] Government policy toward the judiciary underwent a marked change after 1891. President Balmaceda's policies had alerted the local elite about the political importance of courts. In his attempt to expand and modernize state institutions, Balmaceda significantly increased the number of courts and judicial personnel. Between 1882 and 1891 lower courts more than doubled, from just over 40 to 90 (De Ramón 1989:15). After the Civil War, nearly 80 percent of the judges appointed by Balmaceda were removed from office (De Ramón 1989:38). From then on and until the collapse of the parliamentary republic in 1924, political parties closely influenced judicial appointments, and thus, the composition of the judiciary began to reflect the dominant groups within the congress.

Judges appointed between 1890 and 1920 were largely conservative. Indeed, nearly 75 percent of those who openly acknowledged political affiliation were members of the right-wing Conservative or Liberal Parties, while only 18 percent belonged to the reformist-orientated Radical Party. As political parties began to play a role in judicial appointments, corruption and inefficiency became a major problem (De Ramón 1989: 34–36). Judges in rural and mining areas often used their office to obtain financial gain or political advantages (Angell 1972:18; Gill 1966:128; Guerra 1928:129, 1929:452). It is therefore not surprising that one of the objectives of the military movement that brought about the end of the parliamentary republic in 1924 was to cleanse and reform the judiciary. General Ibáñez, however, was characteristically clumsy and heavy-handed in the implementation of this objective. Instead of achieving judicial independence and enhancing the probity of courts, his policy brought about a split within the Supreme Court and generated enormous political controversy. As a consequence, Ibáñez gave up his attempt at judicial reform, but not before removing from office several senior and lower court judges (De Ramón 1989:35;Vergara 1931). Ibáñez's policies, deeply resented by politicians led, in 1933, to another attempt to impeach the Supreme Court. This time the allegation against the members of the Court was that they had failed to defend the integrity of the judiciary against Ibáñez's arbitrary policies.[2] Once again, the impeachment failed, but from then on, the Supreme Court appears to have made every effort to keep a low political profile.

The system of judicial appointments for senior members of the judiciary was not a source of political controversy. The president appointed the members of the Supreme Court and Court of Appeals from lists submitted to him by the Supreme Court. As the scope for political manipulation under this system was limited, it did not create much friction (Fruhling 1980:13–14). This method of appointment, however, guaranteed that those holding senior judicial posts were acceptable to the political elite. As a result, lower court judges who happened to sympathize with either the Socialist or Communist parties would never reach the upper echelons of the judiciary.

Throughout this period, one of the main concerns of the Supreme Court was lack of resources. The Court constantly reminded the executive and the congress that the shortage of resources undermined the quality of judicial services and was a threat to the independence of the judiciary. The amount allocated to the judiciary in the annual budgets was, on average, about half of one percent of the total budget. From 1925 to 1964, the amount assigned to the judiciary only once exceeded one percent of the annual budget (1947 = 1.07 percent) (Rodríguez 1964:72). Since more than 90 percent of the judiciary's budget was spent on salaries, there was little scope for expanding or modernizing court facilities. Indeed, the money available hardly covered the costs of maintaining the existing infrastructure (Rodríguez 1964:73). The congress, however, never seriously debated the financial plight of the judiciary. The relative poverty of the judiciary contributed, albeit perversely, to the safeguarding of its independence. Jobs in the judiciary were not highly sought after because salaries and career prospects were bleak. Political parties were thus not under great pressure from their members to lobby for jobs within the judiciary. Indeed, even an obscure career in the lower grades of the civil service offered more rewards—and less work—than a career in the judiciary.

Legal Reasoning and the Supremacy
of Legislation

The Supreme Court's extreme deference to the political branches of the state had its roots in the prevailing legal culture. The respect displayed by courts toward the legislature and the content of legislative enactments are undoubtedly related to the all-embracing definition of law contained in the opening section of the Civil Code. Law, according to this definition, is "a manifestation of the sovereign will, which, expressed in the manner prescribed by the constitution, orders, forbids or permits." The Civil Code also explicitly excludes custom as a source of law and rejects the notion of binding judicial precedents. The paramount role that the code assigns to the legislature is underscored by the fact that at the time of its enactment in 1857, there was no judicial review of legislation and consequently there was no agency with the power to determine whether a particular law was indeed "expressed in the manner prescribed by the constitution."

The rules on legal interpretation also contributed to keeping judges at a safe distance from politics (Cánovas 1970:139). These rules, set out in the Civil Code, are extremely formalistic (Articles 19–24). They endorse a textual approach to legal interpretation and explicitly discourage any attempt to inquire into the spirit or objectives of the law. The interpreter is expressly forbidden to restrict or to expand the scope of a particular norm, even if the objective is to avoid harmful consequences that could arise from applying a strict textual method of interpretation. Over the years, the Supreme Court relied on these principles of interpretation to distance itself from the social and political consequences of its decisions. Whenever its decisions were criticized, the Court pointed out that judges had a duty to apply the law as they found it and they could not make the law. If court decisions were disappointing it was because the laws were bad, not because of the courts' failings. Thus, according to the Supreme Court, legal progress does not depend on the courts, but on the executive and the legislature.[3] The Court's views about the sanctity of positive law are illustrated in a statement made in response to a charge that, during the 1940s, it had failed to fulfill its role as guardian of the constitution: "If laws cannot be malicious because they are made by the Congress, and aimed at the common good; that is, the well-being of the common people; neither can the judiciary be malicious when it applies such laws."[4] The Court underscores this point when it refers specifically to the charge that it had failed to accept challenges to the constitutionality of the 1948 State Security Act that banned the Communist Party and severely restricted union activities: "[I]f there was a valid law and the government requested the courts to apply it, the courts had no choice but to apply it."[5]

The Court's views about the supremacy of legislation were occasionally expressed with an enthusiasm that went beyond the limits of legal positivism, as illustrated in its written defense in the impeachment proceedings of 1933. The promoters of the impeachment in the chamber of deputies alleged that during the Ibáñez administration in the 1920s, the Court had failed to protect the independence and integrity of the judiciary. During the impeachment debate, parliamentarians defending the Court argued that it should not be held to account, even though its behavior may have been morally objectionable, because, at the time, the Court had no choice but to comply with the law.[6] The Court did not appreciate this type of support. It strongly rejected the characterization of its behavior as morally wrong. The

Court claimed, instead, that its behavior was morally unimpeachable precisely because it had acted in conformity with the letter of the law.[7] The Court's argument thus rejects the traditional legal positivist view regarding the separation of law and morality suggesting instead that positive law determines the content of moral principles.

Guardian of the Constitution

Given the Court's views on the supremacy of legislation and its approach to legal interpretation, it is not surprising that it did not properly fulfill its role as guardian of the constitution. The 1925 Constitution gave the Supreme Court the power to review the constitutionality of legislation, but the introduction of this procedure had little impact, as the Court almost invariably declined to use its newly acquired power (Carvajal 1940:149). Recently compiled statistics show that between 1925 and 1946, almost 90 percent of judicial review cases brought before the Court were dismissed, and this trend continued until the demise of the constitution in 1973 (Valenzuela 1991:160). Two examples of the way the Court approached its role as guardian of the constitution follow.

Delegated Legislation

The 1833 Constitution contained a clause that allowed the congress to delegate legislative power to the president. In 1925, however, after careful consideration, the committee drafting the constitution explicitly excluded this clause from the new text. It was thus clear that those who drafted the constitution regarded the delegation of legislative powers as unacceptable (Evans 1970a:112). The congress, however, did not take notice of this change and continued delegating legislative power. The question as to the constitutionality of this practice soon reached the Supreme Court. It was raised in 1932 in connection with proceedings involving a dispute over mining rights (Carvajal 1940:157–158). The complainant in this case asked the Court to declare unconstitutional a presidential decree that purported to have the force of law by virtue of a previous delegation of power by the congress. The Court, however, refused to rule that this decree was unconstitutional because, in its view, the practice of delegating legislative power was essentially a political matter and, as such, not within the scope of its review powers. According to the Court, compliance with constitutional rules relating to the legislative process was "dependent upon political and social factors which in every respect are alien to legal reasoning," and, consequently, it was not for the Court to tell the congress and the president how they should interpret the constitutional rules governing the legislative process.[8] In this Opinion, the Court, however, was careful to point out that it remained fully committed to the protection of individual rights.[9] An opportunity to test this commitment arose in 1949 in connection with the enforcement of the State Security Act.

Civil and Political Rights

The State Security Act of 1948 banned the Communist Party and cancelled the electoral registration of its members, consisting of approximately twenty-five thousand citizens (Blasier 1950:371–373). René Frías, a communist lawyer affected by these measures, challenged the act as inconsistent with the constitutional provisions that regulated the right to vote.[10] Three articles of the constitution dealt with the right to vote. Article 7 established the requirements: nationality, age, literacy, and registration. Article 8 dealt with the grounds for suspension of this right: physical or mental incapacity or indictment for a serious criminal offense. Article 9 provided that the right to vote was lost upon conviction for a serious criminal offense or loss of nationality. As membership in a political party was not a ground for disenfranchisement, Mr. Frías argued that the 1948 Act was unconstitutional.

The Court acknowledged that, under the constitution, membership in a political party was not a ground for disenfranchisement, but concluded, nonetheless, that act was consistent with the constitution. Its conclusion was based on a narrow textual interpretation of Article 7. According to the Court, the grounds for the loss of the right to vote set out in this Article were merely indicative, not exhaustive. Had the constitution intended these grounds to be exhaustive, Article 9 would have been drafted in a different way. Instead of stating, "the status of citizen with the right to vote is lost . . ." it should have stated that the status of citizen with the right to vote can only be lost in the specified cases. Thus, according to the Court, the constitution did not preclude the legislature from adding new grounds for disenfranchisement in addition to those explicitly mentioned by the constitution. This odd reasoning made a travesty of the principle of constitutional supremacy as it transformed the constitution into little more than a voluntary code of conduct that the legislature was free to supplement, revise, or ignore, depending on circumstances.

It could be argued that in the Frías case, the Court was wise not to accept the challenge to the constitutionality of the State Security Act as the case was politically sensitive and raised an issue about which there was no disagreement between the congress and the president. Yet, even if this cynical argument were accepted, it must be noted that the Court was reluctant to uphold individual rights even in cases where the president and the congress were at odds. A case decided by the Court in 1936 denying a petition of habeas corpus illustrates this point.

The case involved the interpretation of the powers of the president during a state of siege. As explained in chapter 5, the power to authorize the use of emergency powers was vested in the congress. The president, however, was exceptionally allowed to declare a state of siege, but only if the congress was not in session. As the power granted to the president was an exception to the general rule, the constitution also contained a provision that set out the procedure to follow in the event that the state of siege declared by the president was still in force when the congress reconvened. This provision, however, was poorly drafted and it led to conflicting interpretations. It reads as follows: "[I]f the state of siege declared by the president has not expired when the congress resumes its session, the declaration issued by the President of the Republic will be regarded as a government bill."[11] According to the government, a state of siege declared by the president remained in force until the congress explicitly revoked it. The alternative view—favored by the congress—was that as soon as congress reconvened, the state of siege declared by the president would lapse.

In 1936, a major controversy erupted between the president and the congress over the interpretation of this clause. While this controversy was in progress, a man arrested under the state of siege provisions after the congress had reconvened, petitioned for a writ of habeas corpus on the ground that the state of siege had lapsed. The Court of Appeals of Valparaíso granted the writ, but, on appeal to the Supreme Court, denied it (Caffarena 1957:75–77). In its Opinion, the Court endorsed the president's position without even mentioning that what was at issue was a fundamental constitutional right. Moreover, the Court's reasoning suggests that, in its view, presidential decrees can never be struck down, even if they are manifestly inconsistent with the constitution.

The Court's reluctance to make use of its review powers and its lack of concern for individual rights were noted by Karl Lowenstein, an eminent contemporary observer. Upon examining the enforcement of security legislation, Lowenstein concluded that "[I]t cannot be ignored that Law 6,026 and some of the more recent emergency measures permit considerable restrictions on constitutionally granted individual rights. There is, however, no record of objections by the courts on grounds of unconstitutionality." (Lowenstein 1944:372) This view is corroborated by the findings of a well-respected local observer who in an exhaustive review of the case law of the Supreme Court during the 1930s and 1940s, found that the Court almost invariably opted to uphold the powers of the president rather than the rights of the individual (Caffarena 1957:221–227).

Custodian of Judicial Power—the Complaint Proceeding (*recurso de queja*)

Background

The behavior of the Supreme Court as custodian of judicial power contrasted sharply with its behavior as guardian of the constitution. While as guardian of the constitutions the Court was cautious, deferential, and formalistic, as head of the judiciary and custodian of judicial power, it was not restrained either by legal formalities or deference toward the political branches of the State.

As head of the judiciary, the Supreme Court had overall responsibility for the administration and management of all judicial services (Illanes 1966:277). Thus, it had enormous influence over appointments, promotions, and career development of judges. It also had disciplinary power over judges. In the exercise of this power the Supreme Court could act either on its own initiative or at the request of a party in a summary proceeding called "complaint proceeding." Under this proceeding, judges who did not fulfill their duties or who abused their powers faced disciplinary sanctions that included warnings, censures, fines, and even temporary suspension from office. Over the years, the Court (eventually with the acquiescence of the legislature) transformed the complaint proceeding into a form of cassation, thus distorting its original objectives while, in the process, making a travesty of its main function as a Court of Cassation. The Court also interpreted widely its jurisdiction under the compliant proceeding, to include any tribunal or body that exercised judicial power. That is, any tribunal—whether or not formally part of the judiciary—entrusted with the task of deciding disputes brought to it by parties. In doing so, the Supreme Court openly challenged the legislature's attempt to establish administrative tribunals that were not within its supervisory powers. The following paragraphs explain how these changes came about, and assess their implications.

One of the main responsibilities of the Supreme Court was to impose uniformity and coherence on the activities of lower courts. To fulfill this responsibility, the Court had cassation powers, that is, powers to quash judicial decisions based either on a mistaken interpretation of the law or on a failure to observe the rules of procedure. Cassation powers were strictly regulated: decisions had to be reasoned and could only be exercised against a limited number of Court of Appeals' judgments. Thus, cassation powers sought to achieve a balance between ensuring the independence and autonomy of lower court judges and ensuring a degree of uniformity and coherence in judicial decisions. By contrast, the complaint proceeding was a summary proceeding subject to flexible rules that did not require the Court to offer reasons in support of its decisions (Arteaga and González 1986:123). Over the years, the complaint proceeding underwent an important transformation. Instead of a genuine disciplinary proceeding, it became, in practice, an informal type of cassation. How this transformation came about is worth recounting.

Transformation of the Complaint Proceeding

The complaint proceeding dates back to 1875, when the first Judicial Code was enacted. Under that code, a "complaint," as it was then known, was a disciplinary device, not an ordinary civil remedy to challenge judicial decisions (Munita 1955:57). Throughout the nineteenth century, the Supreme Court had consistently resisted attempts by litigants to use the complaint mechanism as a device to review lower court decisions. By the early 1900s, however, the Court had changed its policy. It allowed parties to use the complaint proceeding to overturn lower court decisions and enacted regulations setting out the procedural requirements applicable to it. This decision and the ensuing regulations were strongly criticized by contemporary observers, as the Court did not have the power to amend or supplement the provisions of the Judicial Code (Munita 1955:64–65; Robles 1936:162–163). Four decades later, in 1944, the Court's bold transformation of its disciplinary powers was validated by the legislature through an amendment of the Judicial Code. Although under the terms of the amendment, the complaint proceeding continued to be regarded as a disciplinary mechanism, the Supreme Court soon announced that it could be used to challenge any judicial decision regardless of the availability of other judicial remedies (Munita 1955:61–63, 101). The complaint proceeding as a means to challenge judicial decisions, thus instantly became a more attractive and less cumbersome device than cassation. The Supreme Court also used its expanded disciplinary powers to quash decisions of special administrative tribunals. These tribunals, created by the legislature to resolve disputes in specific areas of public policy, such as labor law or agrarian law, were expressly designed to remain beyond the jurisdictional and disciplinary reach of the Supreme Court. The provisions of the Judicial Code did not apply to these tribunals and the Supreme Court did not play a part in the selection, appointment, or removal of its members. Tribunal members were part of the central administration and so their position was different from that of judges in ordinary courts who were independent of the government, enjoyed security of tenure, and were subject to the disciplinary powers of the Supreme Court (Aylwin 1952:302–310).

The Supreme Court, however, extended the reach of the complaint proceeding to these special tribunals. It did so, based on a broad interpretation of Article 86 of the constitution that entrusted the Supreme Court with disciplinary responsibilities over "all the tribunals in the nation." According to the Court, as special administrative tribunals exercised judicial power, they fell within the scope of its disciplinary jurisdiction. This interpretation enabled the Court to review decisions by special administrative tribunals, which the legislature had established with the express intention of keeping them beyond the reach of the Supreme Court. The Court made ample use of it disciplinary powers to review decisions of labor tribunals, which under the Labor Code were meant to remain outside the framework of the judiciary. The Court's interference with the work of labor courts caused considerable controversy (Aguero 1948). In the end, however, the legislature gave in and formally granted the Supreme Court authority to exercise disciplinary powers over the labor courts (Walker 1965:123). This decision had the unintended effect of strengthening the Ministry of Labor, as workers who had grievances against their employers found the Ministry a friendlier place than labor courts (Ietswaart 1981:657).

By the early 1960s, the Court's expansive interpretation of its disciplinary powers had become generally accepted and the complaint proceeding was available to review decisions handed down by any tribunal, including those that were not formally part of the judiciary, such as the tribunals in the area of price controls, tax administration, competition law, and the special tribunals established under the agrarian reform law.

Legal and Political Impact

The transformation of the complaint proceedings into a form of cassation had a major impact on the Supreme Court's workload.

Statistical evidence shows that by the mid-1950s the complaint proceeding had overtaken cassation as the Court's main area of activity (Arteaga and González 1986:121). This trend continued into the 1960s and early 1970s. Indeed, between 1969 and 1973, the Court handed down approximately 1,700 judgments and decisions per year. Of these, about 50 percent were judgments in complaint proceeding, while cassation judgments amounted to less than 30 percent (Valenzuela 1991: 146–149). The statistics also show that the complaint proceeding was profusely used to challenge labor court decisions. These statistics, however, are not disaggregated, and therefore are not easy to interpret. There is no study analyzing the impact of the complaint proceeding on labor courts or labor law generally. One observer has suggested that, in the area of labor law, the complaint proceeding was largely used to quash labor court decisions that favored workers (Novoa 1970:4–6). This conclusion, however, is based on a very small sample of cases. A statistical survey on the use of the complaint proceeding in the province of Concepción, between 1963 and 1967, indicates that nearly 70 percent of complaint proceedings were rejected (Saavedra and Pecchi 1971:36–39). These figures suggest either that parties were indiscriminately using the complaint proceeding as a third instance, or, that courts showed considerable caution in the exercise of this power. The available evidence on the use of the complaint proceeding against agrarian reform tribunals in the 1960s is also inconclusive. While the complaint proceeding was undoubtedly used by landowners to stop or delay land expropriations, its overall impact was negligible. That the complaint proceeding was not an effective weapon against agrarian reform tribunals is not surprising as their jurisdiction was limited (Thome 1971).

The complaint proceeding was popular with litigants because it became in fact a third instance that allowed parties to challenge otherwise final decisions by ordinary courts or by special administrative tribunals. Thus, the prolific use of the complaint proceeding undermined the authority of lower courts and slowed down the judicial process. But the Court's liberal policy toward the complaint proceeding also had another negative consequence. Because the complaint proceeding was a summary proceeding, the Court was not required to give reasons in support of its decisions (Arteaga and González 1986:123). The prolific use of the complaint proceeding thus undermined the quality of legal reasoning, as well as the independence and autonomy of lower court judges. The Court's reliance on the complaint proceeding to assert its influence on ad hoc administrative tribunals was also deeply resented by the congress and the executive and contributed to reinforcing their tendency to exclude ordinary courts from important areas of public policy.

Administrative Justice

The 1925 Constitution envisaged the establishment of administrative tribunals with general jurisdiction to review administrative action. This provision of the constitution was never implemented and, therefore, the legal system did not have a judicial mechanism of general application to review acts of the administration. These circumstances placed the Supreme Court in an awkward position as citizens aggrieved by acts of the administration often sought judicial relief from ordinary courts. The Supreme Court, constrained as it was by a constitutional provision that allocated jurisdiction to the nonexistent administrative tribunals, was unable to develop a coherent approach to resolve this question. While the Court formally asserted that, pending the establishment of administrative tribunals, ordinary courts did not have jurisdiction to review acts of the administration, in practice, it tried to fashion legal remedies on a case-by-case basis. This approach, based on a retreat to principles of private law, however, offered neither a suitable judicial remedy to individual plaintiffs nor a useful platform to address the numerous problems arising from the absence of an effective system of administrative justice. Instead, it created considerable uncertainty and, once again, confirmed the view held by most politicians that the judiciary was unfit to handle issues of public policy.

A Disjointed System

The failure to establish administrative tribunals was not an oversight. Indeed, between 1925 and 1973 five bills were submitted to the congress providing for the establishment of administrative tribunals (Junta de Gobierno 1982:277–390). These bills, however, were drowned in esoteric legal arguments regarding the nature of the judicial function and the institutional location of the proposed tribunals. Some argued that they should be part of the ordinary judiciary and subject to the supervision of the Supreme Court, while others argued that they should be independent both of the government and of the Supreme Court.[12] Politicians of every persuasion welcomed this doctrinal controversy, which paralyzed the congress, as, one way or another, they all shared the view that judicial control of administrative action was unnecessary and that the most effective restraints on the executive were those generated by the political process.

Failure to establish administrative tribunals did not end issues of administrative justice. Citizens aggrieved by acts of public authorities resorted to ordinary courts only to find the courts declined to accept jurisdiction on the ground that administrative matters should be resolved by the nonexistent administrative tribunals (Silva Cimma 1968:330). Their argument, though consistent with the constitution, was also convenient, as it protected the already overloaded court system from being flooded with administrative law cases (Aylwin 1952:197–298). Yet, as the administrative machinery expanded and state intervention became increasingly more diverse, it became evident that the absence of administrative tribunals amounted to a denial of justice. There thus emerged a disjointed three-prong arrangement that created considerable confusion and failed to get to the root of the problem.

The first prong consisted of areas of administrative practice in which the legislature explicitly gave ordinary courts jurisdiction to review acts of the administration. Thus, for example, ordinary courts were given power to review administrative decision that imposed fines, such as those imposed by the Health and Safety Inspectorate. Courts were also given the power to review certain decisions by local councils (Aylwin 1952:299–302). The second prong consisted of areas of administrative activity assigned to special administrative tribunals that had the power to review administrative action, in areas such as tax administration, customs valuation, competition law, and agrarian reform law (Aylwin 1952:302–310). These special tribunals varied in structure and composition, but their common feature was that their decisions should remain beyond the reach of ordinary courts. This objective was largely frustrated because of the Supreme Court's expansive interpretation of the scope of the complaint proceeding. The third prong comprised administrative activity that had not been expressly assigned to ordinary courts or that did not fall within the jurisdiction of special administrative tribunals. It thus included the bulk, and most sensitive portion, of administrative activity. In formal terms, third-prong activities fell within the jurisdiction of the nonexistent administrative tribunals.

The Court's Dilemma

The third prong presented the Court with a difficult dilemma. What should it do when, as it inevitably happened, individuals aggrieved by administrative acts that fell within this section brought their grievance before ordinary courts? Should the Court direct ordinary courts to accept or to decline jurisdiction? The answer to these questions turned on the interpretation of Article 87 of the Constitution, which reads as follows:

> There shall be administrative tribunals with permanent membership to pass upon claims that may be interposed against arbitrary acts or measures of the political or administrative authorities and the disposition of which has not been entrusted by the constitution or the laws to any other tribunals. Their organization and jurisdiction are matters of law.

According to one interpretation, since the constitution had made special provision for the establishment of administrative tribunals, ordinary courts could not, unless expressly authorized to do so, review acts of the administration (Silva Cimma 1968:330, Silva Bascuñán 1963: 3:440). This interpretation, endorsed by most local administrative lawyers, amounted to a denial of justice, as there was no alternative judicial forum where the aggrieved parties could take their claims. Nevertheless, as ever, an alternative interpretation was available. It was based on Article 5 of the Judicial Code, which sets out the general rule that ordinary courts had jurisdiction over all judicial matters arising within the territory, except those explicitly entrusted by special law to other tribunals. Thus, according to this interpretation, pending the establishment of administrative tribunals, ordinary courts had a duty to assume jurisdiction on claims that challenged acts of the administration (Fontecilla 1953:79–80). This interpretation should have appealed to the Supreme Court, as it was consistent with the expansive notion of judicial power noted in the preceding section. The Supreme Court, however, did not fully embrace it until the eve of the military coup that deposed Allende in 1973, and even then, it did so only temporarily (see chapter 9). Instead, in order to resolve the dilemma posed by the third prong of administrative activity, the Supreme Court resorted to the act of authority doctrine.

The Act of Authority Doctrine

The act of authority doctrine—based on an old French doctrine abandoned in France after the celebrated *Blanco case* in the late nineteenth century (Brown and Garner 1973:64; Dupuis et al. 2004:55, 643)— provided the Court with a simple device to handle cases arising from the third prong of administrative activity, that is, administrative activity that had not been expressly within the jurisdiction of ordinary courts or that did not fall within the jurisdiction of special administrative tribunals. The act of authority doctrine classifies administrative acts into two categories: acts of authority (*autorité*) and acts of management (*gestion*). Acts of authority are broadly acts that involve the use of public authority. Acts of management, on the other hand, are acts of a commercial nature, in which public authorities become involved in connection with their official duties (Aylwin 1952:133). Thus, for example, while a decision to requisition property is an act of authority, the purchase of stationery by a government department is an act of management. Applying this doctrine, the Court would conclude that ordinary courts did not have jurisdiction to review the legality of acts of authority—as, theoretically, these were within the exclusive jurisdiction of the not-yet-established administrative tribunals—but that ordinary courts did have jurisdiction to entertain claims against pubic authorities on matters relating to acts of management (Varas 1940:379–383).

The *Socotransco* case, decided in 1964, illustrates the way the Supreme Court applied the act of authority doctrine.[13] The issue raised in this case was whether ordinary courts could review a presidential decree that had cancelled the legal personality of *Socotransco*, a local transport cooperative. The members of the cooperative sought from the Court a judgment declaring that the president's decree was illegal. The government objected to the jurisdiction of the Court on the ground that the power to grant and cancel legal personality of corporations was vested exclusively in the president. The decree canceling *Socotransco*'s legal personality was, according to the government, an act of authority and, as such, could not be reviewed by ordinary courts. The Supreme Court agreed. According to the Court, in the absence of an explicit grant of jurisdiction, ordinary courts are barred from intervening in matters within the jurisdiction of other organs of the state, even though these courts had not yet been established.

The act of authority doctrine had considerable appeal, as acts of the administration that fell within the category of acts of management were fully within the jurisdiction of ordinary courts. Not surprisingly, private litigants with claims against the government put forward an expansive interpretation of the notion of act of management. However, this doctrine also had some disadvantages. On the one hand, the act of authority doctrine provided an incentive for the government to characterize almost all its decisions as acts of authority to escape from the reach of ordinary courts. On the other hand, and more significantly, the act of authority doctrine did not provide a remedy in cases where administrative acts infringed upon private rights. This issue was raised in the *Socotransco* case. In this case, plaintiff argued—in the alternative—that ordinary courts had jurisdiction because the presidential decree that had cancelled the legal personality of their transport cooperative had financial implications for their members. Although the Court acknowledged that the decree had had this effect, it held nonetheless that ordinary courts did not have jurisdiction either to review the presidential decree or to deal with its financial consequences for the members of the cooperative. Thus, in *Socotransco*, the Court held that the consequences of an act of authority do not alter its nature: once an act of authority, always an act of authority.[14] However, the Court did not always follow this seemingly harsh line of reasoning. Indeed, in some cases where administrative acts had an indirect effect on property rights, the Court attempted to provide a remedy to private parties, while, at the same time acknowledging that ordinary courts could not review acts of authority. Again, drawing loosely on a distinction developed in French administrative law, the court held that where acts of the administration affected assets and liabilities of private parties, ordinary courts had jurisdiction to entertain private claims arising from these acts, although they did not have the authority to review the underlying act of authority.[15] In the *Camus* case,[16] this distinction worked quite well. In this case, the Ministry of Public Works demanded from the residents of a district in Valparaíso a financial contribution to pay for the costs of paving their streets. Mr. Camus along with other local residents refused to pay and instead brought an action asking the court to declare that they were not liable to contribute to the costs of the operation and requesting compensation for damages, which they had sustained as a consequence of alleged negligence attributable to the department. The Supreme Court, while acknowledging that the underlying decision was an act of authority, held that ordinary courts had jurisdiction to deal with the residents' claim because the case involved a dispute between parties over assets and liabilities (*controvesia patrimonial*). In *Camus*, the distinction between the public and the private components of administrative acts seemed to work well because plaintiffs in this case were not directly challenging the decision to pave the street, but merely the government's authority to demand a financial contribution from the local residents.

Courts, however, faced more difficult problems when private parties either directly challenged the legality of an administrative act or raised questions about their legality as an incidental question in the context of cases that were otherwise within the jurisdiction of the courts. These problems raise the difficult issue regarding how to draw the line between the jurisdiction of administrative tribunals and ordinary courts. In general, the solution adopted by most civil law countries with established administrative courts is to reserve to the exclusive jurisdiction of ordinary courts certain category of claims; namely, claims over personal status, individual freedom, or property rights (Brown and Bell 1993:139; Dupuis et al. 2004:646; Szladitz 1984:24–40). In Chile, because of the failure to establish administrative tribunals, the task of drawing the line between the jurisdiction of administrative tribunals and ordinary courts was singularly difficult.

As already explained, one possibility was to argue that pending the establishment of administrative tribunals ordinary courts had full jurisdiction over claims arising from administrative activity. The Court, however, declined to follow this approach. Instead, it adopted a more convoluted approach that, in addition to creating considerable confusion and resentment among government officials, did not resolve the underlying issue of the legality of administrative acts. The following case illustrates this approach.

The Montero *Case*

As explained in chapter 5, DL 520 of 1932 established the Prices and Subsistence Agency (PSA) to control prices of essential consumer goods. The items subject to control were listed in the decree. The PSA, however, interpreting its requisition powers expansively, introduced a rent control system. The objective was to use the government's requisition powers to protect tenants from unscrupulous landlords. This new policy sparked political controversy in the congress, as it was doubtful whether the PSA had the discretion to add new items to those listed in DL 520 (Talesnik 1940:113–1120). The question of the legality of the PSA's rent control scheme soon reached the courts. Mrs. Montero, a landlady from the city of La Serena, challenged the legality of a PSA decree that reduced the rent and extended the terms of the lease in respect of one of her properties. Mrs. Montero requested the court to declare the decree illegal and demanded the immediate restitution of her property. The lower court found that the rent control scheme was ultra vires and declared the requisition order null and void. The Court of Appeals of La Serena affirmed the lower court judgment.[17] The Supreme Court, however, reversed the Court of Appeals decision on the ground that ordinary courts do not have jurisdiction to review acts of the administration.[18] However, while the Court refused to quash the requisition decree, it also provided guidelines to lower courts on how they should decide this type of cases. According to the Court, while ordinary courts were not allowed to invalidate acts of the administration, they were not expected to give effect to illegal acts of the administration. Applying this reasoning to Mrs. Montero's claim, the Court concluded that had the plaintiff requested only the restitution of her property based on the lease agreement, the Court would have been able to decide the case without having to quash an act of the administration. All they had to do was to refuse to apply it; that is, to pretend that it did not exist.

The distinction between quashing an administrative act and refusing to apply it was as a useful device to circumvent the traditional doctrine that ordinary courts could not review acts of the administration. Yet, it was disingenuous because in order to decide whether to give effect to an administrative decree or not, courts had to form a view about its legality. As according to the Supreme Court's approach, courts could not invalidate a government decree, the parties did not litigate this point and courts did not have to offer reasons as to why they refused to apply a particular decree.[19] The Court's approach opened up the possibility that private law could be used indiscriminately to discard or ignore any government decision with which the courts disagreed. The Court's approach was based on the assumption that in the event of a conflict between private and public law principles, private law would always prevail. While most commentators accepted this approach, none raised any questions as to its implications (Aylwin 1952:302; Silva Cimma 1968:259, 329). The political implications of this peculiar doctrinal development were fully felt in the late 1960s and early 1970s when courts were called upon to protect property rights affected by the policies of governments committed to radical structural reform.

Conclusion

The role of the Supreme Court during the party democracy period is somewhat baffling. While on the one hand, the Court and the judiciary were excluded from key areas of public policy; on the other hand courts, were on the whole, able to maintain their independence, partly because of this exclusion. Moreover, the Supreme Court seemed willing to keep a low political profile and defer to the executive and the legislature as evidenced by its refusal to play its role as guardian of the constitution. Yet, under pressure from individuals aggrieved by acts of the administration, the Court responded dynamically and critically as it developed a variety of strategies and subterfuges to review acts of the administration. The practice of the Court in this area, however, was neither consistent nor coherent. Its haphazard doctrinal elaborations undermined the confidence and professional independence of lower courts judges while failing to make judicial decisions more predictable. The behavior of the Court as head of the judiciary was also contradictory. On the one hand, it successfully defied the political branches of the state by asserting disciplinary jurisdiction over special administrative tribunals that the legislature had originally intended should be kept beyond its reach. On the other hand, displaying little concern over the formal limits of its powers and exhibiting an alarming authoritarian streak, it transformed its disciplinary powers into a third instance, thus increasing its capacity to influence the content and direction of judicial decisions. Ironically, the Court's expansive interpretation of its powers replicated the way the executive interpreted its regulatory powers. Yet, in the end, the Court's defiance in some areas of policy did not succeed in fundamentally challenging the political organs of the state, as it had virtually abdicated its role as guardian of the constitution. Its defiance was also largely negative and it failed to improve the quality of legal reasoning. As a result, during this period, the Court failed to persuade skeptical members of the political elites that judicial institutions had a role to play in the democratic process. Thus, deep distrust developed between the judiciary and the political branches of the state that, in later years, would prove fatal for political stability.

Part III

Radical Democracy

Democracy should not depend on elites making a one-time gift to the demos of a predesigned framework of equal rights. This does not mean that rights do not matter a great deal, but rights in a democracy depend on the demos winning them, extending them substantively, and, in the process, acquiring experience of the political, that is, of participating in power, reflecting on the consequences of its exercise, and struggling to sort out the common well-being amid cultural differences and socio-economic disparities.

Sheldon Wolin, "Liberal Democratic Divide,"
Political Theory, 98

Chapter 7

A Revolution in Liberty

Thirty Years In Power

Background

Eduardo Frei won the presidential elections of 1964 by a clear majority. In a three-way contest he polled 56 percent of the vote, while Allende, the runner-up obtained 39 percent and Julio Durán, the candidate of the Radical Party, polled a mere 5 percent of the vote. The scale of the electoral victory undoubtedly gave Frei and his team enormous confidence that they could successfully launch their "revolution in liberty." Indeed, such was their confidence that they predicted that the CDP (*Partido Demócrata Cristiano*/Christian Democratic Party), would remain in office for at least three decades. At the time, this prediction seemed reasonable. The CDP being a new party not heavily contaminated by the discredited coalition politics of the 1940s (Fleet 1985; Grayson 1968). It had a good technical team and hundreds of devoted party workers. Moreover, it also had generous financial support from the United States since Washington regarded Frei as an important partner in the struggle against the spread of Marxism in Chile and the rest of Latin America. Given these circumstances, it is not surprising that the new administration made an auspicious start. During its first two years, the government successfully combined sound economic management with the introduction of structural reforms and major social programs in housing, education, and health. Yet, less than three years later, the government began to lose control and by the end of its sixth year in office, it was politically isolated, deeply divided, and its electoral strength had dropped from 42 percent in 1965 to 28 percent in 1970. Frei's failure was made worse by the fact that in 1970 he had to hand over power to Salvador Allende, the man that both his right-wing supporters and the United States had hoped would never win a presidential election.

Most observers attribute the political failure of the CDP administration to its stubborn refusal to form a broad government coalition for the implementation of its program. CDP opted for an isolationist policy that diluted its electoral support, undermined the spirit of compromise, and brought political polarization (Garretón 1989:14; Valenzuela 1994:128). Left-wing critics of the CDP administration point out that its political failure stemmed from the fact that although its rhetoric was revolutionary, its policies were not. According to this argument, the CDP administration consistently sacrificed its radical programmatic objective in order to satisfy the demands of business associations and other dominant economic groups (Lechner 1970:151–158; Petras 1969:253–255). These views were undoubtedly justified. Instead of seeking political allies, the CDP campaigned vigorously to achieve electoral hegemony across a broad spectrum of classes. This attempt naturally frightened and alienated the rest of the political parties and did nothing to foster the spirit of compromise. Likewise, there is little doubt that the CDP administration was prudent and conservative in managing the economy, as it did not seek to replace the market economy. Yet, these interpretations, though partly correct, do not entirely capture the nature of the dilemma confronted by the CDP administration. While it is true that the CDP did not seek political alliances, there were important political and ideological factors that counseled against such an alliance. An alliance with the Right would have amounted to political suicide as it would have required abandoning the central objective of modernizing the countryside through an agrarian reform and extending union rights to agricultural workers. An alliance with the Left was also unthinkable. The CDP electoral campaign, which had made use of virulent anticommunist propaganda to discredit the left-wing candidate, had deeply scarred the Left. Moreover, as a majority within the new administration genuinely believed that the CDP was an alternative to Marxism, it was unlikely that the idea of inviting the Marxists to join the government would have been seriously considered. The argument that the CDP readily compromised its political program in order to please the private sector is also not entirely accurate. Indeed, although the government was undoubtedly determined to apply sound principles of macroeconomic governance, it never entirely abandoned its commitment to social and economic change. Indeed, as the text that follows show, when confronted with the choice between sound economic management and continuation of its program of structural reform, the government opted for both.

The dilemma that the CDP administration confronted at the outset stemmed from the fact that, although it had won the election by an unusually large margin and, once in office, continued to enjoy enormous electoral appeal, it could not readily transform its electoral strength into political and institutional power to implement its program. If one took into account the strength of the right-wing vote in 1965, at least 20 percent of the CDP's electoral support was from right-wing voters who had opted for Frei as the lesser of the two evils. Moreover, a large proportion of those who stood to benefit from the implementation of the radical reforms advocated by the CDP had voted for Salvador Allende. These circumstances suggest that the CDP urgently needed to broaden its base of support. Yet, instead of doing so by means of political alliances, the CDP opted for electoral competition and political mobilization. As the text that follows show, this strategy produced excellent results. The CDP soon became the single largest party and retained this position until the end of the Frei administration. Yet, its electoral success did not instantly resolve the dilemma of implementation. Although it managed to secure congressional approval for its most important legislative initiatives, it was unable to combine its commitment to sound economic management with the expectations of its heterogeneous constituency.

This chapter examines the dilemma confronted by the CDP administration and explains how it was exacerbated by the attempt to extend political and social rights to rural workers and the urban poor.

The Program

The CDP described its "revolution in liberty" as a process that would usher in a communitarian path to development. On the economic side, as noted in chapter 4, the program sought to radically overhaul the prevailing policy of import substitution by introducing a comprehensive land reform and restructuring the regulatory regime in copper mining. The expectation was that these reforms would provide the foundations for reviving the manufacturing sector and increasing its regional competitiveness. These objectives were combined with a commitment to control inflation to ensure economic growth.

The CDP, however, was not only concerned with economic growth and stability. As a party that drew its philosophical inspiration from the social teachings of the Catholic Church, the CDP was also concerned with social justice. Its program of governance thus placed emphasis on income redistribution and social development, especially in the areas of housing, health, and education. This component of the program was essential since, according to the CDP, underdevelopment could not be tackled merely through the implementation of economic reforms. A truly revolutionary approach required a radical restructuring of the political system. Such a restructuring was necessary because the political system did not adequately represent the claims and aspirations of the majority (Ahumada 1958:136). True democracy, according to President Eduardo Frei Montalva, exists only when the people effectively have access to power and can exercise it (Frei 1967:390). Thus, based largely on the marginality theory developed by Roger Vekemans S. J., a Belgian sociologist, the CDP focused on the issue of political participation. Vekemans's theory of marginality was in fact a precursor of what is today known as "social exclusion" (Vekemans and Giusti 1970). According to Vekemans, "marginals" are people that society treats as outsiders and are permanently excluded from its benefits. Because marginals are weak, disorganized and extremely vulnerable, the state is called upon to play a major role in empowering them so that they can fully exercise their rights as citizens. The marginals that Vekemans had in mind were mainly the urban poor and peasants.

The CDP's objective was ambitious. Its aim was to radically transform the relationship between state and society. Its program envisaged a dynamic role for the state in the management of the economy and the direct involvement of unions in the management of enterprises. This new role of unions called for a redefinition of the relationship between the state and business associations as well as the relationship between management and unions. An indispensable component of this aspect of the program was the introduction of measures to sever the hitherto existing close link between unions and political parties. The aim was to give unions a meaningful stake in the economic process and hence the need to depoliticize them. Accordingly, the CDP set out to become the leading force among workers, peasants, and the urban poor and thus demonstrate that its communitarian path to development was a practical alternative to Marxist socialism.

Given the complexity and scale of the CDP's objectives, it is not surprising that, as the government began implementing its program, sharp disagreements emerged within the party over the meaning of the phrase "communitarian society." It is helpful at this stage to outline the two conflicting interpretations, as they represent the two main political factions within the CDP (Petras 1969:198; Sigmund 1977: 53, 59, 56; Silva Solar and Chonchol 1970; Yocelevzky 1987:307). The moderates—led by President Frei—argued that building a communitarian society was a long-term process that involved two distinct stages. During the first stage—the Frei administration—the state was called upon to play a dominant role through extensive intervention in the economy and the promotion of social programs in favor of the urban poor and rural communities. During the second stage, community organizations would begin to play a more decisive political role thus bringing about genuine social empowerment. The radicals within the CDP rejected this two-stage approach. In their view, the communitarian society envisaged by the party was a truly socialist society. Therefore, the program of structural reforms implemented by the government had to be tailored to this objective. Accordingly, they called for a more extensive and rapid implementation of the process of agrarian reform. They also called for the immediate involvement of workers in the management of industrial enterprises. As they were also skeptical of excessive state intervention, they called upon the government to speedily devolve power to community organizations so as to limit the paternalistic role of the state bureaucracy. Despite its scholastic overtones, this controversy had important practical implications as it influenced the position of party members on key areas of government policy.

Standing for Principles

When the right-wing parties offered their support to Frei to ensure that Allende would not be elected as president, Frei made it clear that their support would not compromise his political platform. After the election he reiterated this view, promising that he would faithfully carry out the promises made during the electoral campaign. Frei's principled stance was not, however, easy to uphold, as the CDP did not control enough seats in the congress to secure approval for its legislative program. Yet, the government decided against forming broad political alliances on the ground that this would compromise its program.

The government's principled stance was greatly aided by the fact that a general election was scheduled for March 1965, only six months after the presidential elections. This election provided the CDP with an ideal opportunity to strengthen its representation in the congress by taking advantage of the favorable political momentum generated by Frei's freshly won victory. The outcome of the elections was encouraging, but not decisive. The CDP secured overall control of the chamber of deputies, but not the senate. The government was confident, however, that through skillful parliamentary maneuvering it would overcome this problem. It expected the congress to approve most of its key legislative initiatives, either with the vote of the Right or the Left. This expectation proved correct. Despite strong opposition by the left-wing parties, the government managed to secure the approval of its copper policy with the votes of the Right. The agrarian reform and peasant unionization bills, vehemently opposed by the right, were approved with the vote of the left (Chonchol 1970:71).

But the CDP's success in the 1965 congressional elections, though impressive, did not fully resolve the government's problems. Although the CDP's share of the vote increased from 15 percent in 1961 to 42 percent in 1965, its new supporters came largely from the middle classes. Indeed the success of the CDP in 1965 was achieved largely at the expense of the vote of the Right and the Radical Party. While the electoral strength of the Right dropped from 30 percent in 1961 to a mere 12 percent in 1965, the Radical Party's share of the vote dropped from 21 percent to 13 percent. By contrast, the electoral support of the Left was not affected by the success of the CDP. Indeed, between 1961 and 1965 the electoral strength of the Communist and Socialist Parties remained virtually unchanged, at around 22–23 percent. Thus, it appeared that the CDP had successfully exploited its popularity to attract middle-class voters, but had not managed to increase its appeal among working-class voters (Zeitlin and Petras 1970:27). The electoral results reinforced the government's view that political alliances were unnecessary. Indeed, since the CDP expected that the implementation of its program would largely benefit groups who hitherto supported the Marxist parties, it did not see any reason to seek an alliance or make any concessions. But the CDP did not passively wait for the reforms to take effect. It immediately launched a well coordinated and effective process of popular mobilization, targeted specifically at voters in urban, mining. and rural areas that were regarded as the natural constituency of the Marxist parties.

The CDP's success in the congressional elections of 1965, combined with its principled stance of not seeking allies was deeply resented and feared by the rest of the political parties. The electoral success of the CDP had so undermined the electoral strength of the Right that in order to survive the Conservative and Liberal Parties were forced merge and form the National Party. This new party was anxious about the CDP's promise of a comprehensive agrarian reform and feared that other sectors of the economy would soon fall within the scope of this reformist zeal. The Radical Party was also on the defensive as it was being displaced from its hegemonic position at the center of the political spectrum by the CDP. Although communists and socialists had managed to retain their electoral strength, they had reason to be concerned because, apart from the vast resources invested by the government in mobilizing subordinate groups, the CDP, as the party of government, was in a position to deliver on its promises. The Marxist parties were also concerned that the CDP's proposals on unions would disrupt their long-standing relationship with the labor movement. Thus, for different reasons, all the parties regarded the CDP with trepidation, as they had grounds for believing that the CDP might achieve its objective of breaking the mould of the prevailing party system. Their anxiety, exacerbated by the tension generated by government policies, fostered a climate of suspicion, corroded the process of political deliberation, and changed the nature of political competition.

Overcoming Hurdles

Economic Reactivation

The initial economic policy of CPD was expansionist and sought to reactivate the economy through a substantial increase in public expenditure. An important component of this policy was an incomes policy aimed at favoring lower income groups. During the first two years, this expansionist policy was successful. It brought about an increase in production, halved the rate of inflation, and did not create a fiscal deficit. Yet, not all went well. The government was unable to fully gain the confidence of the private sector. As a consequence, investment levels were lower than expected and the increase in production was largely based on improved capacity utilization. Even more worrying was the fact that the increase in remunerations between 1965 and 1967 exceeded government targets by more than 50 percent (Ffrench-Davis 1973:59). The inflationary potential of these factors forced the government to seriously reconsider its economic policy.

Since the mid-1940s, inflation had consistently disrupted government programs. Moreover, during the final years of the Alessandri administration, managing inflation became especially difficult as it was compounded with an ever-growing foreign debt. The government's fear of inflation was thus perfectly reasonable. Accordingly, by midterm, it cut public expenditure, restricted credit, and reduced import levels. Although these measures helped to ease inflationary pressures, in the long term they proved ineffective. Public expenditure cuts led to a slight recession that hit mainly employment and income levels of the poorest sections of the population. As the tax system was already overstretched, the government was forced to introduce further cuts in public expenditure and to propose severe austerity measures. Among the measures proposed was a compulsory savings scheme that involved paying 50 percent of the annual readjustment of public sector salaries in government bonds (Molina 1972:139–144). These unexpectedly harsh financial measures were accompanied by a proposal to temporarily suspend the right to strike in support of economic demands. These proposals caused such a political uproar that the government was forced to back down. This policy reversal brought about the resignation of the minister of finance and fatally undermined the government's capacity to control inflation. By the end of Frei's term in office, the annual rate of inflation reached 34 percent; that is, four points higher than in 1964, its first year in office.

The government's defeat on its proposed austerity package was made worse because it exposed deep divisions within the CDP. Indeed, the party, controlled at the time by its radical faction—known locally as *rebeldes*—did not conceal its distaste for the government's proposals and only reluctantly supported them. This attitude caused considerable embarrassment to the president who, in retaliation, used his influence within the party to remove members of the left-wing faction from positions of responsibility. Although Frei managed to reassert control over the party, the cost was high. Shortly thereafter, a small, but influential group of CDP parliamentarians resigned from the party and formed a new political group *Movimiento de Acción Popular Unitaria* (MAPU). The MAPU soon joined the Marxist parties in the establishment of the Popular Unity, the electoral coalition that supported Salvador Allende's successful bid for the presidency.

The government's decision to cut public expenditure and its failure to control inflation had wider consequences. These consequences were not unexpected as a large proportion of public expenditure was devoted to the government's new social programs. Indeed, in 1965, during Frei's first full year in office, more than 50 percent of public investment was allocated to agriculture, housing, and education (Ffrench-Davis 1973:175). The reduction in public expenditure forced the government to scale down these programs. The government, however, refused to abandon them. Not surprisingly, scaling down these programs disappointed its potential beneficiaries and intensified political mobilization. As the CDP would soon find out, the mix of economic austerity with high levels of political mobilization had lethal consequences. In the paragraphs that follow, I examine the government's dilemma in a select number of areas.

Copper—Avoiding Nationalization

Copper policy was a permanent source of frustration for politicians. As explained in chapter 4, copper was explicitly excluded from CORFO's mandate and was left safely in the hands of U.S.-based investors. Yet, revenue from copper exports was subject to sharp fluctuations and, therefore, copper always had the capacity to disrupt the balance of payments and governments' economic policies. Between 1952 and 1970, the annual average fluctuation of the price of copper was 12 percent (Ffrench-Davis 1973:281). The instability of copper revenues was combined with periods when the price was kept artificially low, due to price controls imposed by the U.S. government. Such price controls were strictly enforced during the Second World War and, as a consequence, Chile lost more than five hundred million dollars in revenue from copper exports (Tomic 1974:132). During the Korean conflict in the early 1950s, President González resisted attempts by the U.S. government to impose price controls on copper imports and instead managed to secure a measure of control over the commercialization of copper (Tomic 1974:136). In 1955, however, the Ibáñez administration introduced a new regulatory framework that returned full control over marketing operations to U.S. companies. This new regulatory framework was soon discredited as it yielded greater financial benefits to the companies than to the government (Ffrench-Davis 1974:39–40). Thus, not surprisingly, a new policy on copper was an important component of the CDP's "revolution in liberty."

The objective of the CDP administration was to ensure that copper policy was closely synchronized with national development plans. During its electoral campaign, the CDP had stated that this objective would be achieved through greater state control over copper resources, but its leaders had been studiously ambiguous as to whether this policy entailed the nationalization of U.S. companies operating in the sector. Shortly after taking office, however, President Frei announced the "Chileanization of copper" and presented this policy as a more attractive alternative to full nationalization. The proposed policy involved establishing a joint venture company between CODELCO, the State Copper Corporation, and Kennecott Copper, the owner of one of the country's largest copper mines (Moran 1974:132–138). According to Frei, the proposed joint venture would bring about an increase in production as well as greater control over the country's main natural resource. The government expected that the increased revenue from copper exports would fund other components of its program of structural reforms.

The proposed copper policy was strongly criticized by the Communist and Socialist Parties who demanded instead full nationalization. Several CDP parliamentarians shared this view, but did not oppose the government as they expected, in exchange, that it would sponsor a radical law on agrarian reform (Chonchol 1970:71). The government could afford to ignore the views of the Marxist parties because it could rely on the support in the congress of the National and Radical Parties. Initially, the implementation of the new policy was successful and generated abundant revenue for the government. But, as ever, it was not long before copper once again became the focus of public controversy. Although government revenue increased, the U.S. companies did better than the government. Indeed, not long after the Chileanization was completed and largely as a consequence of the Vietnam war, the price of copper shot up, generating massive windfall profits for the companies. The government's negotiating skills and its ability to look after the country's main natural resources were thus called into question (Ffrench-Davis 1974:40–42). Eventually, the government was forced to take this criticism seriously as some of it came from within the CDP. Accordingly, it took several measures to increase copper revenue. It also entered into a joint venture with Anaconda, the other U.S. company in the sector, which it depicted as agreed nationalization (*nacionalización pactada*). Despite these measures, the government failed to convince its own party about its copper policy. So, in 1970, Radomiro Tomic, the CDP's presidential candidate, called for the full nationalization of copper, thus implicitly repudiating a major plank of Frei's program.

Unions—A New Deal

One of the pillars of the government's program was to eliminate the class struggle through the harmonious integration of capital and labor. To achieve this objective, the program proposed that workers should participate in the management of their workplace. But successful worker participation required unions solely devoted to resolving matters relating to industrial relations, rather than the promotion of political ideology (Yocelevzky 1987:212). In this area, however, the government faced a major difficulty as nearly half the number of union leaders were either members or supporters of one of the two Marxist parties, while only just over 20 percent supported the CDP (Landsberger 1969:129). As a consequence, the main beneficiaries of the proposed enterprise reform would be unions controlled by the Marxist parties. Moreover, as the private sector had shown no enthusiasm for these proposals, the government quietly abandoned them.

The government, however, did not give up on its aim of reducing Marxist influence within the union movement. To this end, it attempted to establish a new labor confederation as an alternative to the Marxist-controlled CUT and introduced a bill proposing the elimination of the prevailing "closed shop" system (Angell 1972:199). The attempt to divide the labor movement through the establishment of a new confederation was strongly criticized by the union movement and leftist groups within the CDP. Realizing that its initiative was doomed to fail the government backed down, and the CDP remained within the CUT umbrella. But the animosity generated by the attempt to divide the union movement had a negative impact on the government's proposal to abolish the "closed shop" system. The "closed shop" had been in operation since 1931, when the Labor Code was formally enacted. Under the Code, the establishment of plant unions (*sindicatos de empresa*) required the vote of at least 55 percent of the workforce. Once the union was established, however, membership became compulsory for the whole workforce. According to the CDP, these provisions unjustifiably restricted workers' freedom of choice, stifled the development of the union movement, and encouraged its politicization. Thus, they proposed a bill to the congress to abolish compulsory union membership and to simplify the procedure for the constitution of unions (Landsberger 1969:130). The bill, however, met with such strong opposition in the congress that the government was forced to withdraw it. Opposition to the bill came not only from the Marxist parties, but also from members of the CDP in the congress (Angell 1972:200). Joining forces with the Marxists, the CDP rebels claimed that the bill would divide and weaken organized labor rather than offer freedom of choice (Yocelevzky 1987:212–220).

Agrarian Reform and Private Sector Confidence

The government, as expected, secured congressional approval for the agrarian reform bill with the vote of the Communist and Socialist Parties. But the process that led to the approval of this bill further exposed the ideological divisions within the CDP and seriously undermined the government's credibility with the business community.

During the electoral campaign, Frei had strongly criticized the limited scope of Alessandri's agrarian reform and had promised that he would promptly introduce a comprehensive agrarian reform law to create 100,000 new property owners. Frei did not act as swiftly as expected. He submitted the agrarian reform bill to the congress only by mid-term; that is, three years after taking office. The delay drafting the agrarian reform bill wasted much precious time and contributed to raising political tension in the countryside. The delay was caused by disagreements within the government regarding the nature of the reform process. Frei and his close advisors wanted a limited agrarian reform, as they did not want to antagonize the private sector. Frei was also keen that the new law should promptly assign property rights to rural workers, so as to fulfill the party's campaign promise. But members of the government's land reform team did not share Frei's concerns. As lead promoters of the process of political mobilization in the countryside, they were in close contact with the mood and demands of agricultural workers. Accordingly, they rejected Frei's proposals and demanded a more extensive land reform. Also, instead of immediately assigning individual property rights, they favored the establishment of cooperatives as a device to organize production in expropriated land. In the event, most of the views espoused by the technical team were incorporated into the agrarian reform law. President Frei, however, continued to have sharp differences with his technical team over the implementation of the agrarian reform law.

Landowners' associations lobbied hard to persuade the government to change some of the bill's provisions, especially those regarding compensation. The spokesman of the Coordination Committee of Agricultural Associations even claimed that the bill would lead the country straight to communism (Kaufman 1972:164–165). Frei had several meeting with representatives of the landowners' associations and he made conciliatory gestures that led them to believe that the government would change the terms of the bill. In the end, however, the bill was approved virtually unchanged (Thome 1989:191–194). The representatives of the landowners were disappointed and frustrated. They regarded Frei's conciliatory gestures as doublespeak and as unequivocal evidence that the CDP could not be trusted.

As the agrarian reform bill undermined the government's credibility with the landowners' associations, relations between the government and business association representing other areas of industry were also deteriorating. Two government policies were a source of special concern to them. First, they were apprehensive about the government's decision to reduce the representation of business associations on the boards of public bodies and state enterprises. This representation had been an important component of the deal that, in the 1940s, paved the way for their acceptance of CORFO's role in the state-led policy of import substitution (Menges 1966:349). Second, they were alarmed at what they regarded as an attempt to divide business associations. This concern stemmed from the government's decision to establish a special committee to handle relations with the private sector (Cusack 1970:112). Business associations correctly interpreted this decision as a device to sidestep established private sector organizations. Interestingly, however, despite their deep distrust of the government, business associations did not seek support from political parties. Instead, they concentrated on strengthening their institutional structures to ensure that they could protect their interests without having to rely on the party system (Cusack 1970). Thus, by the end of the Frei administration the skepticism of the business sector toward the party system was back to the level that prevailed in the early 1950s.

Extension of Rights

One of the central aims of the government was to deepen the process of democratization through the empowerment of groups hitherto excluded from the political system. This process involved mainly the extension of rights to agricultural workers and the development of policies and institutions designed to resolve the housing problems among the urban poor. As this section shows, many of the obstacles encountered by the government in this policy area foreshadowed the problems that the Allende administration was to confront.

Rural Workers

The extension of the right to form unions to rural workers was a natural component of the process of agrarian reform. Yet, this policy soon encountered problems. These problems stemmed largely from the tension between the narrow scope of some of the provisions of the agrarian reform legislation and the broad terms of the law on agricultural unions. The agrarian reform law, though ultimately committed to creating individual property rights, made provision for a transitional arrangement to organize production through cooperatives known as *asentamientos*. But membership of the *asentamiento* was restricted. Only permanent workers in the expropriated farms were entitled to membership. Seasonal and part-time workers were excluded. Permanent workers had special rights, such as the right to cultivate a small plot of land and the right to live in houses provided by the landowner. They were a relatively privileged group compared with the majority of landless peasants who only just managed to scrape a living, often working for permanent workers. Thus by restricting *asentamiento* membership to permanent workers the agrarian reform law unwittingly reproduced the employment stratification of the system of domination it was attempting to replace (Lehmann 1974:82–97). Inevitably, this feature of the agrarian reform law became a source of political tension since the government-sponsored law on agricultural unions gave all agricultural workers the right to form unions.

The law on rural unions, enacted in 1967, was one of the main achievements of the Frei administration, as it reversed the discriminatory policies against agricultural workers, in place since the mid-1930s. The impact of this new law was dramatic. The number of agricultural workers belonging to unions increased from just over 10,000 in 1966 to more than 140,000 in 1970 (Barraclough and Fernández 1974: 176; Yocelevzky 1987:196). The speed of the unionization process reflects the level of political mobilization prevailing in the countryside. Two features of the new law contributed to intensifying this process. First, the new law allowed virtually anyone involved in agricultural activities to establish or join a union. Thus the law gave the right to form unions to peasants who owned or rented small properties (*minifundistas*), as well as to landless agricultural laborers. The institutional framework of participation was thus wider than the somewhat limited production unit envisaged by the agrarian reform law. Second, the law allowed the establishment of more than one union per agricultural enterprise. This feature was introduced by the CDP administration as part of its efforts to eliminate the closed shop system and to depoliticize the union movement. Thus, parallel unionism, which had been rejected for plant unions, was allowed in the agricultural sector. The law on agricultural unions also incorporated several ideas that the government had intended should apply to plant unions, such as the recognition of union federations for the purpose of collective bargaining and legal protection of union officers (Landsberger 1969:131). Ironically, contrary to the CDP's aim of depoliticizing the union movement, the introduction of parallel unions in the countryside, in addition to further worsening the political mobilization process, also provided an incentive for all political parties to become active in the countryside. There thus emerged three major union federations: one controlled by the Communist and Socialist Parties, representing 20 percent of agricultural workers; another established and controlled by landowners and right-wing parties, representing nearly 30 percent of agricultural workers; and a third, the largest of the three, representing some 50 percent of the workers in the sector loyal to the CDP (Barraclough and Fernández 1974:179). The new system of parallel unions in the countryside thus became a vehicle for transferring national political divisions to the rural area.

One of the main achievements of the CDP administration was its serious consideration of the plight of the agricultural sector. It did so by combining a program of land redistribution with the extension of rights to agricultural workers. Despite its many problems, some 1,000 farms were expropriated during the six years of the Frei administration, affecting 15 percent of all agricultural land (Kaufman 1972:97). Yet, agricultural workers were not satisfied either with the form or the pace of the expropriations. Led by CDP and left-wing activists, they demanded speedier and more drastic action. Given these conditions, it is not surprising that rural workers were bitterly disappointed when the austerity measures introduced by the government at mid-term slowed down the pace of expropriations. Indeed rural workers had good reasons to be disappointed—and even enraged—as the publicity machinery of the CDP had led them to expect that there soon would be 100,000 new property owners in the countryside. During the second half of the Frei administration, there was thus a significant increase in the number of strikes in the countryside. While the total number of strikes between 1960 and 1966 was 826, in 1967 and 1968 there were close to 700 per year and in 1969 the number shot up to more than 1,000 (Barraclough and Fernández 1974:194). By the end of the Frei administration political conditions in the countryside were in such a state of ferment that it seemed unlikely that it could be contained within the framework of the prevailing agrarian reform legislation.

Mobilizing the Urban Poor

Popular promotion was the name the government gave to the set of policies that were meant to achieve the objective of social inclusion and empowerment among the urban poor. A distinctive feature of popular promotion policies was its emphasis on the establishment of new mechanisms of participation to ensure that community demands were promptly and effectively channeled to public authorities. These organs of popular participation were also meant to be the foundations of a more democratic institutional order.

The mass of urban poor, many living in subhuman conditions in miserable shantytowns, provided the government with a unique opportunity to implement its programmatic aspirations. Among the many problems affecting the urban poor, housing was the most urgent. Indeed, the country was facing at the time a major housing crisis because of the rapid growth of the urban population during the 1940s and 1950s. While in the 1920s, 40 percent of the population lived in urban centers, in the 1950s this figure had increased to nearly 60 percent, reaching 75 percent in 1970 (Yocelevzky 1987:204). This rapid growth was caused largely by the decline of agriculture, rather than the success of the policy of import substitution. As a consequence, a carefully planned process of urbanization did not accompany the expansion of the population living in cities. There was thus a huge housing deficit, estimated in 1964 to be around 600,000 units (LeGates 974:55). It was made worse by the fact that more than a third of the total urban population lived in Santiago. The mass of homeless urban poor thus became an obvious target of popular promotion policies, and the Ministry of Housing became its main executing agency.

The first step taken by the Ministry of Housing was the launching of a community development program that led to the establishment of more than 3,000 neighborhood committees. These organizations were intended to provide a direct link between the urban poor and the government (Frei 1970:149). Neighborhood committees also played a key role in the implementation of *Operación Sitio*, a self-help program developed by the Ministry of Housing (Cleaves 1974:210–211). Under this program, the government provided an urbanized plot of land to families who agreed to build their own house. The government also supplied building materials and offered technical assistance. Families enrolled on the program had the ultimate responsibility for ensuring that the house was built.

Operación Sitio was well received by the homeless. During its first week, more than 60,000 families enrolled in the program. But politicians were critical of this policy. Communists and socialists dismissed it as a form of welfare provision that had little to do with genuine empowerment. The National Party claimed that the Ministry of Housing was making improper use of state resources for party political purposes. It also condemned the policy as excessively partisan, as it claimed that the government supported only neighborhood committees whose members supported the government (Duque and Pastrana 1972:279–281; Lechner 1970:130–134). Independent observers complained that the policy was badly managed and plagued by bureaucratic problems (Cleaves 1974:284). As criticism against the Ministry of Housing and *Operación Sitio* mounted, the government introduced a bill in the congress to define the powers and regulate the activities of neighborhood committees. The need for regulation was also prompted by the fact that the activities of neighborhood committees and the enthusiasm of Ministry of Housing officials were beginning to create conflicts of jurisdiction between central government and local authorities in the municipalities. The parliamentary debate on the Neighborhood Committee bill was long and acrimonious. The bill was eventually approved, in August 1968, close to the end of the CDP's term in office.[1]

The law on neighborhood committees was a 10,000-word document divided into 65 sections. It was drafted in technical language hardly accessible to shantytown dwellers. The technical complexity of this law was partly a consequence of the strong opposition the government encountered in the congress. Initially, the government had proposed that the Ministry of Housing should have exclusive responsibility for the establishment of neighborhood committees. The congress rejected this proposal and, instead, gave municipalities broad powers to supervise their activities. Thus, municipalities were entrusted with the task of determining the territorial boundaries of committees— a politically delicate task, as the law allowed only one committee per territorial unit. They also authorized any major project undertaken by the committees.

The new law, however, failed to clarify crucial questions concerning the nature of the neighborhood committees. Were neighborhood committees intended to be effective organs of popular representation, or were they merely conduits to facilitate the implementation of government policy? The law provided that neighborhood committees had four main functions (Section 22): to represent the interest of its members in all matters concerning the regularization of property titles; to promote urban development projects in conjunction with the relevant state and municipal authorities; to promote solidarity among its members; and to protect the general interests of the community. The law, however, did not clearly define the political nature of neighborhood committees. One of its sections (Section 1) defined neighborhood committees as local organizations designed to collaborate with state and municipal authorities in defense of the interests of its members. Another section (Section 6), however, defined them as organs of popular representation. Thus, while according to one section, neighborhood committees were little more than local welfare pressure groups, according to another, they were depicted as genuine organs of popular power. During the parliamentary stages of the bill the government unequivocally favored the concept of neighborhood committees as local welfare pressure groups (Vanderschuren 1973:277–278). The constitutional position on this matter was clarified only in 1970, when the CDP sponsored a constitutional amendment that paved the way for Salvador Allende's access to the presidency. This amendment, which purported to regulate the right to participate, provided that neighborhood committees and other organs of popular participation were merely vehicles to facilitate and support the activities of state agencies in the provision of community services. They were not allowed, under any circumstance, to claim the right of popular representation or to attempt to exercise state functions. Thus, after their legalization and subsequent elevation to the status of a constitutional organ, neighborhood committees could hardly be described as organs of social empowerment or self-government.

In practice, however, neighborhood committees did empower the homeless and shantytown dwellers. They quickly acquired enormous prominence due largely to their capacity to represent the demands and aspirations of their members. Neighborhood committees thus had a major role in raising political awareness and confidence among its members. In 1965, before the establishment of neighborhood committees, only 36 percent of shantytown dwellers thought that they could influence government decisions. Four years later after their launch, nearly 80 percent of shantytown dwellers expressed confidence that they could effectively use political pressure to persuade government agencies to act on their behalf or to reverse policies with which they did not agree (Cleaves 1974:282). As political confidence among them increased, so did their expectations. The inability of the government to cope with their new demands created a vicious circle whereby unmet demands from urban groups led to new and more radical demands. This process went far beyond the legal concept of neighborhood committees as mere welfare agencies.

The political potential of neighborhood committees did not go unnoticed by the Marxist parties. They became directly involved in the committees' activities and soon managed to assert considerable influence over them. According to a survey on the composition of neighborhood committees, 30 percent of its members were also union members. This overlap in membership enabled the Communist and Socialist Parties to exert considerable influence on them and to use the process of political mobilization as a political weapon against the government (Duque and Pastrana 1972:288; Vanderschuren 1973:280–281).

As shantytown dwellers became more militant, urban land invasions became more frequent, and, by the end of the CDP administration, they had become a significant political problem. During the first two years of the CDP administration, there were few cases of land invasion: only six cases were registered in Santiago. In 1967, there were

13 and in 1968, there were 8. The number of land invasions, however, grew sharply during the last two years of the CDP administration reaching, 73 in 1969 and more than 200 in 1970 (Duque and Pastrana 1972:263–268). Land invasions generally involved several hundred homeless families and more than 1,000 people (LeGates 1974:60–64). They were complex operations, almost of a paramilitary nature. They were organized by ad hoc committees—known locally as homeless committees—which, invariably, had the support of one or another political party. The Communist and Socialist Parties participated actively in these committees as part of their campaign to recruit members among the urban poor. Eventually, even CDP supporters formed homeless committees and organized land invasions (Landsberger and McDaniel 1976:519).

The government's objective of extending rights and empowering the urban poor undoubtedly contributed to enhancing the political confidence of shantytown dwellers and the urban poor. But the government was unable to control the growing political agitation it had unleashed. Thus, not surprisingly, by the end of his period in office, Frei had lost interest in neighborhood committees and in popular promotion in general (Angell 1972:139).

Revolution Prolonged

Assessment

By the end of Frei's term of office, the government could claim impressive achievements, especially in the area of social development. The improvements in education illustrate this point. During the period, primary school enrolment increased by 40 percent and the provision of meals at schools registered a fourfold increase. Adult education was not neglected, as shown by the significant drop in illiteracy rates from 16 to 11 percent (Ffrench-Davis 185). There were also remarkable improvements in health and social security (Foxley et al. 1980:67–83, 145–182). Income distribution also became more equal as the share of labor in total income went up from 48 percent in 1964 to 53 percent in 1969 (Molina 1972:128). But these achievements conceal a colossal failure: the government's inability to transform its massive electoral majority into a solid coalition for change. Instead, by the end of Frei's period in office the CDP was politically isolated and unable to forge a partnership to extend the "revolution in liberty." Ironically, the plight of the CDP in 1970 was similar to that of the Radical Party in the early 1950s. It was the largest party, but could not find political allies to make a credible bid to stay in power.

As explained above, from the outset the government was as determined to apply sound principles of economic governance, as it was committed to the implementation of its program. But, as the implementation of its policies progressed, it soon had to choose between stabilizing the economy and pushing ahead with its program of structural reforms regardless of economic consequences. After initial hesitation, the government opted for both. It cut public expenditure in order to hold back inflation, but the cuts were insufficient to halt the inflationary pressures. As a result, by the end of Frei's term of office inflation was virtually the same as during the final years of the Alessandri administration. Cuts in public expenditure reduced the funds available for education, health and also had the effect of slowing down the agrarian reform process and the housing program. Yet, despite these cuts, the government did not give up its program of structural reforms. In the end, however, the government's concern with economic stability, combined with its determination to continue pressing for structural reforms, generated a process of political mobilization that had disastrous political consequences.

In political terms the CDP's failure stems largely from its determination to achieve a solid majority for change solely through electoral competition. Initially, this attempt was tactically justified, as evidenced by the impressive performance of the CDP in the general elections of 1965 (42 percent of the vote). But instead of regarding these results as its electoral zenith, the CDP interpreted them as the beginning of an unstoppable trend. Accordingly, it decided to accelerate the process of political mobilization in an all-out effort to increase its electoral strength. The main targets of this effort were the traditional constituencies of the Communist and Socialist Parties. This decision instantly transformed the CDP into the main political adversary of both right and left-wing parties. Thus, not surprisingly, the parties on the extremes of the political spectrum spared no efforts to undermine government policies, even those policies they had supported in the congress. Thus instead of attracting allies to assist in the consolidation of its policies, the CDP converted the process of policy implementation into an arena of discord and political controversy.

The agrarian reform provided the right-wing National Party with an ideal setting to proclaim its commitment to property rights, economic freedom, and middle-class values and thus recover the electoral support that the Right had lost to the CDP in 1964. In electoral terms this strategy was effective. The Right increased its share of the vote from 12 percent in 1965 (combined vote of the Conservative and Liberal Parties) to 20 percent in 1969. The government also had to contend with the growing skepticism of the private sector. Indeed, despite its genuine concern with sound economic governance, the government was unable to persuade business associations that it was serious about protecting property rights. That business associations lost confidence in the government is not altogether surprising. After all, while the government adopted tough measures to stabilize the economy, CDP activists were busy campaigning in support of the ever-growing economic demands of urban and rural workers.

But more damaging than right-wing resistance to economic reform was the government's clumsy attempt to undermine the influence of the Left within the union movement. The government's frustrated attempts to set up a confederation to compete with the CUT were political folly. Communists and Socialists opposed it, and the government was forced to abandon it, as even CDP unionist opposed it. Likewise, the government's attempt to introduce parallel unionism in the mining and manufacturing sectors was resented by the Left and later abandoned because of opposition from within the CDP. Having given up its attempts to redesign the system of industrial relations, the CDP concentrated fully on bolstering its electoral support at the expense of the Marxist parties. Yet, the ensuing electoral competition did more damage to the government than to the Left as it had a general effect of radicalizing popular demands from all sectors, regardless of political affiliation, thus further disrupting the implementation of the program of reforms. As the number of strikes increased and the occupation of land in rural and urban areas proliferated, the attention of the government was diverted to issues of law and order. In the meantime, the main beneficiaries of this incessant electoral competition were the communists and socialists. Indeed, the CDP's decision to pursue the route of electoral competition greatly benefited them. Between 1965 and 1969, the combined vote of the Communist and Socialist Parties increased from 23 percent to 28 percent.

By the end of Frei's term in office, the CDP's expectations of remaining in power for 30 years were shattered. In hindsight it is clear that the government wasted precious time and energy in its hopeless effort to reduce the influence of communists and socialists among urban and rural workers. Why did the government not adopt a more constructive policy toward the left-wing parties? This issue was the main bone of contention between the party's old guard, led by Frei, and the rebel group that managed to control the party for a short period. The rebels demanded closer cooperation with the Left, as in their view the communitarian society that the CDP had promise to build was a socialist society. But Frei disagreed and consistently refused to make any overtures toward the Left. Given prevailing animosities, it is, of course, doubtful that either the Communist or the Socialist Party would have responded positively to an approach from the government. What is certain, however, is that the leadership of the CDP refused to contemplate making such an approach, despite the fact that important sectors within the party advocated it. Indeed, the failure to resolve this issue is what prompted the *rebeldes* to break away from the party.

The government's persistent refusal to broaden its base of support through political alliances reinforced the merciless hostility to government policies by both left-and right-wing parties. The Left, riding on the intense wave of popular mobilization unleashed by the government, did its best to accelerate its pace through the promotion of strike action and the occupation of urban and rural properties. The Right, for its part, continued its support to landowners' resistance to the agrarian reform while bitterly complaining that the government was unable to maintain law and order. As the process of mobilization intensified, the CDP found itself squeezed between two political blocs—one on the right and the other on the left—that sought radical change and shared only one thing in common: their contempt for the CDP. Under these circumstances political discourse was impoverished, as it became largely negative and left no room for negotiation or compromise. In the short term, the main loser of the changes in the structure of the party system was the CDP, which despite being the largest party, remained stubbornly isolated. In the long term, however, these changes played a major part in the collapse of the political regime.

A New Coalition for Radical Change

The foregoing suggests that after the eventful years of the Frei administration a political respite was urgently needed. Yet, the imperatives of the electoral cycle did not allow for a break. As the CDP began to lose its electoral appeal, the Marxist parties emerged as attractive electoral partners to non-Marxist parties. After lengthy political squabbles, the Left established the Popular Unity, an electoral coalition between the two Marxist parties and three social-democratic parties, including the old Radical Party and the MAPU. Meanwhile, the CDP embraced a radical political program, thus distancing itself from the government and implicitly acknowledging the shortcomings of Frei's "revolution in liberty." Yet, despite the party's swing to the left, there were no prospects of an alliance between the CDP and the Marxist parties.

The Popular Unity nominated Salvador Allende as their candidate and called their program a peaceful transition to socialism. Their electoral campaign, however, was uninspiring, as the clear favorite was Jorge Alessandri, the candidate of the Right. After unconditionally supporting the CDP to prevent a Marxist victory, the Right had come to the conclusion that the CDP could not be trusted. Given the persistent division between the parties advocating radical social change and the financial resources commanded by the Right, Alessandri was widely regarded as the strongest candidate. In the event, however, the Popular Unity managed a narrow victory. Allende obtained 36 percent of the vote, while Alessandri obtained 35 percent. The CDP candidate trailed behind with 28 percent of the vote. This unexpected result gave radical democracy a second chance. Yet, although the political slogans and the leading actors had changed, the obstacles to reform had not.

The electoral victory of the Popular Unity, though narrow, confirms that the Marxist parties continued to enjoy the support of a respectable portion of organized workers. But although communists and socialists continued to be a major force within the union movement, their overall influence had decreased. Indeed, the phenomenal expansion of the union movement during the Frei administration brought about a change in the membership of the union movement that significantly reduced the influence of the Marxists parties. In the 1940s and 1950s, when workers from the mining and manufacturing sectors constituted the bulk of the union movement, the communist and socialist had a preponderant influence within it. By the late 1960s, however, as union membership expanded and workers' demands became more radical, neither the Marxist parties nor the CDP could control the activities of unions as they had done in the preceding two decades. The bulk of the newly organized workers were rural workers and workers in the construction and service industries. Although easy to mobilize in pursuit of short-term and sometimes quite radical objectives, they were not as docile or reliable as the members of the old established unions in the mining and manufacturing sectors. During the Frei administration, the main beneficiaries of this volatile workforce were ultraleft movements that were equally critical of the Marxist parties and of the CDP and had no stake in the preservation of the constitutional framework. Thus, even if Allende had presided over an ordinary administration, he would have confronted enormous challenges. He only polled 36 percent of the vote, did not control enough seats in the congress to secure the approval of legislative initiatives, confronted a party system that had lost the habit of compromise, and faced an unusually high level of political mobilization. Allende, however, did not intend to preside over an ordinary administration. He was determined to bring about a real revolution, albeit through peaceful means.

Chapter 8

A Peaceful Revolution

Introduction

Salvador Allende's victory in the presidential elections of 1970 brought about yet another attempt to achieve a social and economic revolution through constitutional means. Allende's program of government, described as "a peaceful road to socialism," was more radical than Frei's "revolution in liberty." It called for the establishment of a dominant state sector comprising large-scale mining, public utilities, and key firms in manufacturing, distribution, and finance. It also called for the rapid implementation of the agrarian reform law and the enactment of comprehensive social programs to benefit the wage earning population. The program also called for an effective transfer of power from the old ruling groups to workers, peasants and progressive sectors of the middle classes (De Vylder 1976:23–40).[1]

The peaceful road to socialism entailed a commitment to total respect for mechanisms and procedures of the political system. Structural reforms would be introduced by means of constitutional or legislative reforms and would be implemented with due respect for the constitutional framework and the principle of legality. In his first annual message to the congress in 1971, Allende reaffirmed his commitment to the institutional framework: "[W]e have promised that our government will put its revolutionary aims into practice with full respect for the rule of law. This is not merely a formal assurance, but the explicit recognition that, in spite of the difficulties inherent in the transition period, the principle of the legality and institutional order are compatible with a socialist regime" (Allende 1973a:149).

These optimistic assertions about the prospects for the new government could not conceal the innumerable obstacles that stood in the way of the peaceful road to socialism. The Popular Unity, Allende's coalition, had won the election by the narrowest of margins (only 1 percent of the vote) and hence its mandate to carry out a revolution through the democratic process was, if not doubtful, at least problematic. The minority position of the Popular Unity parties was reflected in the composition of the congress where they did not have an overall majority. The Popular Unity thus urgently needed to broaden its base of support. Yet, at the time, there were no political partners available. The CDP was unlikely to offer its support, as the Marxist parties had relentlessly opposed the Frei administration and hence were resented by the party's leadership. The National Party, for its part, emboldened by Alessandri's performance, but disappointed with the electoral process that had allowed a Marxist to become head of state, was busy reestablishing and strengthening its links with business associations and was calling for popular mobilization against the new government. There was also a major external obstacle: the Nixon administration in Washington. Indeed, the United States government had embraced ITT's (International Telephone and Telegraph Corporation) plan of action and its goal was, as described by Henry Kissinger, "to make the economy scream" (Kornbluh 2003:2).

Despite these inauspicious conditions, Allende did not scale down his program. Instead, using every jot of power vested in the executive branch and relying on the prevailing high levels of political mobilization, he pressed ahead with surprising vigor and enthusiasm. Initially, the government had some success. The economy grew, inflation was under control, and scores of business enterprises were taken over by the state. The initial success of the government created the impression that it had a carefully planned strategy. But events proved otherwise. As the economy collapsed and inflation began to run out of control, the opposition regained the initiative. Their strategy, which was based on a combination of total opposition in the congress together with popular protests, economic boycotts, and sporadic acts of terrorism made a sham of the government's claim that the Popular Unity represented the majority of the working class; while demonstrating, at the same time, that the government was unable to run the economy and could not be trusted to maintain law and order. In the end, however, Allende's opponents were unable to secure enough seats in the congress to impeach the president and thus secure his removal from office through constitutional means. They thus turned to the military, which, with covert support from the Nixon administration, overthrew the government and destroyed democracy (Church Report 1975; Hersh 1982; House of Representatives 1976).

There is no shortage of contemporary interpretation of the events leading to the military coup that brought an end to the Allende administration and democracy. Some justified the coup while others criticized it. Some attributed the coup to Allende's determination to destroy an otherwise healthy and normal political system; others claimed that Allende failed because he naively believed in the virtues of the democratic process and did not distribute arms to the people, or because he was incompetent and allowed the economy to run out of control (Faundez 1975). Despite their differences, all these interpretations have a grain of truth. Government policy was at times so reckless that it is difficult not to regard it as anything but a conscious attempt to undermine the prevailing institutional framework. There is also plenty of evidence that shows that the government had little or no concern for the devastating inflationary consequences of its economic policies. Yet, there is also evidence that suggests that, even at a very late stage, the government had an inexplicably strong faith in the possibility of resolving the obviously intractable political crisis through compromise and negotiation.

The conflicting interpretations about this period are not merely a result of different ideological perspectives. They stem from the nature of government policies. A careful assessment of these policies suggests that the government never fully reconciled its commitment to revolutionary change with its commitment to respect the procedures and mechanisms of the prevailing institutional framework. This ambiguity pervaded every aspect of government policy. As a consequence, Government policy appeared to respond to a dual strategy: a parliamentary strategy that purported to channel political change through constitutional mechanisms; and a revolutionary strategy that sought to make use of every iota of executive power to implement its program even at the cost of subverting the institutional order. Under the dual strategy, the objective of empowering workers and peasants was subordinated to the objective of asserting control over the commanding heights of the economy. The government, however, soon found out that it could not indefinitely postpone the expectations of greater empowerment and democratization. As this chapter shows, the tragic end of the Popular Unity administration was due largely to its failure fully to grasp the importance of this point.

A Dual Strategy

Origins

There is no evidence that prior to the September 4, 1970 either Allende or the Popular Unity had seriously considered how they would implement their program. This oversight is understandable not only because of the pressures of the electoral campaign, but also because, perhaps with the exception of Allende, the leadership of the Popular Unity had not expected to win. Thus, the new administration confronted the unexpected task of designing a strategy to fulfill its commitment to bring about a transition to socialism within the prevailing institutional framework. Given the novelty of the challenge, the strategists of the new government could neither borrow ideas from the experience of other countries nor could they draw inspiration from Marx and Engels. Indeed, with the exception of a few ambiguous paragraphs, the founding fathers of Marxist revolutionary theory had not seriously envisaged the possibility of a genuine revolutionary transformation without a violent overhaul of the prevailing political institutions (Marx 1969:293, Engels 1970:434, 1976:349). Indeed, the standard-bearers of the Marxist revolutionary tradition had ridiculed and characterized as renegades those who, like Karl Kaustsky and Edward Bernstein, had suggested that a violent political revolution was not the prerequisite for a genuine socialist transformation (Claudín 1977; Hunt 1984:325–362; Moore 1963:65–69). Allende and his political advisors thus had neither a historical blueprint nor a textbook to guide them in the design and implementation of their strategy (Garcés 1972).

Three factors contributed to shaping the political strategy of the Allende administration: the immediate constraints imposed by the institutional framework, the imperative of reactivating the economy, and the ideological assumptions and conflicts between the Communist and Socialist Parties, the leading members of the Popular Unity coalition. The interplay of these three factors brought into being a strategy that simultaneously reaffirmed the commitment to the constitutional framework, while indicating an uncompromising determination to push ahead with revolutionary changes, without any concern for procedural niceties and regardless of consequences.

Allende's electoral victory did not merely pose a novel challenge to left-wing strategists. It also posed a challenge to the opposition parties, the CDP, and the National Party. Their response, however, was remarkably different. The right-wing National Party, together with assorted right-wing extremists and supported by the CIA and a handful of prominent U.S.-based multinationals, were determined to do anything—legal or illegal—to keep Allende from taking office. The constitutional rules offered a unique opportunity to achieve this objective without having to instigate a military coup. It provided that where no candidate in a presidential election obtained more than

50 percent of the vote, it fell upon the two chambers of the congress (in a joint session) to choose the president from the two candidates with the largest number of votes. As Allende had obtained a plurality of the vote, the congress could have chosen Jorge Alessandri, the runner-up, as president. Given that the opposition parties controlled the majority of seats in the congress, they were in a position to block Allende's access to power. This option, however, was politically dangerous as the congress had never before selected the runner-up, and given the intense mobilization prevailing at the time, this option could have easily brought about a breakdown of the political system. The CDP thus rejected this alternative and opted for a different policy. It decided to require Allende to give a further guarantee that his administration would respect the rules and procedures of the democratic process. This guarantee took the form of a constitutional amendment that was hastily negotiated and approved on October 13, 1970, only weeks before Allende was due to take office (Evans 1973: 105–106). This decision prompted disgruntled right-wing groups with links to the CIA, to engage in a variety of terrorist acts, including an unsuccessful attempt to kidnap the commander-in-chief of the army, which resulted in his assassination (Kornbluh 2003:1–115).

The constitutional amendment, known also as the Statute of Democratic Guarantees (SDG), was, ostensibly, meant to strengthen civil and political liberties. It contained detailed provisions dealing with the media, education, freedom of assembly, the right to establish political parties, and the right to participate in grassroot organizations. The Popular Unity regarded the SDG as innocuous because it restated rights already in the constitution—such as freedom of speech and freedom of assembly—and gave constitutional status to principles that had a long tradition in local practice, such as the right to establish political parties and the right to strike. Accordingly, the Popular Unity regarded their acceptance of the SDG as a mere tactical concession (Debray 1971:119–120). As it turned out, however, the SDG became an important weapon in the ensuing political confrontation, as it provided Allende's opposition with a powerful standard to judge and criticize the government. This was a standard that the Popular Unity parties could not easily ignore as they had voted for it in the congress. In strategic terms, the constitutional amendment had a wider significance. It demonstrated that the opposition parties were divided on their policies toward the Popular Unity administration. It also showed that constructive negotiations between the CDP and the new government were possible. These developments strengthened Allende's authority within his coalition, as they appeared to validate his claim that a political compromise with the opposition was possible.

But as the political parties debated the SDG in the congress, events on the ground were moving fast. Allende's election had prompted a new surge of popular mobilization, especially in the countryside where land invasions were proliferating. While left-wing supporters ensured that levels of political mobilization in favor of the government remained high, property owners, frightened by alarmist rumors, brought about a run on the banks. Although the financial panic soon subsided, many industrial firms began to cut production and sack employees and even threatened to shut down altogether, thus raising concerns about a possible investors' strike. In response to the threats of economic boycott, unions promoted a wave of strikes and factory occupations that caused serious concern to the government. Thus, before left-wing political strategists had the time to design a strategy, the government was forced into action. Relying on the extensive regulatory powers vested in the executive, the government intervened to terminate labor disputes and to restore production. The government used two main mechanisms: labor intervention decrees—known also a back-to-work decrees—and requisition decrees (Von Brunn 1972:65–73). Though these decrees placed the enterprise under temporary administration of the government, they did not affect the underlying property rights. The government also launched a policy of economic reactivation that included a massive injection of public funds in labor-intensive projects and an incomes policy in favor of the worst-off wage earners (De Vylder 1976:52–77; Roxborough et al. 1977:71–101).

In the short term, the results of the economic policy were encouraging. Industrial production increased by 12 percent and GDP increased by 8.5 percent. Unemployment fell from 7 to 4 percent and the rate of inflation dropped from 35 percent to 22 percent. The political consequences of the economic policy were also encouraging. In the municipal elections of April 1971, support for the Popular Unity parties increased from 36 percent to a little under 50 percent. The success of these initial measures had the effect of transforming a policy that was meant to be temporary into a permanent feature of the government's strategy. Instead of seeking a negotiated settlement to the congressional impasse, the government began to implement its program relying almost exclusively on its regulatory powers. Thus, back-to-work and requisition decrees enabled the government to take over the administration of scores of industrial and agricultural enterprises. The government also took control of nearly the whole of the banking system through the purchase of shares on the open market and dramatically accelerated the pace of land expropriation under the agrarian reform law.[2] Thus, after ten months in office, almost the whole of the banking sector had been transferred to the state, a large number of business enterprises were under state administration, and the government had expropriated virtually all the land that could be expropriated under the agrarian reform. But while government officials and supporters hailed these achievements as a major step toward the socialist revolution, the president and his cabinet continued to make statements that suggested that they expected a political breakthrough with the Christian Democrats to secure congressional approval for the implementation of their program. Allende thus continuously promised that he would introduce a bill to provide for the nationalization of banks and of the manufacturing sector. Yet, given the pace at which the government was ordering requisitions, expropriating land, and buying out banks, the much-promised nationalization bills were rapidly becoming redundant.

Reconciling Conflicting Ideologies

The government's dual strategy was, undoubtedly, prompted by the need to respond to urgent political and economic pressures. Yet, this strategy was also convenient as it had the virtue of accommodating the conflicting views of the Socialist and Communist Parties over the nature of the Popular Unity's program of government. The socialists argued that the program contained an unequivocal mandate immediately to proceed to the nationalization of the commanding heights of the economy. The communists, adopting a moderate position, argued that the program only called for the nationalization of a select number of enterprises in the mining and manufacturing sectors. The nationalization of the rest of the commanding heights of the economy, according to this interpretation, would take place at a later stage, not within the six-year period of the Allende government. These conflicting interpretations entailed two opposing views on how to strengthen the government's position. The Communist Party argued that the government urgently had to seek support from the CDP in order to persuade the congress to approve their legislative program. The Socialist Party did not agree. It emphatically ruled out any such agreement, as, in their view, the CDP was a bourgeois party committed to the revival, rather than the replacement of, capitalism. They thus argued that the only way to strengthen the government was by immediately beginning the implementation of the program, thus showing determination and commitment to the goal of building a socialist society (Faundez 1980:62–65).

Given these conflicting views, the government's dual strategy played a useful role as both socialists and communists regarded it as an accurate expression of their views. The communists, the main advocates of seeking a compromise with the CDP, regarded the strategy as a useful, albeit temporary, device to soften the hardliners within the CDP, pending a comprehensive agreement with that party over the implementation of the program. The socialists, for their part, embraced the government's strategy because, in their view, its effect would be to bring about a major split within the CDP, thus providing the government with enough votes in the congress to transform the program of requisitions into an effective program of nationalization. Thus, while the communists expected that the CDP would eventually be persuaded to compromise with the government, the socialists did not believe that persuasion would work. They expected that the unfolding of events, mainly the acceleration of the program of requisitions, would make a political compromise unnecessary, as the inevitable split within the CDP would strengthen the position of the Popular Unity in the congress, without having to compromise the program. For the communists, the strategy was a device to push the CDP into negotiations, and for the socialists it was a means of avoiding negotiations—hence their slogan *avanzar sin transar* (move ahead without compromises).

The government's dual strategy was acceptable to both communists and socialists because they shared a common view about their role within the political system. This view, albeit outdated at the time, was based on the assumption that they were the only parties that genuinely represented the interests of the working class and other subaltern classes. It was based on their experience in the 1930s and 1940s when they had a virtual monopoly of the vote of organized workers (Petras and Zeitlin 1967). It led them to believe that workers and other members of the subordinate classes who did not support them were temporarily misguided and, in time, would soon realize that communists and socialists were the only genuine representatives of working-class interests. This view, as explained in chapter 7, made it difficult for the communists and socialists to acknowledge that the CDP had considerable electoral support and influence among workers and peasants. Thus, the government's dual strategy played a useful role, as it was consistent with the Marxist parties' view about their position among workers and other subaltern groups. Indeed, the notion that workers who supported the CDP would eventually gravitate toward the government was consistent with the position of the socialists who flatly opposed any form of negotiation with the CDP. It was also consistent with the position of the communists, because they claimed that as CDP workers began to gravitate toward the Popular Unity administration, the CDP would have no choice but to negotiate with the government. As it turned out, neither the CDP nor its working-class supporters behaved as the communists and socialists expected. Yet, because the dual strategy served to conceal the differences between the two Marxist parties, the government was unable to shift away from it, even after its shortcomings became obvious.

Marxist Orthodoxy and Constitutional Patriotism

The foregoing suggests that what I have described as the dual strategy was little more than a set of tactical decisions aimed at addressing immediate problems and reconciling conflicting ideologies. Yet, at another level, the strategy was consistent with an orthodox Marxist interpretation about the relationship between politics and economics. The dual strategy assigned absolute priority to the immediate takeover of the commanding heights of the economy, thus postponing the political aspiration of effectively transferring power to workers and peasants (Allende 1972:8–11). This orthodox approach to the economy was combined with equally orthodox expectations about the behavior of the main political actors. Indeed, the government expected that as the commanding heights of the economy fell under the control of the state and the agrarian reform abolished large agricultural states, the CDP and other progressive political actors would either willingly join the government, as expected by the Communist Party; or, as expected by the Socialist Party, they would become politically irrelevant because their members would desert them in favor of Popular Unity parties. Throughout this process it was expected that organized workers would remain loyal to the government and the Marxist parties, as the Popular Unity was seen as the natural representative of the interests of subordinate groups. As it turned out, however, the assumptions on which the dual strategy was based were mistaken. Indeed, although the government formally took over a large number of industries by resorting to its administrative powers, it never had effective control over what it described as the commanding heights of the economy. As a consequence, the assumption that other progressive political actors would sooner or later come to recognize the leadership of the Popular Unity was a delusion based on a crude interpretation of Marxist ideology. The most damaging consequence of this interpretation was that it took for granted that workers, peasants, and the urban poor would support government policies, even though their political and economic aspirations had to be postponed (Bitar 1979:278–281; De Vylder 1976:147–148). The government assumed that it could endlessly manipulate and control political mobilization in support of its policies. But, as the government was soon to find out, other political forces also had the capacity to mobilize the population. Moreover, the government also found out that it could not take for granted the loyalty of its own supporters.

Apart from reflecting an orthodox Marxist interpretation of the relationship between economic and political process, the dual strategy was also based upon a fairly conventional view about the nature and attributes of the political and legal systems (Garcés 1972). Indeed, it was based on the view that the prevailing political and legal systems were uniquely stable and could be endlessly stretched (Novoa 1971, 1978, 1992). This assumption, though mistaken, was not surprising given that the formative years of most of the senior leaders of the Popular Unity had been during coalition politics period in the 1940s, when political parties behaved with little regard to constitutional restraints. The revival of the party system in the 1950s, which as explained above, was largely the unintended consequence of the failure to introduce market-based policies, further reinforced the confidence among left-wing leaders that political agency could overcome any obstacle. These two misconceptions—endless flexibility and absolute faith in political agency—were complemented by a commonly held belief that the power vested in the executive was virtually unlimited, as the judiciary was not expected to review acts of authority.

The Popular Unity's views about the flexibility of the political and legal systems were widely shared by other members of the political and intellectual elite. This shared view, which could be described as a form of constitutional patriotism, enhanced the credibility of the dual strategy. It is important to bear this factor in mind, as, otherwise, the political and legal debate during this period becomes incomprehensible. This was Regis Debray's reaction when he visited Chile during the early days of the government. Instead of the familiar revolutionary discourse, he was disappointed to find what he regarded as an obsessive concern with legality and the rule of law. From his privileged standpoint as a theorist of Marxist revolutions, his comments on the political debate were both sarcastic and bitter: "[T]he punctilious prose of speeches, of editorials in the major newspapers, of television discussion, of parliamentary debates and the principal ongoing polemics will thrill no one, unless he is a graduate of Constitutional

Law" (Debray 1971:13). But the fact was that constitutional law graduates, as well as opposition politicians, were, at least initially, genuinely confounded by the government's dual strategy.

Overstretching Institutions

The Economy Screams

In party political terms, the main virtue of the government's dual strategy was that it managed to circumvent the ideological differences within the coalition, while, at the same time, delay the establishment of a unified opposition bloc by the CDP and the National Party. In economic terms the government's dual strategy also seemed to yield benefits. In 1971, GDP increased by 8.5 percent and industrial production increased by 12 percent, while unemployment fell from 7.2 percent to 3.9 percent. Even inflation fell during the first year, from 35 percent to 22 percent. The illusion that the government's strategy was effective could be sustained as long as the economy appeared to be doing well. But, as usual, the economy soon showed signs of weakness. Indeed, as Henry Kissinger had wished, predicted, and done much to ensure it would happen, the economy did scream.

The initial economic policy—which comprised a substantial expansion of demand, strict price controls, and a generous incomes policy—ran into difficulties. The problems faced by the Popular Unity after its first 12 months in office were not unlike those faced by the Frei administration. The incomes policy overreached its target. In one year, labor's share in the national income reached the level it was meant to have reached in six years. Although there was a significant increase in production, the increase was 20 percent below the government's target. Moreover, the incomes policy brought about an unexpectedly high increase in the demand for foodstuffs. The government's plight was made worse by an unforeseen fall in the price of copper. Meanwhile, investment in the private sector declined as the considerable profits generated during the boom of the first year were diverted from productive investments. The government thus had to step in and devote most of its resources to importing foodstuff to satisfy the newly created demand, thus postponing major projects of public investment. Indeed, public investment in 1971 increased by only 1 percent, as most of the growth registered that year was due to the utilization of idle capacity (Behrman 1977:76).

As noted in chapter 7, the Frei administration under similar circumstances had opted for economic stability and had drastically reduced public expenditure. But the Popular Unity did not choose this course of action, as it was unwilling to restrain the political expectations of its supporters. It thus attempted to resolve this problem by relying mainly on the same type of regulatory powers it was using to take over the commanding heights of the economy: strict price and production controls backed by severe sanctions, such as the requisition of goods and the closure of commercial establishments. These measures, however, merely exacerbated inflation.

The government's attempt to fight inflation through administrative measures was a complete failure and led to the breakdown of the price control system. During its first month in office, official prices for basic consumer prices were generally respected, as their supply kept pace with the expansion of demand. As production fell and the capacity to import decreased, however, pressure on prices intensified. This pressure was further aggravated by the determined efforts made by government opponents to withdraw basic goods from the market. The government responded by increasing the number of items subject to price control. This decision did not, however, resolve the problem. As the number of items subject to price control increased, so did the workload of the already overstretched price control agency (Ramos 1979:333–334). Moreover, although the list of consumer goods subject to price control was detailed, it did not include everything and hence, was easily circumvented. Thus, while milk was on the list, but cheese was not. Therefore, there was an abundance of cheese and a shortage of milk. Characteristically, the government responded by imposing price controls on cheese, thus increasing the problem of enforcement.

As the shortcomings of the price control system became evident, the government changed its policy and took direct responsibility for the distribution of essential consumer goods through a network of government-sponsored Price Control Committees (*Juntas de Abastecimientos y Precios*) (Giusti 1975; Meneses 1973). This measure was a total failure and it attracted sharp criticism from government opponents. They depicted the committees as illegal, communist-inspired organizations and as the first step toward the establishment of a totalitarian regime.[3] While the leading retailers' association boycotted them, the opposition claimed that Price Control Committees discriminated against small shopkeepers and were plagued by sectarian practices.[4] The opposition was undoubtedly correct in pointing out some of the deficiencies of the Price Control Committees, particularly with regard to its sectarian practices.[5] The fundamental weakness of this initiative was, however, political. The committees were launched at the worst possible time, when inflation and the black market were already out of control, and hence had virtually no chance of success (Giusti 1975:770).

Aware of the political consequences of the onslaught of inflation, the government attempted, at least twice, to rectify its economic policy so as to bring prices into line with the level of production (Faundez 1988:234–235). These attempts, however, were bound to fail, as they did not reflect a wider political consensus. The government did not consult the opposition and did not take into account the views of its own supporters. Its economic decisions were in fact taken at secret meetings of the Popular Unity leadership and led to the predictable decision to devalue the Escudo (85 percent for imports and 33 percent for exports) so as to halt the flood of imports and redirect resources toward production. The decision to devalue, which under normal political circumstances would have caused serious difficulties, had devastating consequences for the government. Anticipating further price increases, the private sector immediately withdrew basic consumer goods from the market, thus encouraging the black market and worsening the ongoing inflationary process. As inflation began to rise, the government hesitated and eventually gave in, ordering a wage increase to make up for the losses brought about by inflation. After this decision, the government effectively lost control over the economy and inflation shot up from 22 percent in 1971 to 163 percent in 1972 and to more than 500 percent in 1973.

The collapse of the price control system further deepened the public sector deficit, which by 1972 had reached 20 percent of GDP. This outcome stemmed from the fact that the only enterprises that complied with official prices were those under state control. Between November 1970 and July 1972, these enterprises did not increase their prices at all while the general price index increased by 51 percent. To compensate for the financial losses of these enterprises, the government made cash available to them, thus further increasing the public sector deficit. According to some calculations, the deficit of state-controlled enterprises accounted for 35 percent of the public sector deficit (Griffith-Jones 1981:150).

Changing the Rules

As the government began to lose control over the economy, a political settlement with the CDP became urgent. During its first year in office, the government had counted on the fact that the CDP would find it difficult to align itself with the National Party. This expectation was reasonable, as the CDP had a solid base of support among workers and peasants and was reluctant to join the right-wing National Party in its negative campaign against the government. But, as inflation gave way to a flourishing black market and public order began to breakdown, the National Party's allegations that the Popular Unity was unfit to govern and that its real objective was to destroy democracy, began to gain credibility.

As long as Allende's promise to send a nationalization bill to the congress was credible, the CDP sought to keep an independent role as arbiter of the political process. But as time went on, the CDP's position began to shift. In October 1971, after it was obvious that the government was not honoring its commitment to the nationalization bill, the CDP introduced a constitutional amendment that dramatically altered the terms of the political debate. The amendment, though ostensibly designed to regulate the process of nationalizations, was seen by the government as an attempt to undermine it. It contained two main parts: one that divested the executive of the extensive regulatory powers hitherto used by the government to take over the administration of scores of enterprises in the manufacturing and financial sectors; and the other, a set of provisions prescribing the principles that the legislature had to observe in the event it decided to transfer private enterprises into the public sector (Von Brunn 1972:97–111). The government's response took the form of a draft bill delegating broad powers to the president to nationalize enterprises with an authorized capital over a certain fixed amount. According to government estimates, the number of enterprises covered by this measure would have been around 250 (Von Brunn 1972:86–97). Given the balance of forces in the congress, the government bill had no chance whatsoever of securing approval. Congress, however, promptly approved the CDP amendment, leaving the government no option but to use its veto power.

The government's veto provided the basis for negotiations with the CDP. The veto accepted, in general terms, the ideas contained in the amendment, but inserted a clause that provided for the immediate nationalization of 90 enterprises. The figure of 90 was a significant reduction from the government's original proposal of 250. The CDP agreed to negotiate, but insisted that the 90 enterprises would be assessed on a case-by-case basis. After a lengthy process, the negotiations became stuck over seemingly minor procedural wrangles and the inclusion of a handful of firms on the list. Eventually, after six months, in June 1972, the CDP broke off the negotiations. In hindsight, it is clear that if negotiations between the government and the CDP were to have any chance of success, they should have taken place before, not after, the CDP introduced the constitutional amendment. Yet, the CDP introduced the amendment because the government had made no serious attempt to negotiate. After congress approved the amendment, it would have been suicidal for the CDP to climb down and agree to the government's veto, as this would have caused a major split within the party—precisely the outcome expected by some of the parties within the Popular Unity.

Following the introduction of the constitutional amendment by the CDP, its relations with the National Party became increasingly closer. Although in September 1971 the CDP refused to join the National Party in its attempt to impeach the minister of economics, by the end of that year it supported the impeachment of the minister of the interior (Echeverría and Frei 1974:2:34–79). The allegation against the minister was that he had failed to maintain law and order and protect the freedom of assembly of a group of middle-class women who had staged an "empty-pots" demonstration against the government. These circumstances brought the CDP closer to the National Party, and by mid-1972, the two parties had closed ranks to form an antigovernment bloc, which they called the Democratic Confederation (CODE). This realignment of political forces undermined the credibility of the parliamentary prong of the government's dual strategy and strengthened the radical elements within the Popular Unity coalition.

After this first impeachment, there began an incessant round of impeachment of cabinet ministers (Loveman and Lira 2000:376). Although the government responded defiantly, usually reappointing the impeached ministers to another cabinet post, impeachment did prove to be effective, as it kept the government under constant pressure and concentrated the attention of public opinion on alleged unlawful activities of government departments, one at a time. The government complained bitterly that politically motivated impeachments were reviving the discredited parliamentary practices repudiated by the 1925 Constitution. Yet, as previous chapters of this work show, the parliamentary practices of the political elite did not subside after 1925. In any event, the revival of parliamentarism and the consequent weakening of the president were precisely the outcome sought by the opposition.

Impeachments were partly a consequence of the fact that congress had no business to transact. As the opposition parties controlled more than half the seats in both chambers of the congress, the government was unable to secure the approval of any legislation without their agreement. But, because the opposition parties did not have a two-third majority they could not override the president's veto. As a consequence, the government could only secure the approval of those bills essential to keeping the state apparatus functioning, but faced defeat in the case of legislation that purported to introduce changes along the lines envisaged by the government's program. Thus, the congress rejected all government bills, including those designed to deal with illegal occupations of private dwellings, to control hoarding and speculation or to establish a Ministry for the Family. The bill proposing the establishment of informal community-based tribunals to improve access to justice among the poor had to be withdrawn from the congress in order to avoid a humiliating defeat.

In the absence of parliamentary business, the opposition parties in congress kept the pressure on the government in different ways. In addition to continuous round of impeachments, opposition members took the opportunity to use the chamber of deputies and the senate to attack the government for the prevailing climate of social and political unrest. They also appointed special congressional commissions to investigate specific government policies, approached the comptroller general directly to ascertain the legality of government decisions and referred matters to the just then established Constitutional Tribunal (Contraloría General de la República 1971).

But the impeachments and other parliamentary maneuvering were only a sideshow. The key issue arose after the congress rejected the government's veto. This event provoked a major constitutional row that, characteristically, unfolded slowly and was preceded by a heated debate about the correct interpretation of the constitution.

First, there was a Byzantine dispute between the government and the opposition over the number of votes required to override the president's veto. The government claimed that the congress needed a vote of two-thirds while the congress claimed that only a majority was necessary (Silva Cimma 1977:147–202). Then there was a dispute as to whether the Constitutional Tribunal had jurisdiction to resolve this dispute. The government, anxious to prolong the debate, claimed that the Constitutional Tribunal did have jurisdiction. The opposition, acknowledging that their case was weak, disagreed and issued a statement announcing that they would not recognize the Tribunal's decision, were it to assert jurisdiction over this case. Despite this warning, the government submitted the dispute to the Constitutional Tribunal. The Tribunal however, quite sensibly, found the government's request inadmissible. At that stage, the government had the option of either enacting the constitutional amendment approved by the congress or calling a plebiscite. The government chose neither and, as ever, opted for an unconventional solution. It decided to enact only those sections of the amendment that had not been the object of the veto. The opposition—with the backing of the comptroller general—responded immediately, claiming that the partial enactment of the amendment was illegitimate and invalid and demanded the immediate enactment of the text be approved by the congress.[6]

The partial enactment of the amendment trivialized the constitutional process and exacerbated the prevailing political and economic uncertainty. It was yet another sign that the government had lost control over political events and that its dual strategy had collapsed. Shortly thereafter the military deposed the government.

Public Order

The collapse of the price control system hastened the appearance of a black market for basic consumer goods. Government opponents were quick to realize that inflation and market disruption of basic goods were effective political weapons. As political mobilization against the government intensified, the shortcomings of the government's policy on public order became evident.

Upon taking office, the government disbanded the special riot police unit on the ground that it was no longer needed, as the people had acceded to power. This decision was both demagogic and opportunistic because, as already explained, the government took advantage of the militancy of its own supporters during its first months in office to speed up the agrarian reform and takeover of the commanding heights of the economy. As the opposition regained confidence, however, it began to use methods similar to those employed by left-wing supporters. Some involved self-help measures of a paramilitary nature to prevent or repel land or factory occupations. The most important opposition-led protest was a long and costly truck drivers' strike that was followed by a month-long lockout in October 1972 (De Vylder 1976:98). The objective of the lockout was to bring the government down. These events posed a major dilemma for the government. It could not readily used the coercive powers of the state to repress extra-parliamentary activities of its opponents, because it had attempted, albeit unsuccessfully, to control the behavior of its own supporters through persuasion. This weakness played into the hands of the opposition, which described any attempt to restrain antigovernment forces as a sign of the government's totalitarian inclinations and any attempt to resolve conflicts through negotiation as evidence of the government's complicity with the acts of violence.[7]

Aware that these allegations were calculated to create unrest within the armed forces, the government opted for a solution that, in the long term, led to disaster. It increasingly began to call on the military to handle major disruptions of public order, instead of relying exclusively on the police. Thus, the government expected to silence the opposition's allegations, as the professionalism of the army was a myth accepted by all the major political parties. This policy gave the government some breathing space as it enabled it to deal with the opposition-led lockout of October 1972. In the long run, however, the involvement of the army in the enforcement of public order was the beginning of a process that slowly raised the political profile of the armed forces and reassured them of their role as guardians of democracy. After relying on the army to deal with the October events, the government had little choice but to accept military participation in the cabinet. During the period that the military were in the government, the opposition introduced legislation—the Arms Control Act—that gave the armed forces exorbitant powers to conduct searches for weapons and other artifacts allegedly used by terrorist groups.[8] The government was unable to veto this law because it would have been regarded as an affront to the military and as an indication that the government was protecting left-wing terrorist groups. After military participation in the cabinet came to an end, in January 1973, and "normal" politics resumed, the military began vigorously to apply the Arms Control Law to repress and neutralize government supporters.

Legitimacy Eroded

As already noted, one of the key assumptions on which the government strategy rested was that the regulatory powers of the executive branch were virtually unlimited and not subject to any meaningful control from any organ of the state, other than the congress. This assumption was based on the behavior of the courts and other institutions during the period that I have described as party democracy. But the government, however, failed to take into account that legal systems are not static and that legal institutions often shift their position in line with swings in public opinion and the political debate. In particular, it did not seem to have anticipated that individuals and enterprises affected by government measures would make use of the legal system to defend their interests and protect their rights. Thus, courts were soon inundated with complaints against the government. These complaints challenged the validity of requisition decrees and sought to terminate the illegal occupation of factories and rural properties.

Courts responded favorably, albeit slowly, to these legal challenges, and their response infuriated government supporters, thus further raising the stakes of political confrontation. Workers became increasingly more militant and unwilling to make concessions as courts began to issue injunctions that seriously undermined the capacity of government-appointed administrators to manage enterprises under requisition and injunctions that ordered the arrest of the ringleaders of occupations. The government thus confronted a difficult and unexpected dilemma: if it complied with court decisions, it would in effect have to undo some of its policies, thus infuriating its supporters; if it openly took the side of its supporters, it would risk a major confrontation with the judiciary. The government's response to this dilemma was, characteristically ambiguous. While it refused to reverse its policies, it also employed a variety of legal tactics in an attempt to defuse or at least postpone confrontation with the judiciary.

The multitude of legal challenges confronted by the government became yet another issue that diverted its attention from more pressing political and economic problems. Moreover, the mounting legal challenges also undermined the legitimacy of the government—a matter that was skillfully exploited by the opposition—for, it made it possible to raise questions about the constitutionality and legality of every single aspect of government policy, thus reinforcing the impression that the Popular Unity was purposely creating chaos and disorder. Although many of the allegations against the government had solid constitutional and legal bases, there were many that did not. But in terms of the political debate, whether or not these allegations were true was unimportant. As the government began to lose its legitimacy almost any allegation put forward by the opposition seemed credible.

An important component of the opposition's campaign against the government was the Statute of Democratic Guarantees (SDG). The SDG, as explained above, was a constitutional amendment approved by the congress that the Popular Unity had accepted as part of the negotiations that made possible the accession of Allende to the presidency. The Popular Unity regarded the SDG as harmless, as, ostensibly, it was little more than a restatement and further elaboration of civil and political rights already guaranteed by the constitution.

But the Popular Unity soon realized that the SDG had created some unexpected problems. These problems stemmed partly from the fact that the SDG had provided that the exercise of the rights guaranteed by the constitution could only be regulated by legislation. This otherwise reasonable provision was a departure from practice, as hitherto the exercise of some important constitutional rights was regulated by government decrees, not by legislation. Because of the haste with which the SDG was approved, the constitutional amendment did not validate these decrees, so that in constitutional terms, the SDG had implicitly repealed government decrees that imposed restrictions in key areas such as freedom of speech and freedom of the press.

One of the most controversial issues that emerged was whether the government had the power to impose restrictions on broadcasting during national emergencies. This controversy arose as a direct consequence of the SDG. The president's powers to restrict broadcasting during national emergencies had been acknowledged for quite some time and had been widely used in the past. However, these powers were set out in a decree—Decree No. 4,581—enacted in 1949 and not in legislation.[9] Thus, when the government imposed restrictions on radio broadcasting during a major strike in October 1972, a major political row erupted that led to the indictment of a former member of the cabinet.[10] The government claimed that pending the enactment of new legislation, Decree 4,581 should have been deemed as remaining in force. This argument, however, was legally weak, as it failed to take into account the fact that, according to the SDG, only a law could regulate the exercise of rights guaranteed by the constitution.

A similar conflict broke out in connection with the regulation of technical matters relating to television stations. The SDG provided that only universities could establish and operate television stations. Subsequently, new legislation was approved that provided that technical control regarding the allocation of channels was the responsibility of a government agency.[11] When two private universities that ran local TV stations set up a national network, a conflict arose over the scope of the powers of the government agency. While the government claimed that the stations—both notoriously in favor of the opposition—were attempting to launch their own network without complying with the appropriate technical requirements, the managers of the channels claimed that the government was attempting to undermine constitutional rights recognized by the SDG. This dispute raised interesting and difficult problems of interpretation. The parties, however, decided to act unilaterally. The television stations carried on working on the expansion of their networks, and the government, claiming that the TV stations were acting illegally, invoked its regulatory powers and ordered the seizure of the new equipment. The opposition responded immediately, impeaching the minister of the interior for serious breach of the constitution.[12] The official who had ordered the seizure of the equipment was indicted for the crime of false imprisonment.[13]

In the area of education also, the SDG created problems for the government. Here, it substituted three long paragraphs for the two succinct paragraphs that had over the years successfully managed to reconcile state and private education. An interesting feature of the new constitutional clause was that it provided that changes to the prevailing educational system required prior democratic deliberation and decision by the relevant organs, but did not contain any indication as to how to fulfill this requirement. Therefore, it is not surprising that when the government attempted to reform the system of primary education, the opposition dismissed it as undemocratic and as a threat to the cultural values of the nation (Fischer 1979:109–115; Quiros 1973; Smith 1982:196–199).[14]

The SDG created innumerable problems of interpretation that, even under normal circumstances, would have been difficult to resolve. It also provided the opposition with a powerful ideological weapon, as virtually any government decision could, in one way or another, be regarded as a breach of the SDG. As the SDG had been approved with the votes of the Popular Unity, the government could not claim that the opposition was resorting to old bourgeois legislation to obstruct the revolution.

Mobilization without Empowerment

The Popular Unity, as already noted, assigned absolute priority to the objective of nationalizing the commanding heights of the economy. To achieve this objective it not only made ample use of the administrative powers vested in the executive, but also relied heavily on the mobilization of its supporters. Indeed, the wave of strikes and factory occupations that exploded soon after Allende took office was fully exploited by the government to launch a comprehensive policy of intervention and requisition of enterprises in the manufacturing sector. But though the government's approach to taking over the commanding heights of the economy was dependent on workers' militancy, it effectively postponed the Popular Unity's promise to empower workers and other subordinate groups. Although this feature of the Popular Unity's policy was possibly justified in terms of the prevailing balance of forces, it was also consistent with a somewhat orthodox interpretation of Marxism. Indeed, the government's approach assumed that once it secured control over the economy, its political problems would be easily resolved, as the opposition would disintegrate and the vast majority of workers and peasants would support the parties of the Left. The government's overall approach was also orthodox in the way it conceived its relationship with the unions. In line with orthodox Marxist approaches, it took for granted that the interests of the unions had to be subordinated to the overall political strategy, as interpreted by party leaders. This approach proved fatally flawed as instead of bringing about the disintegration of the opposition, it made it more cohesive and militant, and instead of enhancing workers' support for the government, it undermined it.

The Other Civil Society

During the early days of the government, the Popular Unity pursued its objective of taking over the commanding heights of the economy with unexpected determination. It secured the nationalization of copper through a constitutional amendment; it took over virtually the whole banking sector through the purchase of shares; and issued scores of decrees ordering the requisition of firms in the manufacturing sector. In order to allay the fears of the private sector, the government claimed, albeit disingenuously, that the majority of firms had nothing to fear from its policies, as the commanding heights comprised a tiny group of companies—approximately 180 out of a total of 30,000 manufacturing establishments (Allende 1972:16, 24; Bitar 1979:284–285). These arguments failed to appease the private sector. Instead, they prompted a militant response from the opposition. Thus, 18 months after his electoral victory, President Allende was besieged from every direction. While the economy was running out of control and the political system was paralyzed, radical groups within the Popular Unity and within the opposition began to consider alternatives to the democratic process. A regional meeting of Popular Unity parties in the Southern city of Concepción, calling themselves the People's Assembly, demanded the abolition of the parliament and the removal of reactionary judges. This event, which was unequivocally repudiated by Allende, was a sign of the deep fissures that were undermining the government coalition. While the Popular Unity began to disintegrate, the opposition began to coordinate their activities more closely. In April 1972, a meeting that included members of the leading business associations, opposition politicians, and members of extreme right-wing organizations linked to terrorist activities, such as *Patria y Libertad*, met to consider the impact of government policies on family and religious values as well as the declining respect for the fatherland. The government promptly denounced this meeting as subversive. Although the opposition ridiculed these claims, General

Pinochet later disclosed that it was at this time that he and his army colleagues began to seriously consider toppling the government (Faundez 1988:227).

The prevailing political deadlock brought into prominence a variety of civil society groups, mainly associations representing business and liberal professions. These organizations, known locally as *gremios*, assumed a leading role in mobilizing public opinion against the government. As the niceties of constitutional politics did not bind them, they could resort to extreme rhetoric, including calling for the forceful removal of the government. The *gremios* were the leading force behind the long-drawn out truck drivers' strike of October 1972 that prompted a massive lockout that affected industrial enterprises in the major cities of the country (Bitar 1979:163–172; Roxborough et al. 1977:116–117). This movement brought the government to the brink of collapse. In order to remain in office, the government was forced to appoint the heads of the three armed services to the cabinet. These events strengthened the position of the *gremios* and enhanced their influence, not only among the middle classes, but also within organized labor. Indeed, after exploiting a minor labor dispute in the copper industry, the *gremios*, led by affluent University students, managed to stage a spectacular demonstration against the government in support of a segment of the powerful union of copper mine workers. Although the workers who demonstrated against the government represented only a tiny fraction of the workforce, the symbolic impact of this demonstration was formidable. It questioned one of the Popular Unity's most cherished claims—the claim that it was the only and most trustworthy representative of the interests of the working class and other subordinate groups.

The mobilization of white-collar workers against the government was, in many respects, not unexpected, as the government's incomes policy had been purposely designed to favor blue-collar workers and the very poor (Heskia 1973:34–35). Thus, as inflation set in, there was growing resentment and dissatisfaction among white-collar workers. Moreover, given the prevailing turbulence, this group of workers was easily mobilized by slogans that called for effective protection of private property and enhanced respect for family values. What seems surprising, however, is that despite considerable efforts, the government was unable to strengthen and deepen its influence among the working class and other subordinate groups. This failing baffled and frustrated government officials and left-wing activists, as they regarded organized workers were their natural constituency and took their loyalty for granted.

Elusive Loyalty

The difficulties that the Popular Unity faced with the unions stemmed partly from its failure to fully assess the impact of the changes that had taken place among organized workers since the inception of radical democracy. Between 1965 and 1970, the number of workers belonging to unions increased from just over 300,000 to nearly half a million (see appendix C). During the first two years of the Allende administration, an additional 100,000 workers joined unions. Thus, within seven years, the overall rate of unionization had shot up from 10 percent to 22 percent of the workforce (Allende 1973b:793). The majority of the newly unionized workers (60 percent) were agricultural workers who up until 1965 had been denied the right to form unions. This group of workers, along with workers in manufacturing, spearheaded the wave of strikes and land and factory occupations that had prompted the government to use its regulatory powers to take over the administration of large number of rural estates and manufacturing enterprises. The traditional union leadership at the CUT was fully aware of the dangers posed by this seemingly unrestrained process of mobilization. They were confident, however, that as these new groups of workers became politically mature, they would become a formidable force in support of government policies.[15] But the limited scope of the government's program and its failure to confront the question of empowerment frustrated workers and intensified their demands.

The Popular Unity's attempt to soothe the private sector by pointing out that the majority of firms would not be affected by the government's nationalization policy caused serious concern among workers. Indeed, as the nationalization of the commanding heights of the economy comprised a relatively small number of firms, only a small number of workers stood to benefit. Indeed, the government's nationalization program would have affected only 20 percent of industrial workers, representing a mere 5 percent of the total workforce (De Vylder 1976:145–148). As the implementation of the program would have effectively postponed the immediate aspirations of the vast majority of workers, they placed strong pressure on the government to expand it. Because their demands were instigated and supported by the Socialist Party, the government was unable to resist them. But the government also, cynically, took advantage of these demands as it expected—misguidedly as it turned out—that workers' militancy would soften CDP's position and bring about a political compromise. Thus, the government ended up requisitioning scores of firms that under any measure were not part of the commanding heights of the economy, while it was unable to assert control of large firms that should have been part of it (Espinosa and Zimbalist 1978:111; Flores 1973:29–31). Moreover, as the government was carrying out this expanded process of requisitions, it was, at the same time, deeply involved in negotiations with the opposition, in which it was offering to reduce the number of firms covered by its nationalization program from 250 in October 1971, to 90 in June 1972 and then to less than 50 in January 1973. Thus, while the government encouraged workers' mobilization to speed up the takeover of the commanding heights of the economy, it was simultaneously seeking a compromise with the opposition that would have required reversing a process that had generated unrealistic expectations among its supporters. These contradictory signals undermined the political credibility of the government, especially among organized workers. Workers' disappointment was justified as the government, relying on an orthodox Marxist approach, took union support for granted and assumed that unions could be endlessly manipulated to serve its interests. The government's approach to the question of workers' participation illustrates this point.

Limiting Workers' Participation

As noted in chapter 7, the Communist and Socialist Parties were strongly opposed to the CDP's notion of workers' management as they regarded it as little more than a ploy to divert workers from their revolutionary objectives. They also successfully opposed the CDP's attempt to end the closed-shop system in the industrial sector, as they believed that a system of parallel unions would weaken their overall strength. Their concerns, though possibly legitimate, reflected faithfully a fairly orthodox Marxist approach to the relationship between the party and unions. Under this approach unions were expected to subordinate their immediate demands to the enlightened political leadership of the party—the vanguard of the proletariat. That communists and socialists were determined to assert political control over the union movement was amply demonstrated in the 1950s by their ruthless removal of Clotario Blest from the presidency of the CUT. Blest, an independent non-Marxist, had made a major contribution to the rebuilding of the unity of the union movement, but was toppled from office because he was not prepared to subordinate workers' interests to the demands of the Marxist or any other party. In those days, the party line was to contain popular mobilization in order to make a credible bid for the presidency. Thus, it is not surprising that once in office the Marxist parties should have continued to regard the interests of the union movement as absolutely subordinated to its political objectives. But this policy proved unviable for two reasons. First, because, as already explained, the political messages handed down by the government were, if not incoherent, at least contradictory. Second, because the unions soon became aware of the power to bring about political change and thus refused to toe the party line. Indeed, instead of being passive executors of party political decisions, they became actively involved in seeking to influence government policy. Thus, the government's expectation that it could indefinitely defer the empowerment of workers' proved a delusion. That the government was unprepared to deal with this issue is illustrated by its limited and somewhat bureaucratic conception of workers' participation.

The workers' participation schemes proposed by the government assigned a privileged role to the unions and revealed a deep-seated skepticism of workers' ability to manage their own affairs. In the industrial sector, the government proposed two participation schemes: one for firms in the private sector and the other for firms in the state sector (Espinosa and Zimbalist 1978:53–56). The scheme designed for the private sector entailed setting up committees to ensure that production was not disrupted. This scheme was never implemented. The scheme for the state sector envisaged an elaborate structure that included a general assembly, an administrative council, and several production committees. The expectation was that through these organs the voice and interests of workers would be reflected in the management of the enterprise. Yet, the scheme assigned a disproportionate number of seats on the administrative council to government officials, so that in the end, the state-appointed manager always had the final say. Under the government's scheme, the organs of participation were in fact mechanisms of consultation rather than devices for self-management. Underlying this narrow conception of workers' participation was the view that the main conduit to channeling workers' interests and demands was the union—an organ that political parties could easily control. The government proposed an equally narrow scheme for rural areas. It consisted of peasant councils established in various localities. Membership in these councils was, however, restricted to unionized workers. Peasant councils never caught the imagination of peasants (Barraclough and Fernández 1974:198–212).

In the manufacturing sector, the government's scheme of participation was soon swamped by traditional rivalry between the Marxists parties. The Socialist Party regarded the new organs of participation as devices to pressure the government to radicalize its program and to enhance its influence among workers. The Communists were skeptical about these participation schemes, as they continued to regard unions as the main vehicle for channeling workers' interests. But political events soon moved beyond the factory. In their continuing efforts to expand the scope of the government's nationalization program, workers—with the support of the Socialist Party—established new organs of political participation at the local level. They called them *cordones industriales* (industrial belts) (Faundez 1988:267–273). Their objective was to support the efforts of workers in the locality to secure the inclusion of their workplaces into the state sector. Initially, the government strongly opposed the industrial belts, depicting them as divisive and as instruments of the ultraleft. Its views changed, however, when, as a result of the opposition-led strike of October 1972 industrial belts played a major role in ensuring that the supply and distribution of basic goods was not completely disrupted.

The role of industrial belts in support of the government during the October strike was indeed outstanding. Yet, they caused major damage to the government as they consistently opposed its efforts to find a solution to the many problems caused by its misguided dual strategy. However, it would be a mistake to place all of the blame on workers and their organizations. The root cause of the problem stemmed from the government's decision to take advantage of workers' mobilization while failing to take seriously the question of empowerment. Thus, not surprisingly although the majority of workers continued to support the government until the bitter end, their support was not unqualified. A poster carried by a worker at a political rally shortly before the military coup captured the mood of most workers: "[T]his government stinks, but it is my government."

Elections Become Redundant

The Popular Unity was unable to use the political system to further its programmatic objectives, yet it managed to dislocate it. This unintended effect benefited the opposition. The most telling illustration of the dislocation of the political system is reflected in the results of the last general election, held in March 1973, only six months before the military coup. At the time of the election the economic and political situation was bleak and the CDP and the Right had already formed a solid electoral coalition and were determined to remove the government. Given prevailing political conditions, most pollsters predicted an overwhelming victory for the opposition, one that would enable them to secure a two-third majority in the congress to impeach Allende and legally remove him from office. The opposition thus characterized the elections as a referendum on the performance of the government. The CDP was especially hopeful that this strategy would work, as the removal of Allende by constitutional means would pave the way for the election of a Christian Democrat as president.

The electoral results surprised everyone. Opposition parties were disappointed as, although they obtained 55 percent of the vote, they did not gain enough seats to impeach Allende. The Popular Unity, however, was taken by surprise. Its share of the vote increased from 36 percent in 1970 to 44 percent. This was a remarkable performance. The government had faced the elections in the most adverse conditions. During the previous six months, the opposition had promoted systematic campaigns aimed at disrupting the economy and furthering insecurity and chaos. It had encouraged strikes among liberal professionals and white-collar employees and had made full use of its economic power to withdraw consumer goods from circulation, thus creating a profitable black market. At the international level, the government had to contend also with a variety of measures that further disrupted the economy (NACLA 1973:179–208). These measures included a financial blockade instigated by the U.S. government, indirect interference with the commercialization of copper in Europe, and political intrigue and covert activity organized by the CIA. Yet, despite these difficulties, the government not only succeeded in averting the threat of impeachment, but also managed significantly to increase its share of the vote.

But these electoral results, which in a different context would have been hailed as a sign of the maturity and responsibility of the electorate, did not resolve anything. On the contrary, they complicated matters. The results disrupted the opposition's plan to impeach Allende and thus strengthened the position of those who called for a military coup. Within the Popular Unity, the results strengthened the radical groups, as they interpreted them as a mandate to press ahead with the implementation of the program, regardless of legal niceties and without seeking a political compromise. The political crisis made the electoral process redundant, thus foreshadowing the end of democratic politics.

Chapter 9

Legality Defeated

Introduction

During the three decades of party democracy (1932–64), relations between the Supreme Court and the political branches of the state were, on the whole, cordial. The reluctance of the Supreme Court to exercise its powers as guardian of the constitution and its refusal openly to accept challenges to the legality of acts of the administration gave the executive broad discretion to intervene in the economy and other areas of public policy. Although during this period the Supreme Court occasionally accepted challenges to the legality of executive action and managed successfully to bring special administrative tribunals within the scope of its disciplinary powers, these developments did not have a major impact on the form or content of government policy. Relations between the Contraloría and the political branches of the state were also cordial. Although after the impeachment of the comptroller general in 1945, the legality review procedure became more effective as a restraint on the executive, the efficacy of this mechanism was offset by the persistent willingness of the congress to replenish the government's regulatory powers. Thus, while during the party democracy period, both the Supreme Court and the Contraloría had given some indications that they had the power to effectively curb executive action, in practice, their behavior was cautious and deferential so that relations between the main legal and political organs of the state remained cordial.

The inception of radical democracy opened up a new chapter in the relations between the political and legal organs of the state. During this period the Supreme Court and the Contraloría were pushed into the limelight and began to play a role that hitherto they had shunned. The economic and social reforms launched by the Frei administration and further deepened by the Allende administration persuaded an already skeptical private sector that the party system could no longer be trusted to protect property rights. Thus, in their efforts to curb government policies they sought help first from the judiciary and later on from the Contraloría. Given the judiciary's traditional caution, its response was slow and incoherent. The response of the Contraloría was also initially cautious. Yet, as the political struggle intensified, both the courts and the Contraloría attracted considerable political attention as they issued rulings and granted injunctions that appeared to favor one or the other side in the increasingly bitter political confrontation. As the materials in this chapter show, the measures deployed by the courts and the Contraloría to curb government action had all been sporadically used in the past. Yet, in the more tranquil political environment of party democracy, these measures were hardly noticed by the political elite. In the polarized context of the Allende administration, however, these measures became highly contentious. While the opposition welcomed them, depicting the courts and the Contraloría as courageous upholders of the rule of law, the government and its supporters deeply resented them, claiming that the courts and the Contraloría were departing from prevailing practice and shamelessly taking sides in the ongoing political confrontation. There thus followed a cascade of injunctions and counterinjunctions, allegations and counterallegations that trivialized the constitutional and legal processes, destroyed the credibility of legal institutions, and eroded the legitimacy of the government. The defeat of legality was a necessary prelude to the violent overthrow of democracy.

This chapter is divided into three sections. The focus of its first section is on the legal strategies employed by the Frei and Allende administrations to achieve their political objectives. The second and third sections focus exclusively on developments during the Allende administration. The second section examines the controversy between Allende and the Contraloría over the legality of requisitions decrees. The third section explains the complex role that courts played during the period leading up to the collapse of the constitution.

Legal Strategies

Taking Notice of the Judiciary

The judiciary's rise to political prominence began in the mid-1960s during Frei's "revolution in liberty." Although the Frei administration meticulously sought constitutional and legislative authority for its policies, its approach to the implementation of the reform process—consistent with local political practice—was to exclude the judiciary from major areas of public policy. Thus, for example, the amendment that modified the property rights clause of the constitution, as well as the agrarian reform legislation, were carefully drafted so as to exclude the possibility of judicial interference. The constitutional amendment contained detailed provisions on the expropriation of rural properties that were explicitly designed to preclude any interference by the Supreme Court in the agrarian reform process. Moreover, the agrarian reform law established agrarian tribunals with limited jurisdiction to ensure that the implementation of the agrarian reform law would not be delayed by excessive litigation (Avila 1971:92–97).

Despite their limited jurisdiction, landowners made prolific use of agrarian tribunals to challenge government policy. The disciplinary powers asserted by the Supreme Court over these tribunals undoubtedly encouraged private parties to use them. Yet, because the jurisdiction of these tribunals was limited, these challenges had little impact on the pace or direction of the agrarian reform (Thome 1971: 508–509). During this period, landowners and industrialists also made use of the criminal process to protect their property against the proliferation of land invasions and factory occupations. Thus, the structural reforms launched by President Frei and the ensuing political mobilization were useful reminders to members of the economic elite of the crucial role that courts can play in restraining government action.

Ironically, however, by the late 1960s, as political mobilization intensified, the Frei administration was forced to adopt a tough law and order policy, which, naturally, required the cooperation of the judiciary (Roxborough et al. 1977:60–62). Yet, despite its efforts to enlist the support of the courts, the government did nothing to improve the salary and career prospects of judges. Expenditure on the judiciary—as well as the military—had a low priority, as the government had devoted all its spare resources to fund social and economic development programs. The financial difficulties of the judiciary were not new. As explained in chapter 6, the judiciary was almost invariably allocated less than 1 percent of total public expenditure. What was new, however, was the fact that in the late 1960s, lower court judges—inspired by the highly politicized environment—had begun to organize and were more vocal in their demands for better pay and conditions. The situation came to a head when the newly established Judges' Association staged an unprecedented strike in support of judges' pay claims. Initially, the government dismissed these claims, but after a similar type of action by a group of disgruntled military officers, the government gave in and awarded substantial pay increases to the military and the judiciary. While this decision resolved the immediate problem, it did not significantly improve relations between the government and the judiciary. Thus, while the Frei administration tried to play by the rulebook, its ambitious program of structural reforms raised the political profile of the Supreme Court. It also made the private sector aware that, despite the shortcomings of the judicial institutions, they could be used to curb the powers of the executive.

Toward the end of the Frei administration, as the government began to increasingly rely on the courts to contain the process of political mobilization, left-wing parties began to openly criticize the judiciary. A misguided decision by the Frei government to prosecute Carlos Altamirano, a Socialist senator, under the State Security Act provided left-wing parties with an excuse to introduce a motion of impeachment against the entire Supreme Court. The events that triggered the motion of impeachment and its sequel are worth recounting.

Upon returning from a short visit to Cuba, Senator Altamirano gave a public lecture at a provincial university in which he praised Fidel Castro's revolution and violently attacked the mild reformist policies of President Frei. The charges against the senator included making an apologia for violence, insulting the office of the presidency, and behaving disrespectfully toward the armed forces. In order to press charges, however, the government had to request the Court of Appeals to lift the senator's parliamentary immunity. The Court of Appeals declined, but, on appeal, the Supreme Court reversed and the senator was prosecuted and sentenced to a short prison term.[1] The Socialist and Communist Parties were outraged and responded by introducing a motion of impeachment against all the members of the Supreme Court alleging, inter alia, that the judicial system was class biased.

The sponsors of the motion of impeachment claimed that the Supreme Court was class biased because it consistently ruled in favor of landowners and capitalists and had little sympathy for the plight of the working class and the poor. Although the chamber of deputies promptly rejected this motion, it nevertheless provided socialists and communists with an ideal platform to publicize their views about the Supreme Court and the justice system generally. It also prompted the Supreme Court to respond to the claim of class bias. In its response the Court pointed out that class bias was unlikely to occur because judicial conflicts between the wealthy and the poor were infrequent. According to the Court, most cases decided by courts entailed conflict between wealthy parties or between poor parties, not between the wealthy and the poor (Corte Suprema 1967:1461, 1466). The Court complemented this rudimentary sociological analysis with a philosophical argument. In a democracy, the Court claimed, class bias was theoretically and practically impossible, as the only domination allowed was that of the majority of citizens, expressed through the ballot box and embodied in laws made by the elected representatives of the people. Thus, according to the Court, by strictly adhering to the letter of the law, judges were indeed instruments of the only truly dominant group: the electoral majority (Corte Suprema 1967:1468, 1971:XXIV).

The Court's defense against the motion of impeachment was a hopeless attempt to keep the judiciary at a safe distance from the turbulent world of politics. By the late 1960s, this was no longer a realistic alternative. Indeed, the question as to whether courts and other legal institutions were neutral or biased was rapidly becoming an urgent political issue.

Law and the Peaceful Revolution

The controversy between the left-wing parties and the Supreme Court faded as the political debate came to be dominated by the presidential elections of 1970. Moreover, as the electoral platform of the Popular Unity coalition was to bring about a socialist revolution within the prevailing legal framework, they could not afford to appear confrontational toward the judiciary. Yet despite their commitment to legality, the Popular Unity gave no indication as to how they intended to implement their proposed peaceful transition to socialism. Moreover, their program of government contained virtually no information on how an eventual government of the Popular Unity would relate to legal institutions. Indeed, apart from some references to the system of judicial appointments and vague proposals on widening access to justice, the program made no other reference to the legal system. Just before taking office, however, the Popular Unity parties endorsed a constitutional amendment—the Statute of Democratic Guarantees (SDG)—that was generally interpreted as a reaffirmation of their commitment to respect legality and the rules of the democratic process. But, as already noted, the Popular Unity regarded this amendment merely as a tactical concession of little political consequence.

Upon taking office, the government had no time to ponder the intricacies of law and the legal system. During its first months in office, it faced a wave of strikes, factory occupations, and land invasions that demanded immediate action (Barraclough and Fernández 1974:192; Landsberger and McDaniel 1976:519–526; Sader 1973:11–27). Its legal strategy was, consequently, largely shaped by its response to these events. Factory occupations were, at least to start with, a by-product of the government's initial economic policy. Strict price controls combined with large wage increases created enormous hardship on small and medium-sized firms. As a consequence, many firms began to cut their workforce, while others threatened to close down their operations. The unions responded defiantly. The ensuing wave of strikes and factory occupations intensified political polarization. On the left, it strengthened the position of the Socialist Party and the view that prompt and decisive action was required to prevent employers from derailing the government. Among the opposition parties, it strengthened the stand of the right-wing National Party, which claimed that the government was incompetent and could not be trusted with the management of the economy. Thus, while left-wing militant began to promote strikes and occupations as a means of prompting the government into action, landowners and the business community allowed industrial disputes to drag on indefinitely so as to further disrupt economic activity and provoke workers and left-wing activists into action.

The proliferation of strikes and factory occupations posed a serious dilemma for the government. While it could not to allow them to disrupt its economic policy, it could not afford to treat them as mere law and order problems that required heavy-handed measures. The solution was thus to resolve these disputes by resorting to the regulatory powers vested in the executive. The regulatory tools used by the government were mainly two: labor intervention decrees, known locally as back-to-work decrees (*decretos de reanudación de faenas*) and requisition decrees.

The labor code and related legislation gave the government extensive powers to intervene whenever a strike or lockout posed a threat to the health or economic well- being of the community. Government intervention involved issuing back-to-work decrees and appointing a temporary administrator to run the enterprise until the conflict was resolved (Oneto 1971; Yávar 1972). Prior to Allende's presidency, back-to-work decrees were used mainly to break strikes, particularly in the copper industry and in the public sector. The Popular Unity government, however, used them to prevent the disruption of its economic policy. Workers welcomed this form of intervention because government-appointed administrators were invariably sympathetic to their demands. These decrees were also useful because they frustrated attempts by employers to seek remedies through the courts. Indeed, as soon as a back-to-work decree was issued, the factory or agricultural estate was—in legal terms—no longer under occupation and hence judicial remedies to protect property rights could not be used.

Back-to-work decrees, however, posed some difficulties. Under prevailing practice, once the government issued a back-to-work decree, it was required to follow an elaborate procedure aimed at resolving the dispute in question (Contraloría General de la República 1971). Yet, as the disputes were often political, following this procedure would inevitably have led to a decision unfavorable to workers, thus reigniting the conflict. To avoid this problem, the government generally replaced back-to-work decrees with requisition decrees. This move went largely unnoticed by workers, as it did not significantly alter the powers of government-appointed administrators. Requisitions, however, were a useful device because the government could, in theory, keep them in force indefinitely. The rules governing requisition allowed the government to take over the administration of industrial or commercial enterprises whenever a strike, occupation, or lockout seriously disrupted production. Requisition decrees were also attractive because, under prevailing practice, ordinary courts could not review them. Thus, by issuing requisition decrees, the government felt it was beyond the reach of ordinary courts. Accordingly, it soon began to rely almost exclusively on requisition decrees. Thus, the number of enterprises subject to requisition rose from 40 in 1971 to 86 in 1972, while the number of back-to-work decrees during the same period declined from 127 to 75 (De Vylder 1976:146; Instituto de Economía 1973:111; Martínez 1979:268).

The government's willingness to respond to strikes and factory occupations with requisition decrees soon developed a momentum of its own. Workers and party activists realized that all that was necessary to get the government to issue a requisition decree was to start a strike or stage an occupation. As the number of politically motivated strikes and occupations escalated, so did the number of requisition decrees issued by the government. As workers, along with party activists and the left-wing media, regarded these requisitions as full-fledged nationalizations, the government could not easily revoke them. By December 1972, the government found itself administering approximately 40 small and medium-sized enterprises that its supporters regarded as part of the state sector, but which, according to its own program, were not meant to be so (Martínez 1979:268).

Although the government's reliance on the regulatory powers of the executive was, initially, a stopgap measure to deal with strikes and land invasions it soon became the centerpiece of what, in the preceding chapter, I described as the government's dual strategy. Indeed, by relying on the regulatory powers of the executive the government could show determination in the implementation of its program (the revolutionary prong), while making conciliatory gestures that suggested that it was committed to seeking congressional approval for the implementation of its program (the parliamentary prong).

Legal Rationale

Eduardo Novoa is generally credited as the architect of the Popular Unity government's approach to legality. His depiction in the late 1960s of the justice system as class-biased gave him instant access to Allende's inner circle. He became legal advisor to the president and was entrusted with the delicate task of designing the legal strategy for the nationalization of copper. His approach to the wider issue of legality was deceptively simple. He argued that the government's regulatory powers had been on the statute books for many years, had been widely used, and hence were legally and constitutionally indisputable (Novoa 1971, 1978,1992). Novoa's argument was based on a thorough diagnosis about the malaise affecting the legal system. In this study he argued that the failure of the legal system to play a meaningful role in economic development stemmed from a distorted conception of the law (Novoa 1963/64, 1968). In his view, judges and lawyers, obsessed with the rules and principles of private law, failed to give due consideration to the array of public law rules that gave the state the power and responsibility to promote economic development. According to Novoa (1963/64), one of the factors that contributed to maintaining this distorted perception about the legal system was the fact that public law rules were scattered in hundreds of laws and regulations and, as such, were not easy to find. As a first step toward resolving this problem, he suggested that these rules be adequately systematized and codified. This somewhat crude legalistic diagnosis of the weaknesses of the legal system was consistent with Novoa's claim in 1971 that the Popular Unity administration had adequate legal tools to begin the implementation of the peaceful road to socialism Novoa 1971. The opposition flatly rejected this argument, pointing out that the government was acting in bad faith as it was relying on legal instruments that were meant to preserve, not overturn the prevailing economic system (Echeverría and Frei 1974: 3:108–122, 129–150). Novoa and his more politically minded colleagues were naturally aware that these legal instruments had not been intended as tools for overhauling the economy. They claimed, however, that the electoral victory had given the Popular Unity a mandate to interpret existing laws and regulations in line with the aims of its program (Garcés 1973; Viera-Gallo 1972).

In practical terms, the strategy proposed by Novoa rested on the peculiar features of the prevailing system of administrative law characterized by the absence of judicial review of administrative action. The government, as well as Novoa, were well aware of the risks involved in this course of action, but do not appear to have fully anticipated the pace and direction of the confrontation with the opposition over the issue of legality (1972). At first, the government was confident. It managed to successfully overcome some objections by the Contraloría to the legality of its decrees and found means to circumvent court injunctions. The government's initial success in defeating legal challenges astonished many local lawyers, as it created the impression that it had a carefully planned legal strategy (Eluchans 1972). It also encouraged those affected by government policies to creatively search for legal devices and remedies to defend against government policies. Thus there developed a series of skirmishes that escalated into a full-scale war over the legality of government action. The government's response to the avalanche of legal challenges was incoherent and contradictory, thus confirming that it did not have a strategy for the implementation of its program. Instead, it responded to these challenges with a variety of subterfuges and techniques that, apart from trivializing the legal process, failed to resolve the underlying political problem. One of these subterfuges involved developing a new doctrine about the enforcement of judgments. This ill-considered doctrine provoked a major confrontation that lent credibility to the Supreme Court's allegation that the government was in breach of the principle of the separation of powers and had thus flouted the constitution and the rule of law. Ironically, what this legal confrontation shows is that those affected by government policies had learned Novoa's lesson: legal systems are complex edifices that have many cracks. These cracks, however, were used as much to further as to resist government policy. The following sections offer a detailed analysis of different aspects of the confrontation that led to the defeat of legality and opened the way for the violent overthrow of democracy.

Contraloría versus Allende

By the time the Allende administration came into office, the Contraloría's approach to the legality review procedure, as explained in chapter 5, was well established. Although the Contraloría continued to characterize it merely as a jurisdictional check involving an abstract comparison between two legal texts, in practice, the legality review procedure involved a scrutiny of the findings of fact by the administration. But, while the Contraloría had unequivocally extended the scope of its review powers, it had not developed clear guidelines regarding what the review of facts entailed—the so-called standard of review. Moreover, its practice was not consistent. In some areas, such as state security, its approach was relatively lenient. In matters relating to labor and economic regulation, however, the Contraloría invariably scrutinized the facts underlying government decrees. Given the government's reliance on the regulatory powers of the executive for the implementation of its program, it is not surprising that there soon developed a conflict between Allende and the Contraloría.

The Allende administration behaved as if it had assumed that the Contraloría's review of its back-to-work and requisition decrees would be largely formal and that any legal objection could be easily overridden by means of a *decreto de insistencia* (Novoa 1971). These assumptions proved wrong. First, the Contraloría did not treat the review of government decrees as a formality. On the contrary, it zealously focused on the facts invoked by the government as predicate for its actions and in some instances went well beyond the scrutiny of facts, extending its reach to areas of policy. Second, the government did not find it easy to use *decretos de insistencia*. Its reliance on them in 1971 and the first half of 1972 provoked major political rows with the congress, which culminated with the impeachment of cabinet ministers. After the truck drivers' strike in mid-1972, the military agreed to accept cabinet posts on certain conditions, one of which was that the government cease to use decretos de insistencia. Thus, while the military were in the cabinet (from September 1972 to January 1973) the government had to avoid using them. As a consequence, the government became entangled in a long and debilitating controversy with the Contraloría. In the end, however, the government could not escape issuing the much-dreaded decretos de insistencia. This section examines aspects of the conflict between Allende and the Contraloría, with special reference to the legality review of requisition decrees.

Regulatory Requisitions

Under the requisition legislation, the government could take over the administration of industrial and commercial enterprises to prevent disruptions in the production or distribution of essential consumer goods (Von Brunn 1972:68–73). In the past, there had been doubts about the legality of this type of requisition because under the terms of DL 520 (1932), the government was allowed to requisition only essential consumer goods. As explained in chapter 5, in the 1940s the government expanded the scope of its requisition powers to include the takeover of the administration of enterprises. These regulations provoked a major political row and were cited as one of the grounds for the impeachment of the comptroller general in 1945. Any doubts about the legality of regulatory requisitions were dispelled in the 1960s when the Contraloría, subject to certain conditions, confirmed their legality.[2] During the early months of the Allende administration, the Contraloría, though objecting on formal grounds to the legality of a decree that had ordered the requisition of a textile company, confirmed nonetheless that regulatory requisitions were well within the powers of the executive. But on this occasion the Contraloría also reminded the government that it had to produce evidence of the underlying facts and that requisitions were temporary measures that did not affect property rights.[3]

The government accepted, in general terms, that the Contraloría was entitled to scrutinize its requisition orders. Accordingly, it submitted to the Contraloría documentary evidence that purported to establish either a disruption in the distribution channels of specific consumer goods or a standstill in production caused either by a strike, lockout, or workers' occupation. The evidence of these facts consisted of technical reports and certificates on market conditions and on the factors that had brought about the standstill in production. The officials attesting on these facts were civil servants, duly empowered, from the Ministry of Labor or Ministry of Economics. The government expected that the Contraloría would carry out a purely formal assessment of the evidence, checking the accuracy and authenticity of the dates, signatures, and seals of the documents. The scope of the Contraloría's review, however, went beyond the government's expectations.

One of the facts that the government found almost impossible to establish was the existence of a standstill in production. The Contraloría generally objected to the certificates issued by Ministry of Labor officials on the ground that they were based on statements made by workers and, as such, only proved that the statements had been made, not that they were true.[4] On the surface, this objection was reasonable, except that in most instances the standstill was such a well-publicized fact that it was hardly necessary to establish it through documentary evidence. The government was thus justified in regarding the Contraloría's rejection as politically motivated and unfair. But what caused more irritation to the government was that the Contraloría did not provide any hints as to how facts such as a standstill of production could be accredited. The meaning of the phrase "standstill in production" is not self-evident and the requisition statute did not define it. It could be said to include different factual situations ranging from the complete shutdown of operations to various degrees of partial decline of a company's activities. Thus, it is reasonable to expect that any attempt to define it would lead to a genuine difference of opinion. In its legal Opinions, however, the Contraloría seemed to assume that there was an authoritative definition that the government had failed to apply. This approach enabled the Contraloría to frame its objections in purely negative terms. It merely stated that the government had failed to establish that there was a standstill in production, without giving any indication as to how this fact could be established. The government attempted to meet the Contraloría's objections by improving the formal presentation of its documentary evidence. But as the government improved on the formal presentation of the evidence, the Contraloría would raise the standard of evidence. Thus, for example, apart from requiring clear evidence about the standstill in production, the Contraloría also began demanding that the government show evidence of a causal link between the standstill in production and market disruption.[5] The Contraloría also often rejected government evidence by using information, generally contradictory, supplied by the owners of enterprises, without indicating why their evidence was more credible than that offered by the government (Espinoza 1972a:24).

As the conflict with the government intensified, the Contraloría's objections increasingly began to include policy, rather than purely legal matters. Thus, in some cases the Contraloría objected to the legality of a requisition decree on the ground that the government could have resolved the underlying problem by requiring the enterprise to meet production targets.[6] Likewise, where the standstill of production was caused by a factory occupation, the Contraloría's view was that requisitions were inappropriate because factory occupations were illegal.[7] In another case, although the Contraloría approved the legality of a decree that ordered the requisition of a firm that manufactured tinned foods, it nonetheless excluded from the scope of the requisition decree units within the firm, which, according to the Contraloría, were not directly responsible for the alleged market shortages. In this case, the units that the Contraloría excluded from the scope of the requisition order were those devoted to servicing and repairing tools and machinery.[8] As the Contraloría was aware that these decisions constituted a departure from its practice, it formally announced that it had abandoned its formalistic approach to legal interpretation. It embraced instead a teleological approach, one concerned with the objectives of the law, rather than with its literal meaning.[9]

A Procedural Gap

As explained in chapter 5, the general rule was that government decrees could not be enforced until the legality review procedure was finalized. But requisition decrees were exempted from the general rule. Because they were meant to deal with an emergency, they could be implemented before the legality review procedure was completed. The law, however, did not set a time limit for the completion of the legality review procedure, nor did it set a deadline for the issuing of the decretos de insistencia. This procedural gap was fully exploited by the government, making it possible to prolong its exchanges with the Contraloría, while at the same time indefinitely postponing the decision to issue decretos de insistencia.

A controversial ruling by the Contraloría eventually forced the government to resort to the much-dreaded decretos de insistencia.[10] In its ruling the Contraloría held that requisition decrees that did not pass the legality review procedure were illegal and therefore the government had an obligation to immediately revoke them, unless it chose to override objections by issuing a decreto de insistencia. The accuracy of this interpretation was doubtful, as both the law and practice of the legality review procedure allowed the government an unspecified amount of time to respond to the Contraloría's objections and did not set a fixed time for the government to issue a decreto de insistencia. But the question as to whether the Contraloría's interpretation was constitutionally and legally correct was beside the point. It was welcomed by the opposition who, aware of the distaste of the military for decretos de insistencia, demanded that the government should either immediately revoke requisition decrees questioned by the Contraloría or issue decretos de insistencia. The government rejected this interpretation, but soon had to face the consequences of the Contraloría's ruling.

Early in 1973, an overzealous employee of the post office in the province of Concepción, who also happened to sympathize with the opposition, apparently puzzled by the dispute over the legality of the requisition decrees, asked the Contraloría for guidance: should he deliver the mail of requisitioned enterprises to the owners of the enterprise or to the state-appointed administrator? Not surprisingly, the Contraloría replied that given the illegality of the requisition, the mail had to be delivered to the owners of the enterprise, not to the state-appointed managers.[11] This response posed a major threat to the government's ability to manage requisitioned firms, as it required state employees to redirect orders, thus discontinuing the delivery of spare parts and disrupting distribution networks. State employees who failed to comply with the Contraloría's ruling faced disciplinary sanctions that were also administered by the Contraloría. In an attempt to prevent a "lawful" boycott against enterprises under requisition, the government issued a single decreto de insistencia that had the effect of ratifying the requisition of 42 firms. This decree effectively removed the issue of the legality of requisition decrees from the jurisdiction of the Contraloría.[12]

The Role of Courts

The government's approach to legality rested on the assumption that courts would not interfere because, under the prevailing system of administrative law, they did not have jurisdiction to review acts of the administration. According to Eduardo Novoa, the government was merely taking advantage of the loopholes and contradictions in the legal system (Novoa 1971). But the government failed to anticipate that those affected by government measures would make use of other loopholes and contradictions within the legal system to defend their interests and protect their rights. Thus, courts were soon flooded with complaints that challenged the validity of requisition decrees and that sought to terminate the illegal occupation of land and factories. Courts responded by granting injunctions that restrained the powers of state-appointed managers and by ordering the arrest of the ring-leaders of occupations. The injunctions presented the government with a dilemma: if it complied, it would infuriate its supporters; if it refused, it would provoke a major confrontation with the judiciary. The government's response to this dilemma was, characteristically, ambiguous: it refused to reverse its policies, but at the same time it employed a variety of legal tactics to avoid a damaging confrontation with the judiciary. In the end, however, the government was unable to avert confrontation with the judiciary. This section explains the various stages of this confrontation, illustrating both the legal and political issues arising from it.

In Search of Remedies

The main targets of judicial challenges were requisition orders that placed commercial and industrial enterprises under the temporary administration of state-appointed managers. As already noted, this type of requisition was described as regulatory requisition in order to distinguish it from the requisition of essential consumer goods. The Directorate of Industry and Commerce (DIRINCO), a department of the Ministry of Economics, issued requisition decrees. A special administrative tribunal—the Commerce Tribunal—heard appeals against decisions taken by DIRINCO. It consisted of three members: a lawyer from the Ministry of Economics appointed by the minister; a lawyer from the Consejo de Defensa del Estado (the government's legal advisors and attorneys); and a lawyer appointed by the National Association of Merchants (Eluchans 1972:50–51).

The Commerce Tribunal was thus the natural forum to challenge the validity of requisitions. The first to resort to it were the owners of a textile company requisitioned by the government in 1971. The tribunal, however—with the dissenting vote of the member appointed by the National Association of Merchants—declined to accept jurisdiction. In its decision, the tribunal pointed out that while it had jurisdiction to review requisition of essential consumer goods, it did not have jurisdiction to review regulatory requisitions, as these were acts of authority (Espinoza 1972b). The case eventually reached the Supreme Court, which exercising its disciplinary jurisdiction, ordered the Commerce Tribunal to hear the appeal.[13] The tribunal did so, but was unable to reach a decision. At first its meetings were delayed as the member of the tribunal appointed by the Ministry of Economics boycotted its sessions. Eventually, when the tribunal finally met, its three members could not agree on a decision.[14]

The deadlock of the Commerce Tribunal paved the way for a direct confrontation with the judiciary, as those who sought to challenge requisition decrees had no alternative but to seek remedies through ordinary courts. But because courts did not have general jurisdiction to review acts of the administration, the option of resorting to the courts was not straightforward. It was thus that the owners of enterprises under requisition came to rely on the possessory actions, which enabled them to resort to the courts to demand the recovery of possession over their assets. Possessory actions were accompanied by a request for provisional remedies.[15] Lower courts generally accepted jurisdiction and immediately granted provisional remedies. Provisional remedies (granted ex parte, that is without a hearing) were generally injunctions that froze the bank accounts of the enterprises under requisition and prohibited state-appointed administrators from selling the goods produced by the enterprise. Courts also often appointed an administrator to look after the interests of the company. Court injunctions posed a major problem for the government. In political terms, the government could not afford to comply, as this would have alienated its supporters and would almost certainly cause a rift within the Popular Unity coalition. Thus, the government circumvented the injunctions. This was, initially, relatively easy. For example, an order freezing bank accounts could be circumvented by withdrawing funds in advance, and the prohibition from entering into contracts for the sale of goods could be circumvented simply by transferring the goods to a state agency. As most injunctions were specifically addressed to state-appointed managers, the government developed the practice of appointing new managers, thus forcing the owners of the enterprises to start new proceedings. But this type of maneuvering could not last forever, as it led to ever-stronger responses from the courts and strident reactions from the opposition. As the battle over court injunctions intensified, the government was placed on the defensive and slowly, but consistently, began to lose control over the behavior of its supporters. The case of *Empresa de Maderas Prensadas Cholguán* (hereafter Cholguán) illustrates this point.

The Requisition of Maderas Prensadas Cholguán

Cholguán, located in one of the southern provinces, was a relatively large enterprise that manufactured chipboard and other timber products.[16] The government was aware of the potential of timber as an export and was keen that Cholguán should expand its operations. It thus began to explore the possibilities of establishing a joint venture with the owners of Cholguán in which the state, through CORFO, would become a minority partner, in exchange for an important injection of public funds. To secure workers' support, Cholguán's management entered into an agreement with its unions under which the unions accepted, in principle, the idea of the joint venture and agreed that questions concerning the eventual incorporation of Cholguán into the state sector would be resolved through direct negotiations between Cholguán and CORFO officials. Negotiations between CORFO and Cholguán did not, however, make progress. The unions attributed the delay to bad faith on the part of management. Thus, after a wait of nearly seven months for a decision on the proposed joint venture, the unions repudiated the agreement, occupied the factory, and demanded its nationalization.

Unwilling to antagonize the unions, the government issued a back-to-work decree and appointed a state official to manage the enterprise.

As this decree failed to pass the Contraloría's legality review, it was promptly replaced by a requisition decree. The owners of Cholguán responded by bringing a possessory action before a lower court, accompanied by a request for provisional remedies, which was duly granted. The provisional remedies enjoined the state-appointed administrator from entering into any contract or carrying out any activity without prior approval by the court-appointed administrator.

The state-appointed administrator did not comply with the injunctions, aware that the unions would have strongly resisted it. He thus proceeded to arrange for several shipments of chipboard from Cholguán's warehouse to clients in Santiago. On that same day, however, the owners of the company brought proceedings against the state-appointed administrator for contempt of court and asked the court to immediately issue an injunction prohibiting the removal of products from the warehouse. The police was duly notified of the injunction. However, following instructions from the intendant of the province, they did not enforce it. Thus, the government-appointed administrator was able to resume delivering orders, although he could not use the firm's logo on the invoices as the injunctions were still in force. As criminal proceeding against the state-appointed managers were going through the courts, the opposition parties initiated impeachment proceedings against the intendant, accusing him of violating the principle of judicial independence and of the crimes of usurping judicial functions and denial of justice. The senate approved the impeachment and the intendant was removed from office.[17]

Arguments about Possessory Actions

The opposition welcomed the court injunctions against state-administrators of enterprises under requisition, as it confirmed their view that the government was openly in breach of legality and the rule of law. The government, for its part, vigorously rejected them, claiming that they were illegal and inconsistent with prevailing judicial practice. The legal arguments in support of the government's position, though not compelling, were not altogether unfounded. Indeed, they were consistent with the position held by most its predecessors, including the Frei administration. Yet the Allende government appears not to have noticed that only three years before the Popular Union came into power, the Supreme Court had taken the view that possessory actions could indeed be used to challenge government decrees deemed illegal. In order to fully understand the strength and weakness of the position of the Allende government on the issue of possessory actions, it is helpful briefly to examine a case decided by the Supreme Court in 1967.

In order to resolve a strike in a large agricultural estate that had escalated into a full-blown land occupation, the Frei administration issued a back-to-work decree and appointed a government official to take over the administration of the farm. As the landowner feared that this decision was a prelude to expropriation, he challenged it through the courts. As ordinary courts could not directly review the legality of the decree, he brought, instead, a possessory action to recover possession. The lower court accepted jurisdiction and granted a provisional remedy, enjoining the state-appointed administrator from taking up his job. The government strongly objected on the familiar ground that ordinary courts did not have jurisdiction as they could not review acts of the administration. The Supreme Court disagreed. By a narrow majority of 6 to 5, the Court held that the lower court had jurisdiction. Hereafter I refer to this case as the *Conflict of Jurisdiction* case.[18]

In the *Conflict of Jurisdiction* case, the Supreme Court followed the reasoning of the *Montero* case (see chapter 6). It began by restating the general proposition that courts do not have jurisdiction to review acts of the administration, but pointed out that courts, nonetheless, have a duty to uphold property rights. Because the dispute in the *Conflict of Jurisdiction* case involved an action to recover possession, the lower court could not decline to exercise jurisdiction. The Supreme Court then went to state that, if, in order to resolve a claim to recover possession, judges are required to apply a decree that in their view is either unconstitutional or illegal, they should refuse to apply it. According to the Court, by refusing to apply such a decree lower courts were not invalidating it, but merely refusing to acknowledge its efficacy. Toward the end of the Allende administration, the Supreme Court employed the same reasoning—in the *Rayonhil* case[19]—to hold that courts were not required to give effect to requisition decrees in proceedings where owners affected by requisition asserted a private right.

Given the similarities between the *Conflict of Jurisdiction* case and the *Rayonhil* case, it is not surprising that the arguments of the Frei and the Allende administrations were almost identical. They both pointed out that the distinction between invalidating and refusing to apply a decree was unconstitutional because, in order to refuse to apply a government decree, courts had to form a view about the decree's validity, a matter that was solely within the jurisdiction of administrative courts. Apart from this general argument, they also put forward an argument that related specifically to the nature of possessory proceedings.

The argument about the nature of possessory proceedings pointed out that this mechanism was a public order device aimed at ensuring peaceful relations among individuals and, as such, could not be used to challenge acts of the administration. According to this argument, possessory actions are designed to protect de facto possession over immovable or chattel interests, either by restoring possession or by protecting it from eventual disturbance. The aim of possessory actions is to discourage self-help. Therefore, plaintiff in these proceedings only needs to prove de facto possession for one year. Moreover, in these proceedings, neither property rights nor the intentions of the disturber are at issue; and they are not contingent on the initiation of further proceedings, where questions concerning property rights or criminal responsibility may be raised. On the basis of this analysis, the Frei and Allende governments argued that possessory proceedings were designed to govern relations among individuals and were not a device to challenge acts of the administration. This argument was persuasive, but it posed difficult doctrinal issues regarding judicial practice, which neither the Supreme Court nor government lawyers were interested in exploring.[20]

The five dissenting Supreme Court Justices in the *Conflict of Jurisdiction* case agreed with the Frei administration that possessory actions could not be used to challenge administrative acts. Allende made a similar argument, which was accepted by the Court of Appeals of Santiago in 1972 in the *Rayonhil* case. Rayonhil was a textile company requisitioned by the government and placed under the administration of a state-appointed manager. Rayonhil brought a possessory action requesting provisional remedies against the state-appointed administrator. The lower court and the Court of Appeals declined to hear the case, pointing out that ordinary courts could not grant Rayonhil's request because it required the court to decide upon the legality or otherwise of the underlying administrative act—a matter which was not within the jurisdiction of ordinary courts.[21] The Supreme Court, however, disagreed. According to the Court, what was at issue here was not the validity of administrative acts, but the protection of plaintiff's property—a right protected by the constitution. The Court—relying on the reasoning of the *Montero* case—held that ordinary courts were not required to give effect to illegal acts of the administration. Therefore it sent the case back to the lower court with instructions to assert jurisdiction over Rayonhil's claim. While it is difficult to quarrel with the outcome of this case, the Court's reasoning is unpersuasive, as it is based on the assumption that private rights can always be invoked to override acts of the administration.

Because the Court does not acknowledge the possibility of a genuine conflict between private and public law, it does not offer any indication as to how state action could ever be justified. This failing in the Court's reasoning, as explained in chapter 6, can be traced to the peculiar features of the legal system and its seriously flawed system of administrative justice.

But if the reasoning of the Supreme Court was unpersuasive, so was the reasoning of the plurality of the Court of Appeals in the *Rayonhil* case, as well as its reasoning in the *Conflicts of Jurisdiction* case decided in 1967. In these two cases, the Court of Appeals merely reaffirmed the well-rehearsed, but unrealistic view that pending the establishment of administrative tribunals, ordinary courts did not have jurisdiction to review acts of the administration. In practical terms, this argument transformed every act of the administration into an unassailable act of authority. Absent from the Court of Appeal's reasoning was any attempt to acknowledge the need to develop a legal discourse that would seek to reconcile private and public interests. It is thus not surprising that courts were, generally, unable to play a constructive role in deciding this type of cases.

Public Order and the Criminal Process

Possessory actions, though effective devices to disrupt the administration of enterprises, did not immediately bring about a return of the requisitioned enterprises to their owners. Indeed, as the *Rayonhil* case shows, it merely remanded the case to the lower court for further lengthy proceedings. Thus, the enterprises affected by requisition orders sought protection from the criminal law. But this approach also presented difficulties.

Criminal trespass was an offense defined in section 457 of the Penal Code as the unlawful occupation of realty. The penalty for this crime was only a small fine that increased slightly if force against persons had been employed. The reported cases suggest that criminal trespass was mainly intended to discourage self-help, especially in disputes between small farmers over the delimitation of boundaries or the use of water resources (Etcheberry 1987:1–7). An interesting feature of the case law was that courts generally held that the offense required a profit motive (*animus lucrandi*), even though this was not mentioned in the definition of the offense (Labatut 1964:363). Thus, government lawyers naturally argued that land and factory occupations did not fall within the scope of the notion of criminal trespass, as they were politically motivated. Courts, however, departing from their previous practice, rejected this argument and asserted jurisdiction over politically motivated factory occupations and land invasions.

The Supreme Court, while acknowledging that under normal circumstances politically motivated occupations would not fall within the scope of offense of trespassing, emphatically stated, in a case decided in July 1972, that "as long as property rights are recognized by the constitution . . . courts have a duty to protect them."[22] Earlier, the Court had urged lower courts to adopt tougher measures to bring occupations to an end. Until then, courts had relied on the police to secure the end of occupations and land invasions.[23] The Supreme Court, however, decided that, given prevailing political conditions, courts could order the arrest of ringleaders of factory or land occupation and keep them in detention for up to two months as a means of compelling the others to bring the occupation to an end. Interpreting broadly other provisions of the criminal law, the Court also decided that persons excluded from possession of their property because of illegal occupations could, at any stage of the criminal process, request provisional measures (*precautorias*) to compel occupiers to vacate the property. These provisional measures were all the more drastic as they could be ordered without a hearing (ex parte). The Supreme Court also issued special instructions urging courts to deal swiftly with complaints arising out of factory occupations and land invasions.[24]

Occupation of the Court
of Melipilla

As courts became stricter in their interpretation of the crime of trespass, workers became increasingly more militant. Thus, the government found itself once again caught between the pressure of militant workers who refused to comply with court orders and judges who demanded the enforcement of their decision. The occupation of the court of Melipilla, a small farming community in the vicinity of Santiago, illustrates the government's plight.[25]

Melipilla had its fair share of rural labor disputes. In April 1972, one such dispute involving six workers at a small farm, led to its occupation. The landowner initiated criminal proceedings against the workers, accusing them of trespassing and requesting, as a provisional remedy, their arrest. As consequence, five workers were arrested. Upon hearing about these events, workers in neighboring farms occupied the farm in solidarity with their colleagues. The landowner went back to the court and obtained another arrest warrant against the occupiers.

Shortly before the police were due to begin enforcing the court order, the intendant of the province arrived at the farm and held discussions with the occupiers. According to the intendant, the purpose of his visit was to advise workers not to use force against the police. The landowner, however, claimed that the intendant had gone there to alert the occupiers of the imminent arrival of the police and to advise them to hide. In the event, the occupation was brought to an end and 39 workers were arrested.

The workers remained in custody despite the fact that the occupation had come to an end and that the penalty for trespassing was only a fine. Lawyers representing workers unsuccessfully requested the local judge to release them, even though they had been in detention for more than a month. The plight of these 39 workers soon became a huge political issue in the locality. It prompted a large demonstration outside the court by hundreds of workers from the region who demanded the immediate release of their colleagues. In the course of this demonstration, 60 odd workers marched into the court and assembled outside the judge's office chanting slogans against the judge and the judicial system. The judge immediately telephoned the president of the Supreme Court to report the events and called upon the local chief to evict the occupiers.

The local police chief could not comply with the judge's request because his unit was small and it needed reinforcement. In the meantime, however, the intendant of the province and the undersecretary of state of the Ministry of Justice arrived on the scene. After separate meetings with the judge and the demonstrators, they persuaded the demonstrators to leave the building peacefully, thus avoiding police intervention. The behavior of the intendant came under close scrutiny, although the president of the Supreme Court acknowledged, in a statement issued shortly after the event, that timely intervention by government officials had made it possible to avoid violence. Nevertheless, the judge appointed to investigate the Melipilla events requested the senate to lift the immunity of the intendant so that he could be tried for the crime of "failure to assist the public authority" (Penal Code: Article 253). The request was based on an allegation that the intendant had ordered the police not to comply with the judge's request for assistance. The intendant, for his part, argued that the removal of the demonstrators from the court had been achieved with the agreement of all parties concerned and that neither he nor the undersecretary of justice had, at any time, ordered the police not to comply with the judge's request. The senate, quite unexpectedly, refused to lift the immunity.[26]

Delaying the Enforcement
of Judgments

The tough measures announced by the Supreme Court to secure the end of occupations encouraged property owners affected by land or factory occupations to make use of criminal proceedings. This development posed a difficult problem for the government. As criminal courts could directly request assistance from the police to enforce their decisions, the government feared that the enforcement of eviction orders would provoke violent clashes. The government's response to this new situation was original. The minister of the interior, General Carlos Prats—who was also the commander in chief of the army— issued detailed instructions to the police on how to respond to a request for eviction orders. Under these instructions, police officers were required temporarily not to enforce them if, in their judgment, the matter raised serious issues of public order. Where the police opted for suspending the execution of the eviction order, they were required to notify the minister of the interior who, if in agreement with the police decision, would endorse it in writing. If the minister did not respond within a prescribed period of time, the eviction order had to be enforced.[27]

The government justified these instructions on public order grounds. The enforcement of court orders, according to the government, often had political and social consequences that could lead to serious disruption of public order. Hence, it claimed, the decision as to the timing and opportunity for the enforcement of court orders had to rest with the government. The instructions were intended to assist police officers on the ground, as it established that the enforcement of court orders could only be delayed if the minister of the interior issued a written order to this effect. The instructions thus distinguished between the operational responsibility of police officers and the political responsibility of the minister of the interior. The government was convinced that the indiscriminate enforcement of eviction orders would merely intensify social unrest.[28]

The government instructions on the enforcement of court orders provoked a political and constitutional dispute that culminated in an acrimonious exchange of letters between Allende and the Supreme Court.[29] The Supreme Court wrote several letters to Allende expressing its concern about the policy on the enforcement of eviction orders. Allende responded by restating the view that, in the interest of public order, it was legitimate for the government to delay the implementation of court orders. Allende also pointed out that by indiscriminately granting eviction orders, courts were abusing their power and worsening a highly volatile political situation.[30] The Supreme Court dismissed Allende's argument about the behavior of courts claiming it to be sociological speculation devoid of any legal meaning.[31] But the Court also admitted, albeit implicitly, that judges had expanded their power to grant injunctions. It argued, however, that the prolific use of injunctions was a legitimate judicial response to the government's abuse of power. According to the Court, it was the duty of courts to do everything within their power to protect property rights.[32] The Supreme Court had undoubtedly drawn inspiration from the government's view that political events continuously renewed the content and spirit of the law.

Conclusion

The drive toward radical democracy was carried out without careful consideration of the response of courts and other legal institutions. Indeed, both the Frei and Allende administrations seemed to assume that their radical policies would not clash with prevailing principles of legality. This assumption was based on the practice that prevailed during the party democracy period, when courts and the Contraloría maintained a deferential attitude toward the executive and rarely challenged administrative decisions. During the radical democracy period, however, both courts and the Contraloría became more assertive and more willing to accept claims from private parties that sought to restrain the scope of government action. While the Frei administration accepted these institutional restraints, the Allende administration did not. Under pressure from his supporters, facing a hostile congress and high levels of political mobilization, the Allende administration pressed ahead with the implementation of its programs making use of every scrap of power vested in the executive branch. In hindsight, the notion that in a democracy a socialist program of reforms could be launched through the backdoor by means of administrative decrees is bizarre. Yet, as explained above, this policy was only intended as temporary, pending the approval of comprehensive legislation for the nationalization of the commanding heights of the economy. In practice, however, because the government's political strategy proved unworkable, this bizarre legal policy became permanent.

The political stalemate between Allende and the opposition raised the political profile of the Contraloría and the courts, as parties aggrieved by government policy demanded swift remedies to undo what they claimed were arbitrary decisions by the government. The government argued, however, that it was acting within the letter of the law, as it was merely applying decrees and regulations that had been on the books for years and had been profusely used by previous administrations. Although, this argument was politically disingenuous, in strictly legal terms, it was not unsound. Indeed, the government was merely taking advantage of a fundamental weakness of the legal system: the absence of an adequate system of administrative justice. In the past most administrations had invoked this weakness to claim that their decisions were beyond the reach of the courts and that the legality review of the Contraloría was a mere formality. Given the nature of the policies implemented by the Allende administration, these arguments sounded hollow and lacked any credibility. Nevertheless, as this chapter shows, the response by the Contraloría and the courts to the policies of the Allende government was slow and not entirely coherent. While the Contraloría openly announced a shift from a formalistic to a purposive approach to the legality review, the Supreme Court deployed a variety of doctrines that successfully disrupted the implementation of government policies. But the Supreme Court's shift from a passive to more active and rights-orientated approach was prompted more by immediate political considerations than by a genuine transformation in the way it conceived its role as guardian of constitutional rights. Thus, it is not surprising that after Allende was safely out of the way, the Supreme Court reverted to type, refusing to question the atrocities committed by the Pinochet regime and thus, implicitly endorsing them. Even today, after nearly 15 years of democracy, the Court continues to regard executive action as virtually unassailable (Couso 2005). Sadly, the Supreme Court's appalling record on human rights during Pinochet's dictatorship appears to have vindicated Allende's bizarre legal policies, as well as his skepticism toward the courts.

Concluding Comments

My study has adopted a historical approach with a focus on institutions, using the process of democratization as its unifying thread. The historical perspective has enabled me to explain the interplay between enduring institutional structures on the one hand, and political action, on the other. Thus, this study acknowledges both the capacity of institutions to constrain political action and the power of individuals and groups to transform society. The historical approach, combined with the multilevel focus of the enquiry has, hopefully, enabled me to relate the uneven advances and frequent setbacks in the democratization process to the complex interplay of political, economic, and legal processes. The concluding comments that follow highlight some of the themes of the book.

Institution Building

State building and regime building in Chile were arduous processes in which amazing political and economic achievements were combined with formidable and persistent failures. The success of the elite during the nineteenth century is generally seen as a by-product of their integration and cohesion. Yet, neither integration nor cohesion of the elite was spontaneous. They were objectives that the elite relentlessly and ruthlessly pursued and the elite did not hesitate to crush any challenge to the supremacy of the central government. However, they were not only obstinate and ruthless; they were also pragmatic and flexible as they promptly incorporated their former opponents into their circle, shifted the balance of power from the president to the congress, and spearheaded a process of political liberalization that recognized basic civil and political rights and expanded the franchise. Thus toward the end of the nineteenth century the domestic and international legitimacy of the state and regime seemed firmly established.

The economic prosperity brought about by the acquisition of nitrate mines following the war against Perú and Bolivia seemed to reinforce the virtues of the political regime. Yet, the newly acquired wealth brought about a major rupture among the elite and in 1891, plunged the country into a Civil War that deposed President Manuel Balmaceda, and brought presidentialism to an end. The controversy that led to the military confrontation was about how to use the abundant revenue flowing from the ever-expanding nitrate exports. Balmaceda's administration sought to devote the bulk of the newly acquired export revenue to building the infrastructure to facilitate the development of a national market. His opponents, however, preferred the easier option of relying on the newly acquired revenue to ease the tax burden of the elite. This option also entailed bringing the incipient process of democratization to a halt. Thus the regime that emerged after the Civil War embraced economic liberalism—insofar as it lowered tariffs for luxury goods and handed over the exploitation of nitrates to foreign investors—but shunned political liberalism, as the self-styled parliamentary regime that emerged after the Civil War was unwilling to incorporate new social forces—miners, and urban workers—into the political system.

The institutions of the legal system had no difficulty accommodating to these new conditions. After all, the tough law and order measures against the emerging working class were not inconsistent with Bello's oligarchic conception of "limited freedom." According to this concept, law was seen as guarantor of rights, but only on condition that public order was not threatened. The ruthless use of the law against subordinate groups was also consistent with the narrow conception of political rights held by most members of the political elite during the nineteenth century. Indeed, even the most prominent liberals of the time had serious reservations about democracy and would have agreed with Diego Portales, who regarded democracy as wholly inappropriate to the conditions prevailing in the country.

What confounds most observers, however, is that although the regime that emerged from the Civil War effectively brought to a halt the incipient process of democratization, the formal trappings of constitutionalism and democratic procedures were scrupulously observed. The old 1833 Constitution remained in force and there were regular elections for presidents and members of the congress. Moreover, the political parties established in the nineteenth century—which were the only parties that participated in the electoral process—soon acquired a taste for the sophisticated maneuvering generally associated with genuine parliamentary regimes. Thus there developed a modern party system, but one that did not reflect or represent the needs and aspirations either of the mining and industrial proletariat or of the middle classes. It is thus not surprising that when nitrate revenue became unstable and workers' organizations became more assertive, the much-revered 1833 Constitution collapsed without a shot being fired.

The crisis of the regime in the 1920s presented the elite with a problem that, so far, had been neglected: the inclusion of new social forces into the political system. The two political options on offer—Arturo Alessandri's liberal populism and General Carlos Ibáñez's authoritarianism—proved unsatisfactory. The main reason for their failure was that both Alessandri and Ibáñez were reluctant to fully incorporate the emerging social groups into the political system. Despite his considerable electoral appeal, Alessandri turned to the military instead of seeking a broad political alliance with parties that represented working- and middle-class interests. Ibáñez, who sought to restore the old presidential regime, but was also concerned with the modernization of the economy, manipulated and repressed workers' organizations, while attempting to establish an authoritarian regime with fascist overtones. The failure of both Alessandri and Ibáñez to expand the scope of the political system and to accept the legitimacy of workers' demands exacerbated and prolonged the political crisis. Indeed, the four military juntas that attempted to govern the country between July 1931 and the end of 1932—some of which had a marked leftist orientation—reflect the prevailing confusion, suggesting that the pragmatism characterizing nineteenth century elite had long vanished.

Given the political chaos and persistent economic crisis of the 1920s and early 1930s, the return to constitutional democracy in 1932 is a surprising outcome that calls for an explanation. I reject as simplistic the explanation the claims that in the 1930s, the political elite recovered their pragmatism and taste for political compromise and established a regime, which some describe as the *"estado de compromiso"* (Garretón 1989). I have argued that it was neither the democratic proclivities of the elite nor their addiction to the principles of constitutionalism that brought about and sustained the regime after 1932. Instead, the consolidation of the regime that I characterize as party democracy should be attributed to three closely connected factors: the purge of the army, the incorporation of the Socialist and Communist Parties into the political system, and the consensus among the main political actors on a limited state-led policy of import substitution.

In hindsight, the purge of the army—carried out during the early stages of the second Alessandri administration—seems a relatively simple process. Indeed, after the debacle of the Ibáñez administration and the disarray brought about by the four military juntas in 1932, the army was deeply divided and politically exhausted. It was also politically discredited as the brunt of the impact of the Great Depression was felt during the Ibáñez administration and attributed to government incompetence. It is important to note that it was Arturo Alessandri, a prominent member of one of the two leading right-wing parties, who led the purge of the army. Alessandri, moreover, carried out this task with the support of the Republican Militia—a 15,000 strong paramilitary organization—originally established by right-wing sympathizers in 1932 to resist the short-lived Socialist Republic. From the perspective of the Right, the decision to send the military back to the barracks was understandable as events in the early 1930s suggested that important elements within the armed forces were either dangerously attracted to the Left (as was the case of Marmaduque Grove, member of the first Military Junta in 1932 and later founding member of the Socialist Party), or were interested in political modernization and had little sympathy for the established oligarchy—as was the case of Ibáñez. The right-wing parties' decision to purge the army under the leadership of Alessandri signaled their commitment to seek a political solution to the prevailing crisis.

The second factor that accounts for the consolidation of party democracy was the emergence of the Popular Front coalition as a major political force. This coalition brought together for the first time parties representing middle- and working- class interests. Several factors made its creation possible: the meteoric electoral growth of the recently established Socialist Party; the Communist Party's decision—following the line set by Moscow—to seek alliances with reformist parties; and the Radical Party's desperate search for allies in its efforts to become the leading representative of middle-class voters. It was thus that the Popular Font coalition came into being and in 1938 achieved an unexpected victory in the presidential elections. The third factor that contributed to the consolidation of party democracy was a consensus on the policy of import substitution. This policy had been partially implemented by several administrations since the mid-1910s, after nitrate revenue became unstable. By the late 1930s, however, political conditions were ripe and all major political parties signed up to it. But, this policy had severe limitations, as it was largely circumscribed to the industrial sector, thus excluding the all-important mining and agricultural sectors.

Given the political and economic disruption caused by the Great Depression, the return to constitutional government was not an outcome that could have been predicted in the early 1930s. It was also an outcome that, initially, the main political actors accepted with serious reservations as neither the Right nor the Left regarded each other as trustworthy partners. Nonetheless, the three factors identified above persuaded these reluctant democrats to play by the rules of the constitution.

Embracing Constitutionalism

A remarkable feature of the period I characterize as party democracy is the way the reluctant democrats of the 1930s appeared to abandon their distrust of the democratic process and embraced the principles of constitutional government. Was this a genuine shift or one that was opportunistic and determined largely by circumstances? Can this shift be attributed to the long-term impact of institutions? There can be no precise answer to these questions as both short-term considerations and institutional factors played a role in the stability of the regime. Yet, it is significant that the 1925 Constitution, which at the time of its adoption was almost unanimously rejected by the main political parties, was, by the early 1960s, embraced by all political parties as an emblem of legitimacy and stability. Despite embracing constitutionalism, the main political actors remained skeptical about the virtues of the democratic process.

The commitment of the main political actors to compromise was as shaky as the consensus on the new economic policy. Although, initially, the Left agreed to exclude the agricultural sector from the reach of the state-led policy of import substitution, it never fully agreed to exclude it from the reach of democratic politics. Accordingly, the communists, prompted partly by their intense electoral competition with the socialists, made a decisive move to promote the unionization of agricultural workers. The parties of the Right regarded this move as political heresy as they viewed the introduction of democratic institutions in the countryside as tantamount to social revolution. They thus did everything within their power—including supporting a law that banned the Communist Party from politics and severely restricted union rights—to retain the long-standing veto on agricultural unions. Meanwhile, the implementation of the restricted import substitution policy was causing further disruption to the political order. The consequences of the exclusion of copper from the scope of the new economic policy were fully felt during the run-up to World War II, when the price of copper in international markets soared, while Chilean copper was sold at subsidized prices to support the Allies' war effort.

The considerable loss of export earnings was not compensated and, unsurprisingly, was deeply resented. This explains why in 1952, the government was so keen to have greater control over the marketing of copper exports. But the more immediate problem was caused by the exclusion of agriculture, as the inefficiency of the sector put enormous pressure on the balance of payments and greatly contributed to fueling of inflation. The economic policy implemented during this period thus had devastating political consequences. It fragmented the party system, destroyed the unity of the labor movement, and fueled strong authoritarian and antiparty sentiments among the electorate. Indeed, by the late 1940s, the political system was on the brink of collapse. That it did not do so was largely due to Carlos Ibáñez who, in his reincarnation as a 75-year-old populist candidate, brought about, unintentionally, a revival of the party system, which, in turn, reinvigorated the decaying process of democratization.

It is ironic that it should have been Ibáñez, the authoritarian figure of the 1920s and indefatigable plotter against the constitutional government, who inadvertently created the conditions that gave the political regime a new lease of life. In addition to restraining the political ambitions of the military, his failure to shift from a state-dominated import substitution policy toward a market-friendly policy opened the door to a further process of political liberalization that was to radically alter the terms of political competition in favor of the parties of the Left. By the early 1960s, the popular discrediting of market-based policies was so overwhelming that the right-wing parties, having abandoned any hope of winning a presidential election, were forced to support Eduardo Frei, their archrival, who promised to implement a program of reforms diametrically opposed to their most cherished values. The electoral decline of the right-wing parties also prompted the business community to question whether they were really capable of representing their interest. Thus, not surprisingly, as the power base of the parties of the Right was eroded, their confidence in the democratic process declined. The picture on the Left was totally different. As the party system regained its strength and the unity of the labor movement was reestablished, the left-wing parties became increasingly convinced about the virtues of constitutional government and of the democratic processes. Accordingly, they spared no effort to contain the militancy of the labor movement so as to give credibility to their bid to achieve power through democratic means. The positive attitude of the left-wing parties toward constitutional democracy is not surprising as they had greatly benefited from the electoral reforms of the mid-fifties. Thus, even the most militant supporters of the Marxist parties began to accept that achieving socialism through democratic means was both possible and desirable.

It is important to emphasize that the neutralization of the military both at the beginning and toward the end of the party democracy period was due to an unexpected sequence of events. The purge of the military in the 1930s was possible because the armed forces were largely blamed for the economic consequences of the Great Depression and, as a consequence of their failure in government, were deeply divided. Likewise, in the late 1940s, when the political regime came under severe strain and the prestige of political parties was at its lowest, General Ibáñez capitalized on the antidemocratic sentiment; in order to preserve his status as a constitutionally elected president, he managed to deflect the growing political dissent within the armed forces. Thus, to a significant extent, the much-hailed professionalism of the armed forces was brought about by a fortunate and unexpected sequence of events.

Institutions Matter

As this book has shown, institutions and institutional practices played an important role in shaping both the advances and setbacks to the process of democratization. In political terms, what is most noteworthy is the belated acceptance of the controversial presidential regime. Since the mid-nineteenth century, the presidential regime was regarded as the embodiment of authoritarian and arbitrary rule. The process of political liberalization in the nineteenth century involved largely a transfer of power from the president to the congress. Indeed, so powerful was the sentiment against presidentialism, that it was the detonating factor in the dispute that led to the Civil War in 1891. Thus, it is not surprising that in the 1920s, despite the obvious failure of the parliamentary republic, virtually all the political parties opposed the 1925 Constitution because it proposed a presidential regime. Yet, they soon tamed the new regime and presidents had to concede that political parties had a major say in the appointment and removal of cabinet ministers. Political parties thus found it easy to accept this modified form of presidentialism, which, in turn, was consistent with well-established practices developed during the parliamentary republic.

Having tamed presidentialism, the parties had no difficulties reverting to the old tradition of rallying around the political center in order to enable the government of the day to effectively respond to political and economic emergencies. Thus, the ruthless use of regulatory powers, so prevalent during this period, was not exclusively brought about by the unilateral action of autocratic presidents. On the contrary, the extraordinary expansion of executive power was carried out with the active involvement of the congress and the acquiescence of the Supreme Court. Thus, governments during this period enjoyed widespread institutional legitimacy, despite paying scant attention to legal and constitutional niceties. Paradoxically, however, despite the congress's willingness to delegate legislative power and tolerate constitutional delinquencies in the drafting of regulations, most presidents felt powerless and some vigorously campaigned to secure a further expansion of their powers. This perception of powerlessness is also surprising as presidents were effectively beyond the reach of ordinary courts because of the failure to establish administrative tribunals. The Supreme Court was not especially concerned by this state of affairs, as it had a misplaced aversion to exercising its role as guardian of the constitution. In any event, the Court did not have much room to maneuver because the constitutional provision that explicitly provided for the establishment of administrative tribunals made it difficult for the Court to develop a coherent approach to provide effective remedies to individuals aggrieved by acts of the administration.

In the absence of judicial review of administrative action, the legality review administered by the *Contraloría* assumed enormous importance. This unlikely mechanism, which was a preventive type of review and which took place before administrative decisions took effect, did—on the whole—restrain the executive, as evidenced by the level of compliance with the comptroller general's decisions. It also made an important contribution to the improvement of the quality of governance as it instilled in government officials the habit of publicly giving reasons for their decisions. Yet, because the legality review procedure was merely an administrative check, governments retained an enormous discretion to act in areas that they deemed urgent and important.

These features of the legal system—though seemingly incongruous—were not irrational. They were the product of a process of accommodation between the executive and the congress, on the one hand; and the Supreme Court and the *Contraloría*, on the other. Together they enabled governments to respond swiftly to economic and political emergencies, while claiming full adherence to the constitution and to the principle of legality. Thus, these features served to enhance the legitimacy of the regime and contributed to the reinforcement of the general perception that it meticulously respected the constitution and the principle of legality.

Ideology Also Matters

The process of accommodation between political and legal institutions had a counterpart in legal reasoning that was reflected in the sharp distinction between public and private law and in the somewhat obscure notion of the act of authority. This feature of legal reasoning, often invoked in attempts to justify the expansion of regulatory powers, also encouraged political parties to believe that popular mandates were not restrained by constitutional and legal procedures. This self-styled version of popular constitutionalism also explains the inordinate optimism underlying the efforts of the two administrations that in the 1960s and early 1970s sought to radically transform democratic governance.

Governments, as well as courts, invoked the act of authority doctrine to justify and explain why certain acts of the government were beyond the reach of ordinary courts. This doctrine, which effectively gave judicial immunity to the executive, led in turn to the development of a sharp distinction between public and private law. While civil law systems generally draw a distinction between public and private law, in Chile the distinction was stretched to absurd limits. Given the absence of judicial control of administrative action, public law was effectively regarded as an autonomous sphere having no bearing on the realm of private law. Thus, instead of regarding public and private law as different dimensions of the same legal order, they were regarded as tightly sealed compartments. This conception of the public/private divide was expedient, as it enabled the political system to expand without taking notice of the courts.

As noted above, although the Supreme Court was not overly concerned by this state of affairs, it did not have room to maneuver and develop strategies to protect rights of individuals aggrieved by administrative action. The sharp line that divided public from private law further compounded the Court's difficulties. Yet, while acknowledging these difficulties, the Court's attempt to resolve this problem was clumsy and counterproductive. Indeed, as explained in chapter 6, the Court proposed that whenever lower courts were called upon to apply illegal acts of administration they should ignore them; that is, refuse to apply them and treat them as nonexistent. From the perspective of the executive, this approach was seen as arbitrary as it enabled courts to effectively annul administrative acts without having to give reasons. Given this clumsy approach, it is not surprising that governments and most politicians tended to regard the Court and the judiciary as untrustworthy and unable to understand policy issues. As a consequence, the judiciary, though independent, was irrelevant in terms of public policy. The exclusion of the judiciary from key areas of public policy had fatal consequences. Indeed, during the Allende administration, legal discourse proved divisive and instead of providing a common ground to resolve disputes, it exacerbated them. The government and the Court, adducing plausible arguments, firmly believed the interpretation of the law of was correct. Thus, unwittingly the poverty of legal discourse contributed to the ongoing political dispute.

It should also be noted that the judicial immunity enjoyed by the executive and the broad notion of the act of authority also played a role in shaping political leaders' perception about the possibility of achieving revolutionary outcomes through the procedures of the political system. Indeed, both Frei and Allende had an excessive, if not naïve, faith in the strength and flexibility of the political and legal systems. They both believed that the prevailing institutional framework was resilient and capable of withstanding the pressure of massive social and economic change. This belief—shared by most of the members of the political elite—stemmed from their own experience as leaders of progressive political movements. They both began their political careers in the 1930s, when the country managed an unexpected return to democracy. During this period they both served as cabinet ministers and were soon elected to the congress. As senators in the 1950s, they played an important role in the reconstitution of the union movement and in diverting the Ibáñez administration from its authoritarian aim. They were also closely involved in challenging the right-wing government of Jorge Alessandri. Thus, from their perspective, as well as from the perspective of their parties and the organizations that supported their programs, the political system had demonstrated an extraordinary capacity to accommodate the political interests they espoused. Thus, it is not surprising that they should have believed that a peaceful revolution was both desirable and possible. Even Allende's legal strategy, though in hindsight bizarre, had the hallmark of the regime, as it was based on a plausible interpretation of the regulatory powers of the executive shared by many lawyers and senior judges.

Empowerment and Rights

An upsurge of popular mobilization, political polarization, and the erosion of centrist positions accompanied the emergence, in the 1960s, of two strong political movements that proposed radical reforms. The erosion of the political center is often regarded as a factor that contributed to the collapse of democracy. Yet, the disappearance of the center was a symptom, rather than the cause, of the malaise affecting the political regime. A key factor leading to the radicalization of politics was the discrediting of market-based policies, which, in turn, was due largely to the stubborn refusal by right-wing forces and the business community to resolve the agricultural question. They failed to impose market discipline on agricultural enterprises and refused to carry out a meaningful agrarian reform. The failure to resolve the agricultural question, combined with the liberalization of the electoral system, had fatal consequences for the right-wing parties. The discrediting of the market and the subsequent collapse of the right-wing vote created a political imbalance, which, though not perceived as such at the time, had a hugely detrimental impact on the political regime. Indeed, after Frei's victory in 1964, the only two credible political actors on the electoral scene were the CDP on the one hand, and the Socialist and Communist Parties, on the other. As a consequence, these two progressive forces, mistakenly confusing the electoral decline of the Right with its disappearance, became mortal enemies. Their antagonism not only debilitated them, but also greatly deteriorated the political system. The CDP, which had planned to govern for 30 years, was unable, in 1970, to muster enough votes to beat a resurgent Right, which was beginning to turn toward neoliberalism. The socialists and communists concentrated more on eroding the electoral strength of the CDP than on working toward broadening their electoral and political appeal.

While the self-destructive competition between the CDP and the Marxist parties can, to some extent, be attributed to the logic of electoral competition, their inability to develop a coherent policy to further democratization through the extension of rights to subordinate groups raises more fundamental issues. There is little doubt that, on paper, Frei's policy on popular promotion was both persuasive and attractive. It was based on a diagnosis of the impact of social and economic exclusion, which it sought to remedy through the establishment of grassroots organizations. The policy was well received and it greatly benefited shantytown dwellers by providing them not only with material support to resolve basic needs, but also, more importantly, with the means to enhance their political awareness and self-respect as citizens. It soon became clear, however, that the government did not assign priority to these lofty objectives. Indeed, as soon as the economy showed signs of instability, the government's interest in Popular Promotion policies declined. But the government's loss of interest in Popular Promotion also reflects a profound distrust of autonomous grassroots organizations. The ambiguity reflected in the law that established Neighborhood Committees concerning the nature of these organizations and the government's failure to act on its promise to empower unions through workers' management schemes suggests that, while the CDP had carried out a correct diagnosis of the problem of social and economic marginality, it failed to fully gauge its political consequences.

The Popular Unity's approach to empowerment and the extension of rights to subordinate groups also had serious shortcomings. The Popular Unity took full advantage of the intense process of mobilization, using it as a mechanism to take over the administration of industries. Yet, its proposals and policies on workers' participation revealed a deep mistrust in the ability of workers and the urban poor to run their affairs. The participation schemes proposed by the government gave overriding decision-making power to government officials, while relegating workers' representatives to an advisory role. Implicit in this approach was the assumption that popular empowerment was not a government priority. The priority was the takeover of the commanding heights of the economy. According to this view, only after the government was firmly in control of the commanding heights of the economy could issues of participation and empowerment be considered. Despite their tactical disagreements, the Socialist and Communist Parties shared this orthodox conception about the relationship between economics and politics. They both agreed that taking over of the commanding heights of the economy was an absolute priority. It is not, however, easy to reconcile this orthodox Marxist approach with the government's claim that it was attempting a new and unconventional transition to socialism—one that sought to reconcile socialist economic policies with prevailing democratic structures.

It could be argued that the government's orthodox Marxist approach to the question of empowerment pervaded the whole strategy of the Popular Unity. Indeed, the government's overall strategy seemed to rest on the assumption that its programmatic objectives could be achieved through the manipulation of administrative mechanisms rather than through democratic deliberation and political compromise. From this perspective, Allende's claim that his government was committed to a transition to socialism through democratic means seems purposely designed to conceal his real intention and to confound the electorate. Yet, as this work has shown, the Popular Unity's program, its strategy, as well as its virtues and failings, were deeply embedded in the country's political history.

Chile had a reputation for political stability and adherence to the principle of legality. This book has shown law's contribution to shaping the political regime, as well as the impact of the political process on legal and institutional development. The legal system undoubtedly had many failings, but it also had some outstanding features. It is an open question whether timely legal reform would have simultaneously improved the legal system and the quality of the democratic process. It could well be—as I have argued—that what I have called the judicial immunity of the executive was crucial in sustaining political stability during the early years of democratic consolidation, in the 1930s and 1940s. It is thus debatable whether a more creative and daring Supreme Court would have effectively contributed to the protection of the rights of citizens. It is likely that a more dynamic Court would have provoked a political backlash that would have undermined judicial independence and perhaps even destabilized the democratic process.

I hope also that the contents of this book contribute to the debate on the breakdown of democracy. By 1970, standard political indicators—such as electoral participation, levels of unionization, freedom of the press, and freedom of assembly—suggested that the process of democratization had reached a peak. Yet, only three years later, the Pinochet dictatorship launched a massive and brutal process of dedemocratization that was warmly welcomed by those who had opposed Allende on the ground that his government had failed to respect the rule of law and the principles of democracy. In order to understand the double standards of Pinochet's supporters, as well as the efficacy of Pinochet's policy of dedemocratization, it is necessary to relate the political squabbles that preceded the breakdown of the regime to its historical evolution. This book has shown that the radicalization of the democratic process was mainly rooted in policy failings, rather than in right- or left-wing ideology. While the political liberalization of the 1950s was carried out without corresponding economic reform, the substantive economic reforms of the 1960s were not accompanied by equivalent changes at the political level. Thus while in the 1950s there was political democratization without economic change, in the 1960s there was economic change without corresponding political and institutional change. Under these circumstances, the breakdown of the political regime in 1973, though by no means inevitable, was not wholly unexpected.

Appendix A

Presidents and Administrations between 1831 and 1973

1831–1925

1831–41	General José Joaquín Prieto
1841–51	General Manuel Bulnes
1851–61	Manuel Montt
1861–71	José Joaquín Pérez
1871–76	Federico Errázuriz
1876–81	Aníbal Pinto
1881–86	Domingo Santa María
1886–91	José Manuel Balmaceda
1891	Civil War
1891–96	Jorge Montt
1896–1901	Federico Errázuriz (son of President Federico Errázuriz [1871–76])
1901–06	Germán Riesco
1906–10	Pedro Montt (son of President Manuel Montt)
1910–15	Ramón Barros
1915–20	Juan Luis Sanfuentes
1920–25	Arturo Alessandri

1925–32

Between the second resignation of President Alessandri in October 1925 and the restoration of constitutional government in December 1932, there were 15 administrations, some of which were elected:

October 1–December 23, 1925	Vice Presidency of Ramón Barros
December 23, 1925–April 7, 1927	Presidency of Emiliano Figueroa (elected)
April 7, 1927–July 21, 1927	Vice Presidency of Carlos Ibáñez

July 21, 1927–July 26, 1931	Presidency of Carlos Ibáñez (elected)
July 27–August 20, 1931	Vice Presidency of Juan Esteban Montero
August 20–November 15, 1931	Vice Presidency of Manuel Trucco
November 15– December 4, 1931	Vice Presidency of Juan Esteban Montero
December 4, 1931–June 4, 1932	Presidency of Juan Esteban Montero (elected)
June 4– June 13, 1932	First Military Junta
June 13–June 16, 1932	Second Military Junta
June 16–June 30, 1932	Third Military Junta
June 30–July 8, 1932	Fourth Military Junta
July 8–September 13, 1932	Provisional Presidency of Carlos Dávila
September 13–October 2, 1932	Provisional Presidency of General Bartolomé Blanche
October 2–December 24, 1932	Vice Presidency of Abraham Oyadenel

1932–73

1932–38	Arturo Alessandri
1938–41	Pedro Aguirre
1941–46	Juan Antonio Ríos
1946–52	Gabriel González
1952–58	Carlos Ibáñez
1958–64	Jorge Alessandri (son of President Arturo Alessandri)
1964–70	Eduardo Frei
1970–73	Salvador Allende

Appendix B

Presidential Elections 1932–70

Date	Number of Registered Voters and Registered Voters as Percentage of Total Population	Participation Rates of Registered Voters	Percentage of Vote for Each Candidate
October 30, 1932	464,879 (9.5%)	74%	A. Alessandri 55% M. Grove 18% H. Rodríguez 14% E. Zañartu 12% E. Lafferte 1%
October 25, 1938	503,871 (10.3%)	88%	P. Aguirre 50% G. Ross 49% C. Ibáñez 0.02%
February 1, 1942	581,486 (11.1%)	80%	J. A. Ríos 55% C. Ibáñez 44%
September 4, 1946	631,257 (11.2%)	76%	G. González 40% E. Cruz-Coke 30% F. Alessandri 30% B. Ibáñez 3%
September 4, 1952	1,105,029 (17.6%)	87%	C. Ibáñez 47% A. Matte 28% P. E. Alfonso 20% S. Allende 5%

Continued

Appendix B Continued

Date	Number of Registered Voters and Registered Voters as Percentage of Total Population	Participation Rates of Registered Voters	Percentage of Vote for Each Candidate
September 4, 1958	1,497,902 (20.5%)	84%	J. Alessandri 31% S. Allende 29% E. Frei 20% L. Bossay 15% A. Zamorano 3%
September 4, 1964	2,915,121 (34.8%)	87%	E. Frei 56% S. Allende 39% J. Durán 5%
September 4, 1970	3,539,747 (36.2%)	83%	S. Allende 36% J. Alessandri 35% R. Tomic 28%

Source: Correa et al. 2001:192–193; Borón 1971b:51.

Appendix C

Union Membership and Rates of Unionization 1932–73

Year	Number of Members	Unionization as Percentage of Workforce	Percentage of Unionized Workers in Agriculture
1932	54,801	–	–
1938	125,972	–	–
1946	251,774	–	–
1952	282,383	13.20	0.4
1953	298,274	12.17	0.6
1954	299,364	11.88	0.7
1955	305,192	12.08	0.7
1956	317,352	13.90	0.7
1957	300,040	13.00	0.7
1958	276,346	11.90	0.7
1959	282,498	10.30	0.7
1960	232,417	10.10	0.6
1961	257,563	10.60	0.6
1962	247,007	10.00	0.6
1963	262,498	10.30	0.6
1964	270,542	10.30	0.7
1965	292,653	10.90	0.7
1966	350,516	12.80	3.0
1967	406,186	14.64	11.5
1968	499,761	17.48	16.7
1969	530,984	18.20	19.7
1970	551,086	19.40	20.7
1971	586,600	20.63	21.7
1972	632,485	22.00	21.6
1973	934,335	30.80	24.6

Source: Allende 1973b:858; Correa 2001:78; Sader 1973: 29,32; Scully 1992:156.

Appendix D

Comptroller Generals 1927–77

Pablo Ramirez R.	March 26, 1927–July 21, 1927
Kenneth Page	July 22, 1927–December 14, 1927
Rodolfo Jaramillo	January 5, 1928–January 8, 1929
Edecio Torreblanca	January 9, 1929–November 5, 1929
Miguel Solar	November 7, 1929–February 22, 1932
Gustavo Ibáñez	February 23, 1932–December 31, 1938
Agustin Vigorena	January 5, 1939–December 18, 1945
Humberto Mewes	February 7, 1946–June 14, 1952
Enrique Bahamondes	September 16, 1952–May 11, 1959
Enrique Silva Cimma	September 16, 1959–January 31, 1967
Héctor Humeres	August 11, 1967–December 31, 1977

Notes

Translations into English are by the author, unless otherwise stated.

1 Building a Strong State

1. For the text of the 1833 Constitution and its amendments see, http://www.historia.uchile.cl/ (last accessed March 13, 2006).

2 Political Liberalization and Civil War

1. The text of Article 82 paragraph 6 reads as follows: "Son atribuciones especiales del Presidente: . . . (6) Nombrar y remover a su voluntad a los Ministros del Despacho y oficiales de sus secretarías a los Consejeros de Estado a los Ministros Diplomáticos a los cónsules y demás agentes exteriores, y a los Intendentes de provincia y Gobernadores de plaza;" at www.historia.uchile.cl (last accessed March 13, 2006). [The special powers of the President include the prerogative: . . . (6) To appoint and remove, at his discretion, Cabinet Ministers, senior officers of Government Departments, Members of the Council of State, Ambassadors, Consuls and other diplomatic agents, and Intendents and Governors.]
2. Courcelle-Seneuil lived in Chile between 1855 and 1863. He worked as consultant to the Ministry of Finance, established the first economics course at the University of Chile and influenced a generation of intellectuals and politicians (Martner 1929: 274–278).

3 Transition to a Modern State

1. For the text of the 1925 Constitution and its amendments see, http://www.historia.uchile.cl/ (last accessed 13 March, 2006).

5 Governance and Accountability

1. *Boletín de la Cámara de Diputados*, Sesión 3, January 29, 1969.
2. See the *Contraloría's* Annual Reports (*Memoria Anual de la Contraloría General de la República*) 1964–70.

3. *Diario de Sesiones del Senado*, Sesión 21, (Legislatura Extraordinaria) December 17, 1945, p. 691.

4. Ibid., p. 705.

5. On the impeachment of the comptroller general, see, *Boletín de la Cámara de Diputados*, Sesións 10 and 11, on November 22, 1945, pp. 603–621, 623–698; and *Diario de Sesiones del Senado*, Sesiones No. 14 to 25 held between December 4 and 27 and December 14 and 25, 1945, pp. 469–489, 499–523, 537–553, 566–590, 596–621, 629–659, 663–688, 691–719, 723–738, 748–770, 831–832.

6. *Diario de Sesiones del Senado*, Sesión 21, December 17, 1945, pp. 695, 705.

7. Ibid., p. 692.

8. Ibid., p. 705.

9. *Diario de Sesiones del Senado*, Sesión 29, January 2, 1946, p. 953.

10. *Diario de Sesiones del Senado*, Sesión 30, January 8, 1946, pp. 995–1019.

11. See the *Contraloría's* Annual Reports (*Memoria Anual de la Contraloría General de la República*) 1963–69.

12. *Contraloría General de la República*, Oficio 77516, October 21, 1965, Oficio 915, June 27, 1966 and Oficio 51559, July 9, 1966. Source: *Contraloría General de la República, Secretaría General*.

13. Dictámen No. 41,164 (July 16, 1968) *Boletín de Jurisprudencia* (7) July 1968, pp. 52–53.

6　The Supreme Court

1. *Cámara de Diputados, Boletín de Sesiones*, 20a Sesión, June 28, 1933, p. 1000.

2. *Cámara de Diputados, Boletín de Sesiones*, Sesión 13a Ordinaria, June 19, 1933, p. 625; Sesión 19a Ordinaria, June 27, 1933, pp. 931–975 ; Sesión 20a Ordinaria, June 28, 1933, pp. 995– 1057.

3. For the Supreme Court's response to the allegations contained in the articles of impeachment, see *Cámara de Diputados, Boletín de Sesiones*, Sesión 16a, November 14, 1967, pp. 1451–1473. For the congressional debate on the impeachment, see *Cámara de Diputados, Boletín de Sesiones*, Sesión 16a, November 14, 1967, pp 1487–1552; and Sesión 17a, November 14, 1967, pp. 1562–1608.

4. *Cámara de Diputados, Boletín de Sesiones*, Sesión 16a, November 14, 1967, p. 1468.

5. Ibid., p. 1463.

6. *Cámara de Diputados, Boletín de Sesiones*, Sesión 19a Ordinaria, June 27, 1933, p. 934.

7. Ibid., p. 948.

8. De Castro (inaplicabilidad e inconstitucionalidad), Corte Suprema September 13, 1932, *Revista de Derecho y Jurisprudencia*, Vol. 30 (1933), pp. 36–45.

9. Ibid.

10. Frías Ojeda, René (inaplicabilidad), Corte Suprema, February 3, 1949, *Revista de Derecho y Jurisprudencia*, Vol. 46 (1949), pp. 618–640.

11. Article 72 (17) reads as follows: "Si a la reunión del Congreso no hubiere expirado el término señalado, la declaración que ha hecho el Presidente de la República, se entenderá como una proposición de ley." [In case of internal unrest, the prerogative to declare a state of siege rests with the Congress; but if Congress is not in session, the President of the Republic may declare a state of siege for a specific period. If the state of siege ordered by the President has not expired by the time the Congress reconvenes, the state of siege declared by the President will be regarded as a legislative bill.]

12. For a sample of these views, see Junta de Gobierno 1982: 25–184.

13. Sociedad Cooperativa de Compraventa de Transportes Colectivos Ltda (*Socotransco*) con Fisco, Corte Suprema, January 9, 1964, *Revista de Derecho y Jurisprudencia*, Vol. 61 (1964), pp. 7–14.

14. Ibid., p. 13.

15. See Dupuis et al. 2004: 647 on what French administrative law characterizes as *l'emprise irréguliere* (irregular seizure or expropriation).

16. Camus V., Alfredo y otros con Dirección de Pavimentación, Corte Suprema, May 23, 1961, *Revista de Derecho y Jurisprudencia*, Vol. 58 (1961), pp. 144–150.

17. Montero con Comisariato Departamental de Subsistencias, Corte de Apelaciones de La Serena, March 2, 1945, *Revista de Derecho y Jurisprudencia*, Vol. 42 (1945), pp. 3–16.

18. Montero con Comisariato Departamental de La Serena, Corte Suprema, October 14, 1947, *Revista de Derecho y Jurisprudencia*, Vol. 45 (1948), pp. 248–250.

19. For an early statement of this doctrine, see Fernández Concha con Municipalidad de Ñuñoa, Corte Suprema, June 14, 1909, *Revista de Derecho y Jurisprudencia*, Vol. 14 (1916), pp. 112–116.

7   A Revolution in Liberty

1. Ley de Junta de Vecinos y Demás Organizaciones Comunitarias, Ley No. 16,880, *Diario Oficial*, No. 27113, August 7, 1973.

8   A Peaceful Revolution

1. For the Popular Unity's Program of Government see, Zammit (1973), pp. 255–286.

2. Copper was nationalized in 1971 by means of a constitutional amendment that had the support of all the parties.

3. *El Mercurio*, January 15, 1973, p. 21.

4. *El Mercurio*, January 18, 1973, p. 12; *El Mercurio*, January 29, 1973, p. 17.

5. See debate on the impeachment of Orlando Millas, minister of economics: *Cámara de Diputados, Boletín de Sesiones*, Sesión 51, May 17, 1973, pp. 2833–2852; *Diario de Sesiones del Senado*, Sesión 27, July 3, 1973, pp. 1075–1110; Sesión 29, July 4 , 1973, pp. 1155–1188; Sesión 30, July 5, 1973, pp. 1193–1195.

6. Dictámen No. 50,782 (July 2, 1973) *Contraloría General de la República, Boletín de Jurisprudencia* (6–10) June–October 1973, pp. 461–465.

7. See, for example, the senate debate on the impeachment of Hernán del Canto, minister of the interior, *Diario de Sesiónes del Senado*, Sesión 37, July 24, 1972, pp. 2016–2050; Sesión 39, July 25, 1972, pp. 2116–2149; Sesión 42, July 26, 1972, pp. 2272–2288 and Sesión 44, July 27, 1972, pp. 2334–2366.

8. Ley No. 17,798, *Diario Oficial*, No. 28,383, October 21, 1972.

9. Decreto No. 4,581, *Diario Oficial*, No. 21,588, February 23, 1949.

10. *El Mercurio*, January 27, 1973, p. 12.

11. Ley No. 17,377, *Diario Oficial*, No. 27,779, October 24, 1970.

12. *Diario de Sesiones del Senado*, Sesión 42, July 17, 1973, pp. 1465–1498; Sesión 46, July 18, 1973, pp. 1607–1618; Sesión 47, July 19, 1973, pp. 1627–1630.

13. Ministro en Visita Extraordinaria (Corte de Apelaciones), Contra Jaime Schatz Prilutzky, July 11, 1973, *Revista de Derecho y Jurisprudencia*, Vol. 70 (1973), pp. 70–77.

14. "La Escuela Nacional Unificada y la Constitución Política" *El Mercurio* (editorial), March 20, 1973.

15. *El Siglo*, June 27, 1971, p. 4.

9 Legality Defeated

1. Corte Suprema (desafuero) Contra Carlos Altamirano Orrego, September 12, 1967, *Fallos del Mes*, Vol. 9 (107) 1967, pp. 228–230 and Corte Suprema (desafuero apelado) Contra Carlos Altamirano Orrego, September 14, 1967, *Fallos del Mes*, Vol. 9 (107) 1967, pp. 231–232.

2. Dictámen No. 60,058 (October 30, 1962) in Soto 1974: 253–255 and Dictámen 81, 916 (December 30, 1968) *Contraloría General de la República, Boletín de Jurisprudencia* (12) December 1968, p. 63.

3. Dictámen No. 43,315 (June 29, 1971) *Contraloría General de la República, Boletín de Jurisprudencia* (5–6) May–June 1971, pp. 349–351; and Dictámen No. 58,371 (August 20, 1971) *Contraloría General de la República, Boletín de Jurisprudencia* (7–8) July–August 1971, pp. 472–473.

4. Dictámen No. 87,708 (December 7, 1971) *Contraloría General de la República, Boletín de Jurisprudencia* (11–12) November–December 1971, pp. 721–722.

5. *Contraloría General de la República, Memoria de la Contraloría General de la República Correspondiente al Año 1973*, p. 46.

6. Dictámen No. 18,447 (March 15, 1972) *Contraloría General de la República, Boletín de Jurisprudencia* (3–4) Marcho–April 1972, p. 198.

7. Dictámen No. 1638 (January 8, 1973) *Contraloría General de la República, Boletín de Jurisprudencia* (1) January 1973, pp. 16–18.

8. *Contraloría General de la República, Memoria de la Contraloría General de la República Correspondiente al Año 1973*, p. 44.

9. *Contraloría General de la República, Memoria de la Contraloría General de la República Correspondiente al Año 1971*, pp. 9–10; *Contraloría General de la República, Memoria de la Contraloría General de la República Correspondiente al Año 1972*, pp. 10–13; *Contraloría General de la República, Memoria de la Contraloría General de la República Correspondiente al Año 1973*, p. 10.

10. Dictámen No. 50,782 (July 2, 1973) *Contraloría General de la República, Boletín de Jurisprudencia* (6–10) June–October 1973, pp. 461–465.

11. "La Contraloría Ignora Oficialmente las Objeciones del Ministro Millas" *El Mercurio*, March 14, 1973, p. 8; "Ministro Millas Insiste ante Contralor para que Enmiende un Dictámen" *El Mercurio*, March 21, 1973, p. 16.

12. Decreto No. 206, *Diario Oficial*, No. 28,543, May 4, 1973, pp. 2–3.

13. Corte Suprema (recurso de queja) S.A. Yarur Manufacturas de Algodón, January 4, 1972, *Revista de Derecho y Jurisprudencia*, Vol. 69, Sección Sexta (January–April 1972), pp. 1–7.

14. Corte Suprema (recurso de queja) S.A. Yarur Manufacturas de Algodón, November 15, 1972, *Revista de Derecho y Jurisprudencia*, Vol. 69, Sección Primera (December1972), pp. 195–197.

15. According to records held at the Consejo de Defensa del Estado in 1973, 26 possessory actions were pending before civil courts (*juzgados civiles*) in Santiago (information on file with the author).

16. The account that follows is taken from *Diario de Sesiónes del Senado*, Sesión 31, July 9, 1973, pp. 1209–1219.

17. *Diario de Sesiónes del Senado*, Sesión 34, July 10, 1973, p. 1277.

18. Corte Suprema, (contienda de competencia) Juez de Letras de Melipilla con S.E. el Presidente de la República, May 3, 1967 in *Junta de Gobierno* 1982, pp. 223–239.

19. Corte Suprema (casación de fondo) Rayonhil Industria Nacional de Rayón SA con Director de Industria y Comercio y Otros, September 5, 1973, *Revista de Derecho y Jurisprudencia*, Vol. 70, Sección Primera, pp. 66–71. See also, Corte Suprema (*recurso de queja*) Juan Bravo Ramos, 27 September 1972 in *Junta de Gobierno* 1982, pp. 240–248.

20. It should be noted that the argument that possessory actions were designed to govern relations among individuals and not designed to challenge administrative acts could well be consistent with the intention of the legislature, but it is not consistent with judicial practice. Arturo

Alessandri and Manuel Somarriva, the leading authorities on this subject, provide useful background on this issue, but do not resolve it. They explain that before the adoption of the 1925 Constitution (which arguably divested ordinary courts from jurisdiction to review acts of the administration), possessory actions were frequently used to challenge and invalidate administrative acts. They cite very few cases after 1925 where possessory actions were successfully used to oppose acts of public officials. This shift in the case law should, presumably, be attributed to the provision in the constitution on administrative tribunals. The authors, however, do not make this point (Alessandri and Somarriva 1957, pp. 829–845).

21. On May 31, 1972, the Sexto Juzgado Civil decided that it did not have jurisdiction to resolve the possessory action brought by Rayonhil on May 18 (Rol 684–72) of the same year. On November 28, 1972, the Court of Appeals (Santiago) affirmed the lower court's decision. The Court of Appeals decision was not reported (photocopy of the judgment on file with the author).

22. Corte Suprema (recurso de queja) Gerardo Garrido Rojas, July 26, 1972, *Revista de Derecho y Jurisprudencia*, Vol. 69, Sección Cuarta (July–December 1972), pp. 98–102.

23. Corte Suprema (recurso de queja) Empresa Nacional de Construcciones, August 3, 1972, *Revista de Derecho y Jurisprudencia*, Vol. 68, Sección Cuarta (July–August 1971), pp. 156–157.

24. Circular No. 664, March 20, 1972, *Fallos del Mes*, Vol. 13 (164), p. 48.

25. For the events in Melipilla see, "Antecedentes Relacionados con los Sucesos Acecidos en el Juzgado de Letras de Melipilla el 9 de Mayo de 1972," *Revista de Derecho y Jurisprudencia*, Vol. 70 (7/8) 1973, pp. 157–161.

26. *Diario de Sesiones del Senado*, Sesión 27, July 7, 1972, pp. 1792–1800.

27. Circular Confidencial No. 3 de 19 Enero 1973 del Ministro del Interior (General Carlos Prats) "Sobre Procedimiento a Seguir en Caso de Cumplimiento de Ordenes Judiciales de Desalojo de Determinados Establecimientos Industriales," *Revista de Derecho y Jurisprudencia*, Vol. 70 (7/8), p. 203.

28. See, for example, the statement by Hernán del Canto, minister of the interior, explaining that the government often delayed the enforcement of judgments in order to prevent a disruption of public order. *Diario de Sesiones del Senado*, Sesión 3, July 24, 1972, p. 2026.

29. For the exchange of letters between the Supreme Court and President Allende, see *Revista de Derecho y Jurisprudencia*, Vol. 70 (7/8) 1973, pp. 206–211, 215–240.

30. Ibid., pp. 216–226.

31. Ibid., p. 229.

32. Ibid., p. 235.

Bibliography

Abbott, Roger S. (1951) "The Role of Contemporary Political Parties in Chile," *American Political Science Review*, Vol. 45 (2), pp. 450–463.

Affonso, Almino (1972) "Esbozo Histórico del Movimiento Campesino Chileno," *Revista Latinoamericana de Ciencias Sociales*, No. 3 (June), pp. 37–69.

Affonso, Almino, Sergio Gómez, Emilio Klein, and Pablo Ramírez (1970) *Movimiento Campesino Chileno* (2 vols.) (Santiago: ICIRA).

Agor, Weston H. (1971) *The Chilean Senate* (Austin: University of Texas Press).

Aguero, Luis (1948) "Sobre la Improcedencia del Recurso de Queja con que se Pretende Invalidar las Sentencias Definitivas de las Cortes del Trabajo," *Revista de Derecho y Jurisprudencia*, Vol. 46, pp. 50–56.

Ahumada, Jorge (1958) *En Vez de la Miseria* (Santiago: Editorial del Pacífico).

Alessandri, Arturo and Manuel Somarriva (1957) *Curso de Derecho Civil (Volume 2) De los Bienes* (Santiago: Editorial Nacimento).

Alexander, Robert J. (1962) *Labor Relations in Argentina, Brazil and Chile* (New York: McGraw Hill).

Allende, Salvador (1972) "Segundo Mensaje del Presidente Salvador Allende al Congreso Pleno," *Sesiones del Congreso Nacional, Legislatura 316a Ordinaria, Sesión del Congreso Pleno, May 21, 1972*, pp. 5–28.

——— (1973a) "The Chilean Road to Socialism—First Annual Message to the Congress, 21 May 1971," in Salvador Allende, (ed.), *Chile's Road to Socialism* (London: Penguin Books), pp. 138–166.

——— (1973b) *Mensaje del Presidente Allende ante el Congreso Pleno, 21 de Mayo 1973* (Santiago).

Alvarez, Oscar and Moisés Poblete (1924) *Legislación Social Obrera Chilena* (Santiago: Imprenta Santiago).

Angell, Alan (1972) *Politics and the Labour Movement in Chile* (Oxford: Oxford University Press).

Anonymous (1868) *La Acusación a la Corte Suprema* (Santiago: Imprenta del Ferrocarril).

Aramayo, Oscar (1964) *Régimen Legal del Comercio Interior Chileno* (Santiago: Editorial Jurídica).

Arellano, José Pablo (1985) "Social Policies in Chile: An Historical Review," *Journal of Latin American Studies*, Vol. 17 (2), pp. 397–418.

Arendt, Hannah (1973) *On Revolution* (London: Penguin Books).

Arteaga, Angela and Benito González (1986) "Corte Suprema: Tribunal de Casación?" *Revista Chilena de Derecho*, Vol. 13, pp. 101–142.

Atria, Raúl (1983) "Tensiones Políticas y Crisis Económica: El Caso Chileno 1920–1938" *Estudios Sociales*, March, pp. 177–218.

Avila, Alamiro (1971) "Chile," in Andreas F. Lowenfeld (ed.), *Expropriation in the Americas* (New York: Dunellon), pp. 83–111.

Aylwin, Mariana and Ignacia Alamos (1979) "Los Militares en la Epoca de don Arturo Alessandri" in Claudio Orrego (ed.) *Siete Ensayos Sobre Arturo Alessandri Palma* (Santiago: Instituto Chileno de Estudios Humanísticos), pp. 303–390.

Aylwin, Patricio (1952) *Manual de Derecho Administrativo* (Santiago: Editorial Jurídica).

Barraclough, Solon and José Antonio Fernández (1974) *Diagnóstico de la Reforma Agraria Chilena* (México: Siglo Veintiuno Editores).

Barrera, Manuel (1971) "Perspectiva Histórica de la Huelga Obrera en Chile," *Cuadernos de la Realidad Nacional*, No. 9 (March), pp. 119–155.

——— (1979) *Desarrollo Económico y Sindicalismo en Chile: 1938–1970* (Santiago: Vector—Centro de Estudios Económicos y Sociales).

Bauer, Arnold (1975) *Chilean Rural Society from Spanish Conquest to 1930* (Cambridge: Cambridge University Press).

——— (1990) "Industry and the Missing Bourgeoisie: Consumption and Development in Chile, 1850–1950," *Hispanic American Historical Review*, Vol. 70 (2), pp. 227–253.

Behrman, Jere (1977) *Macroeconomic Policy in a Developing Country: The Chilean Experience* (New York: Elsevier/North-Holland).

Bello, Andrés (1982) *Obras Completas de Andrés Bello—Vol. XVIII: Temas Jurídicos y Sociales* (Caracas: Casa Bello).

Bengoa, José (1985) *Historia del Pueblo Mapuche* (Santiago: Editorial Sur).

Bitar, Sergio (1979) *Transición, Socialismo y Democracia* (México: Siglo Veintiuno).

Blakemore, Harold (1974) *British Nitrates and Chilean Politics 1886–1896: Balmaceda and North* (London: Althone Press).

——— (1986) "Chile from the War of the Pacific to the World Depression, 1880–1930," in Leslie Bethell (ed.), *The Cambridge History of Latin America, Volume V* (Cambridge: Cambridge University Press), pp. 499–551.

Blasier, S. Cole (1950) "Chile: A Communist Battleground," *Political Science Quarterly*, Vol. 65 (3), pp. 353–375.

Bollen, Kenneth A. (1980) "Issues in the Comparative Measurement of Political Democracy," *American Sociological Review*, Vol. 45 (3), pp. 370–390.

Borchard, Edwin M. (1917) *Guide to the Law and Legal Literature of Argentina, Brazil and Chile* (Washington: Government Printing Office).

Borón, Atilio (1971a) "La Evolución del Régimen Electoral y sus Efectos en la Representación de Intereses Populares: el Caso de Chile," *Revista Latinoamericana de Ciencia Política*, Vol. II (3), pp. 395–436.

———— (1971b) "Movilización Política y Crisis Política en Chile (1920–1970)," *Aportes*, No. 20, pp. 41–69.

Borzutzky, Silvia (2002) *Vital Connections—Politics, Social Security and Inequality in Chile* (Notre Dame, IN: University of Notre Dame Press).

Bowman, John R. and Michael Wallerstein (1982) "The Fall of Balmaceda and Public Finance in Chile: New Data for an Old Debate," *Journal of Inter-American Studies and World Affairs*, Vol. 24 (4), pp. 421–460.

Bravo, Bernardino (1976) "Los Estudios Sobre la Judicatura Chilena de los Siglos XIX y XX," *Revista de Derecho Público (Separata)*, No. 19–20, pp. 89–116.

———— (1978) *Régimen de Gobierno y Partidos Políticos en Chile 1924–1973* (Santiago: Editorial Jurídica).

———— (1982) "La Difusión del Código de Bello en los Países de Derecho Castellano y Portugués" *Revista de Estudios Histórico-Jurídicos*, Vol. 7, pp. 71–106.

———— (1986) *Historia de las Instituciones Políticas en Chile y en Hispanoamérica* (Santiago: Editorial Jurídica).

Brown, L. Neville and J. S. Bell (1993) *French Administrative Law* (4th edition) (Oxford: Oxford University Press).

Brown, L. Neville and J. F. Garner (1973) *French Administrative Law* (2nd edition) (London: Butterworths).

Bulnes, Gonzalo (1980) *Los Mapuches y la Tierra* (Rotterdam, Instituto Nuevo Chile: Pequeñas Ediciones).

Burr, Robert N. (1965) *By Reason or Force: Chile and the Balancing of Power in South America, 1830–1905* (Berkeley: University of California Press).

Cabrera, Patricio (1971) "Derecho Laboral," in Universidad Católica, *Orientaciones del Derecho Chileno* (Santiago: Editorial Jurídica), pp. 241–286.

Caffarena, Elena (1957) *El Recurso de Amparo Frente a los Regímenes de Emergencia* (Santiago, No Reference to Editorial).

Campbell, Margaret V. (1959) "Education in Chile, 1810–1842," *Journal of Inter-American Studies*, Vol. 1 (3), pp. 353–375.

Campos, Fernando (1963) *Historia Constitucional de Chile* (3rd edition) (Santiago: Editorial Jurídica).

Canovas, José (1970) "Actitud Actual del Juez Frente a la Ley y el Derecho" *Revista de Derecho y Jurisprudencia*, Vol. 67, pp. 134–142.

Cariola, Carmen and Osvaldo Sunkel (1977) "Chile: Ensayo de Interpretación" in Roberto Cortés Conde and Stanley J. Stein (eds.), *Latin America: A Guide to Economic History 1830–1930* (Berkeley: University of California Press).

———— (1990) *Un Siglo de Historia Económica de Chile 1830–1930* (Santiago: Editorial Universitaria).

Carrière, Jean (1981) *Landowners and Politics in Chile—A Study of the "Sociedad Nacional de Agricultura" 1932–1970* (Amsterdam: Centre for Latin American Research and Documentation).

Carvajal, Horacio (1940) *La Corte Suprema* (Santiago: Imprenta El Esfuerzo).

Castedo, Leopoldo (1954) *Resumen de la Historia de Chile* (3 Vols.) (Santiago: Editorial Zig-Zag).

Cavarozzi, Marcelo José (1975) "The Government and the Industrial Bourgeoisie in Chile: 1928–1964," (PhD dissertation, University of California).

Chonchol, Jacques (1970) "Poder y Reforma Agraria en la Experiencia Chilena," *Cuadernos de la Realidad Nacional*, No. 4, pp. 50–87.

Church Report (1975) *Covert Action in Chile 1963–1973, 94th Congress 1st Session Staff Report of the Select Committee to Study Governmental Operations with respect to Intelligence Activities* (United States Senate, December 18, 1975) available at http://foia.state.gov/Reports/ChurchReport.asp (last accessed May 17, 2007).

Cleaves, Peter S. (1974) *Bureaucratic Politics and Administration in Chile* (Berkley: University of California Press).

Claudín, Fernando (1977) "Democracy and Dictatorship in Lenin and Kaustky," *New Left Review* No. 106 (November/December), pp. 59–76.

Collier, Simon (1985) "Chile from Independence to the War of the Pacific," in Leslie Bethell, (ed.), *The Cambridge History of Latin America, Volume III* (Cambridge: Cambridge University Press) pp. 583– 613.

——— (2003) *Chile: The Making of a Republic, 1830–1865* (Cambridge: Cambridge University Press).

Collier, Simon and William F. Sater (1996) *A History of Chile, 1808–1994* (Cambridge: Cambridge University Press).

Contraloría General de la República (1971) "Procedencia Jurídica de las Intervenciones Decretadas por el Ejecutivo a Partir del Primero de Septiembre 1970 en Fundos, Fábricas, Industrias, Bancos u Otras empresas Privadas, y Facultades que Tienen los Interventores Designados," *Boletín de Jurisprudencia* (Oficio No. 17,785) (3/4) March–April, pp. 154–162.

Correa, Sofía, Consuelo Figueroa, Alfredo Jocelyn-Holt, Claudio Rolle, and Manuel Vicuña (2001) *Documentos del Siglo XX Chileno* (Santiago: Editorial Sudamericana).

Corte Suprema (1967) "Respuesta de la Corte Suprema a la Acusación Constitucional," *Cámara de Diputados, Boletín de Sesiones*, Sesión 16, Tuesday, November, 14, 1967, pp. 1451–1473.

——— (1971) "Memoria Leída por el Presidente de la Corte Suprema en la Inaguración del Año Judicial 1971," *Revista de Derecho y Jurisprudencia*, Vol. 68 (January–April), pp. V–XXXII.

——— (1972) "Memoria Leída por el Presidente de la Corte Suprema en la Inaguración del Año Judicial 1972," *Revista de Derecho y Jurisprudencia*, Vol. 69 (January–April), pp. V–XXXII.

——— (1973) "Memoria Leída por el Presidente de la Corte Suprema en la Inaguración del Año Judicial 1973," *Revista de Derecho y Jurisprudencia*, Vol. 70, pp. V–XXV.

Couso, Javier (2005) "The Judicialization of Chilean Politics: The Rights Revolution that Never Was," in Rachel Sieder, Line Schjolden, and Alan

Angell (eds.), *The Judicialization of Politics in Latin America* (New York: Palgrave Macmillan), pp. 105–160.

Culver, William C. and Cornel J. Reinhart (1989) "Capitalist Dreams: Chile's Response to Nineteenth Century World Copper Competition," *Comparative Studies in Society and History*, Vol. 31 (4), pp. 722–744.

Cusack, David F. (1970) "The Politics of Chilean Private Enterprise under Christian Democracy" (PhD dissertation, University of Denver).

Debray, Regis (1971) *The Chilean Revolution—Conversations with Allende* (New York: Vintage Books).

De Ramón, Armando (1989) *La Justicia Chilena Entre 1875 y 1924* (Santiago: Escuela de Derecho Diego Portales, Cuadernos de Análisis Jurídico No. 12).

De Shazo, Peter (1979) "The Valparaíso Maritime Strike of 1903 and the Development of a Revolutionary Labor Movement in Chile," *Journal of Latin American Studies*, Vol. 11 (1), pp. 145–168.

——— (1983) *Urban Workers and Labor Unions in Chile, 1902–1927* (Wisconsin: University of Wisconsin Press).

Deutsch, Sandra McGee (1999) *Las Derechas: The Extreme Right in Argentina, Brazil, and Chile, 1890–1939* (Stanford: Stanford University Press).

De Vylder, Stefan (1976) *Allende's Chile* (Cambridge: Cambridge University Press).

Donoso, Crescente (1976) "Notas Sobre el Orígen, Acatamiento y Desgaste del Regimen Presidencial, 1925–1973," *Historia*, No. 13, pp. 271–351.

Drake, Paul W. (1978) *Socialism and Populism in Chile, 1932–52* (Urbana: University of Illinois Press).

——— (1989) *The Money Doctor in the Andes* (Durham, NC: Duke University Press).

Dunlop, Sergio (1970) "El Juez en la Sociedad Chilena Presente," *Revista de los Jueces*, No. 3, pp. 17–22.

Dupuis, Georges, Marie-José Guédon, and Patrice Chrétien (2004) *Droit Administratif* (9th edition) (Paris: Armand Colin).

Duque, Joaquín and Ernesto Pastrana (1972) "La Movilización Reivindicativa Urbana de los Sectores Populares en Chile, 1964–1972," *Revista Latinoamericana de Ciencias Sociales*, Vol. 4 (December), pp. 259–293.

Echeverría, Andrés and Luis Frei (1974) *1970–1973 La Lucha por la Juridicidad en Chile* (3 Vols.) (Santiago, Editorial del Pacífico).

ECLA (1949) *Economic Survey of Latin America* (New York: United Nations Economic Commission for Latin America).

Edwards, Agustín (1932) *Cuatro Presidentes de Chile 1841–1876* (2 Vols.) (Valparaíso: Sociedad Imprenta y Litografía Universo).

Edwards, Alberto (1972) *La Fronda Aristocrática* (Santiago: Editorial del Pacífico).

——— (1976) *Bosquejo Histórico de los Partidos Políticos Chilenos* (Santiago: Editorial del Pacífico [1903]).

Ellsworth, P. T. (1945) *Chile: An Economy in Transition* (New York: Macmillan).

Eluchans, Edmundo (1972) "Recursos Legales de los Afectados Respecto de una Resolución que Dispone la Requisición de un Establecimiento Industrial o Comercial," *Estudios Jurídico*s, Vol. 1 (1), pp. 48–64.

Encina, Francisco A. (1934) *Portales* (Santiago: Editorial Nascimento).

——— (1952) *La Presidencia de Balmaceda* (Santiago: Editorial Nascimento).

Engels, Frederick (1970) "A Critique of the Draft Social Democratic Programme of 1891," in *Karl Marx and Frederick Engels Selected Works*, Vol. 3 (Moscow: Progress Publishers), pp. 429–439.

——— (1976) "Principles of Communism" in *K. Marx and F. Engels, Collected Works*, Vol. 6, *Marx Engels 1845–48* (London, Lawrence and Wishart), pp. 341–375.

Espinosa Juán G. and Andrew S. Zimbalist (1978) *Economic Democracy: Workers' Participation in Chilean Industry 1970–1973* (New York: Academic Press).

Espinoza, Raúl (1972a) "La Contraloría General y el Proceso de Cambios," *Revista de la Universidad Técnica del Estado*, No. 8 (May–June), pp. 15–33.

——— (1972b) "La Requisición de los Monopolios Textiles y un Fallo de la Corte Suprema," *Revista de la Universidad Técnica del Estado*, No. 7 (March–April), pp. 91–100.

Estelle, Patricio (1970) "El Club de la Reforma 1868–187," *Revista Historia*, Vol. 9, pp. 111–135.

Estévez, Carlos (1949) *Elementos de Derecho Constitucional* (Santiago: Editorial Jurídica).

Etcheberry, Alfredo (1987) *Derecho Penal en la Jurisprudencia* (Vol. 3), Santiago: Editorial Jurídica.

Evans, Enrique (1970a) "La Delegación de Facultades Legislativas," in Eduardo Frei, et al. (eds.), *Reforma Constitucional 1970* (Santiago: Editorial Jurídica), pp. 109–154.

——— (1970b) *Relación de la Constitución Política de la República de Chile* (Santiago: Editorial Jurídica).

——— (1973) *Chile, Hacia una Constitución Contemporánea—Tres Reformas Constitucionales* (Santiago: Editorial Jurídica).

Faundez, Julio (1975) "The Chilean Road to Socialism," *The Political Quarterly*, July–September, pp. 310–325.

——— (1980) "The Defeat of Politics: Chile under Allende," *Boletín de Estudios Latinoamericanos y del Caribe*, No. 28 (June), pp. 59–75.

——— (1988) *Marxism and Democracy in Chile: From 1932 to the Fall of Allende* (New Haven: Yale University Press).

Feliú, Guillermo (1951) "Durante la República. Perfiles de la Evolución Política, Social y Constitucional," in *La Constitución de 1925 y la Facultad de Ciencias Jurídicas y Sociales* (Santiago: Facultad de Derecho, Universidad de Chile) pp. 59–305.

Fernández, Elisa (1996) "Beyond Partisan Politics in Chile: The Carlos Ibáñez Period and the Politics of Ultranationalism between 1952–1958" (PhD dissertation, University of Miami).

Fernández, Enrique (2003) *Estado y Sociedad en Chile, 1891–1931* (Santiago: Editorial LOM).

Ffrench-Davis, Ricardo (1973) *Las Políticas Económicas en Chile 1952–1970* (Santiago: Ediciones Nueva Universidad).

——— (1974) "La Importancia del Cobre en la Economía Chilena," in Ricardo Ffrench-Davis and Ernesto Tironi, (eds.), *El Cobre en el Desarrollo Nacional* (Santiago: Universidad Católica, Vice-Rectoría de Comunicaciones), pp. 23–50.

Ffrench-Davis, Ricardo and Ernesto Tironi (1974) *El Cobre en el Desarrollo Nacional* (Santiago: Universidad Católica, Vice-Rectoría de Comunicaciones).

Fiamma, Gustavo (1977) "Apreciación de los Hechos o Interpretación del Derecho?" in *La Contraloría General de la República—50 Años de Vida Institucional* (Santiago: Facultad de Derecho, Universidad de Chile), pp. 191–202.

Fischer, Kathleen B. (1979) *Political Ideology and Educational Reform in Chile, 1964–1973* (Los Angeles: UCLA Latin American Center).

Fleet, Michael (1985) *The Rise and Fall of Chilean Christian Democracy* (Princeton: Princeton University Press).

Flores, Fernando (1973) "Interview," *Chile Hoy*, No. 31, pp. 29–31.

Fontecilla, Mariano (1953) "Facultad o Jurisdicción de los Tribunales Ordinarios para Conocer de Ciertas Materias Relacionadas con Decretos del Presidente de la República," *Revista de Derecho y Jurisprudencia*, Vol. 50, pp. 75–84.

Fox-Przeworski, Joanne (1980) *The Decline of the Copper Industry in Chile and the Entrance of North American Capital, 1780–1916* (New York: Arno Press).

Foxley, Alejandro, Eduardo Aninat and José Pablo Arellano (1980) *Las Desigualdades Económicas y la Acción del Estado* (México: Fondo de Cultura Económica).

Frei, Eduardo (1964) "Mensaje de S.E. el Presidente de la República, 1 de Deciembre 1964," *Cámara de Diputados—Sesión Extraordinaria*, Vol. 1, pp. 280–292.

——— (1967) "The Role of Popular Organizations in the State," in Paul E. Sigmund, (ed.), *The Ideologies of Developing Nations* (revised edition) (New York: Frederick A. Praeger), pp. 390–392.

——— (1970) *Sexto Mensaje del Presidente Eduardo Frei Montalva al Congreso Pleno*, May 21, 1970.

Frei, Eduardo, Gustavo Lagos, Sergio Molina, Alejandro Silva, Francisco Cumplido, and Enrique Evans (1970) *La Reforma Constitucional 1970* (Santiago: Editorial Jurídica).

Friedman, Lawrence M. (1975) *The Legal System: A Social Science Perspective* (New York: Russell Sage Foundation).

Fruhling, Hugo (1978) "Liberalismo y Derecho Durante el Siglo XIX," *Ensayos*, No. 1, pp. 7–46.

——— (1980) *Poder Judicial y Política* (Santiago: Facultad Latinoamericana de Ciencias Sociales).

Galdames, Luis (1964) *A History of Chile* (New York: Russell and Russell).

Galecio, Rubén (1966) "El Juez en la Crisis," *Revista de Derecho y Jurisprudencia*, Vol. 63 (5), pp. 121–140.

Garcés, Joan E. (1972) "Chile 1971: A Revolutionary Government within a Welfare State" in Kenneth Medhurst (ed.), *Allende's Chile* (London: Hart-Davis MacGibbon), pp. 27–50.

——— (1973) "Vía Insurreccional y Vía Política: Dos Tácticas" *Revista de la Universidad Técnica del Estado*, Nos. 13–14 (Marcho–June), pp. 7–38.

——— (1976) *Allende y la Experiencia Chilena* (Barcelona: Editorial Ariel).

García, Norberto (1972) "Algunos Aspectos de la Política de Corto Plazo de 1971" in Instituto de Economía (ed.), *La Economía Chilena en 1971* (Santiago: Universidad de Chile, Facultad de Economía Política), pp. 47–270.

Garretón, Manuel Antonio (1989) *The Chilean Political Process* (Boston: Unwin Hyman).

Gazmuri, Cristián (1998) *El 48 Chileno* (Santiago: Editorial Universitaria).

Gil, Federico G. (1966) *The Political System of Chile* (Boston: Houghton Mifflin Company).

Giusti, Jorge (1975) "Participación Popular en Chile: Antecedentes para su Estudio. Las JAP," *Revista Mexicana de Sociología*, Vol. 37 (4), pp. 767–788.

Gomez, Juán Carlos (2004) *La Frontera de la Democracia* (Santiago: Editorial LOM).

Góngora, Mario (1986) *Ensayo Histórico Sobre la Noción de Estado en Chile en los Siglos XIX y XX* (Santiago: Editorial Universitaria).

Grayson, George (1968) *El Partido Democratacristiano Chileno* (Buenos Aires: Editorial Francisco de Aguirre).

Griffith-Jones, Stephany (1981) *The Role of Finance in the Transition to Socialism* (London: Francis Pinter).

Guerra, José Guillermo (1928) *Temas Constitucionales* (Santiago: Imprenta Universitaria).

——— (1929) *La Constitución de 1925* (Santiago: Establecimientos Gráficos Balcells).

Guzmán, Alejandro (1982) *Andrés Bello Codificador Tomo II—Fuentes* (Santiago: Ediciones Universidad de Chile).

——— (1988) *Portales y el Derecho* (Santiago: Editorial Universitaria).

Halperin, Ernst (1965) *Nationalism and Communism in Chile* (Cambridge, MA: MIT Press).

Hanisch, Hugo (1982) "Contribución al Estudio del Principio y de la Práctica de la Fundamentacón de las Sentencias en Chile durante el Siglo XIX," *Revista de Estudios Histórico-Jurídicos*, Vol. 7, pp. 131–173.

Haring, Clarence H. (1931) "Chilean Politics, 1920–1928," *Hispanic American Historical Review*, Vol. 11 (1), pp. 1–26.

———— (1933) "The Chilean Revolution of 1931," *Hispanic American Historical Review*, Vol. 13 (May), pp. 197–203.

Heise, Julio (1954) *Historia Constitucional de Chile* (Santiago: Editorial Jurídica).

———— (1960) *150 Años de Evolución Institucional* (Santiago: Editorial Andrés Bello).

Hersh, Seymour M. (1982) "The Price of Power—Kissinger, Nixon, and Chile," *The Atlantic Monthly* (December), pp. 31–58.

Heskia, Isabel (1973) *La Distribución del Ingreso en Chile* (Santiago: CEPLAN, Documento No. 31).

Hirschman, Albert O. (1963) "Inflation in Chile," in Albert Hirschman (ed.), *Journeys toward Progress* (New York: Twentieth Century Fund).

House of Representatives (1976) *United States and Chile during the Allende Years, 1970–1973, Hearings before the Subcommittee on Inter-American Affairs of the Committee on Foreign Affairs* (Washington, DC).

Hughes, Steven Wirth (1971) "Governmental Decision-Making in Chile: The Relative Decisional Positions of the Executive and the Legislature" (PhD dissertation, University of North Carolina).

Humeres, Héctor (1971) "Reanudación de Faenas en Ciertos Conflictos Colectivos," in Antonio Oneto (ed.), *Tratado General Sobre Reanudación de Faenas* (Santiago: Ediciones Revista Técnica del Trabajo y Previsión Social), pp. 209–211.

Huneeus, Jorge (1891) *La Constitución Ante el Congreso—Tomo 2* (Santiago: Imprenta Cervantes).

Hunt, Richard N. (1984) *The Political Ideas of Marx and Engels: Classical Marxism 1850–1895*, vol. 2 (London: Macmillan).

Hutchinson, Elizabeth Quay (2001) *Labors Appropriate to Their Sex—Gender, Labor and Politics in Urban Chile, 1900–1930* (Durham: Duke University Press).

Ietswaart, Heleen F. P. (1978) "Labor Law and Labor Relations in Chile 1900–1970: A Case Study of Law as a Means of Social Control," *Verfassung und Recht in Überese*, Vol. 11, pp. 283–304.

———— (1981) "Labor Relations Litigation: Chile, 1970–1972," *Law and Society Review*, Vol. 16 (4), pp. 625–668.

Illanes, Osvaldo (1966) "The Supreme Court of Justice of Chile," *International Commission of Jurists Journal*, Vol. 7, pp. 269–277.

Instituto de Economía y Planificación (1973) *La Economía Chilena en 1972* (Santiago: Universidad de Chile, Facultad de Economía Política).

Insunza, Sergio (1966) "Como Escoger y Utilizar las Fuentes Jurídica," *Revista de Derecho y Jurisprudencia*, Vol. 63 (4), pp. 97–120.

Izquierdo, Gonzalo (1976) "Octubre de 1905, Un Episodio en la Historia Social Chilena," *Historia*, Vol. 13, pp. 55–96.

Jaksić, Iván (1998) *Selected Writings of Andrés Bello* (New York: Oxford University Press).

———— (2001) *Andrés Bello: Scholarship and Nation-Building in Nineteenth-Century Latin America* (Cambridge: Cambridge University Press).

Jocelyn-Holt, Alfredo (1997) *El Peso de la Noche* (Buenos Aires: Ariel).

Joxe, Alain (1970) *Las Fuerzas Armadas en el Sistema Político Chileno* (Santiago: Editorial Universitaria).

Junta de Gobierno (1982) *Los Tribunales Contenciosos Administrativos—Antecedentes para su Estudio* (Valparaíso: Instituto Hidrográfico de la Armada de Chile).

Kaufman, Robert R. (1972) *The Politics of Land Reform in Chile, 1950–1970: Public Policy, Political Institutions, and Social Change* (Cambridge: Harvard University Press).

Kay, Cristobal (1977) "The Development of the Chilean *Hacienda* System," in Kenneth Duncan and Ian Rutledge (eds.), *Land and Labour in Latin America* (Cambridge: Cambridge University Press), pp. 103–139.

Kinsbruner, Jay (1973) *Chile a Historical Interpretation* (New York: Harper Torchbooks).

Kirsch, Henry W. (1977) *Industrial Development in a Traditional Society* (Gainsville: University of Florida Press).

Kornbluh, Peter (2003) *The Pinochet File—A Declassified Dossier on Atrocity and Accountability* (New York: The New Press).

Labatut, Gustavo (1964) *Derecho Penal—Tomo II* (4th edition) (Santiago: Editorial Jurídica).

Landsberger, Henry A. (1969) "Ideology and Practical Labor Politics," in Mario Zañartu and J. J. Kennedy, (eds.), *The Overall Development of Chile* (Notre Dame, IN: University of Notre Dame Press), pp. 113–145.

Landsberger, Henry A. and Tim McDaniel (1976) "Hypermobilization in Chile 1970–1973," *World Politics*, Vol. 28 (4), pp. 502–541.

Lavrin, Asunción (1989) "Women, Labor and the Left," *Journal of Women's History*, Vol. 1 (2), pp. 88–116.

Lechner, Norbert (1970) *La Democracia en Chile* (Buenos Aires: Ediciones Signos).

LeGates, Richard T. (1974) "A Decade of Struggle for Housing in Chile," *Inter-American Economic Affairs*, Vol. 28 (2), pp. 51–75.

Lehmann, David (1974) "Agrarian Reform in Chile, 1965–1972: An Essay in Contradictions," in David Lehmann (ed.), *Agrarian Reform and Agrarian Reformism* (London: Faber and Faber), pp. 71–120.

Loveman, Brian (1976) *Struggle in the Countryside: Politics and Rural Labor in Chile, 1919–1973* (Bloomington: Indiana University Press).

——— (1979) *Chile—The Legacy of Hispanic Capitalism* (New York: Oxford University Press).

Loveman, Brian and Elizabeth Lira (2000) *Las Ardientes Cenizas del Olvido—Vía Chilena a la Reconciliación Política 1932–1994* (Santiago: LOM).

Lowenstein, Karl (1944) "Legislation for the Defense of the State in Chile," *Columbia Law Review*, Vol. 44, pp. 366–407.

Lowenstein, Steven (1970). *Lawyers, Legal Education, and Development: An Examination of the Process of Reform in Chile* (New York: International Legal Center).

Macías, Leopoldo (1946) *Los Decretos de Insistencia* (Santiago: Universidad de Chile, Facultad de Ciencias Jurídicas y Sociales).

Makluf, José (1973) *La Regulación Jurídica del Comercio* (Santiago: Editorial Jurídica).

Mamalakis, Markos J. (1976) *The Growth and Structure of the Chilean Economy: From Independence to Allende* (New Haven: Yale University Press).

Manin, Bernard (1997) *The Principles of Representative Government* (Cambridge: Cambridge University Press).

Martínez, Alberto (1979) "The Industrial Sector: Areas of Social and Mixed Property in Chile," in Sandro Sideri (ed.), *Chile 1970–1973: Economic Development and Its International Setting* (The Hague: Martinus Nijhoff), pp. 221–274.

Martner, Daniel (1929) *Historia de Chile, Historia Económica, Tomo I* (Santiago: Balcells).

Marx, Karl (1969) "The Hague Congress," in *Karl Marx and Frederick Engels Selected Works*, Vol. 2 (Moscow: Progress Publishers), pp. 292–294.

Matus-Valencia, Juán G. (1958) "The Centenary of the Chilean Civil Code," *American Journal of Comparative Law*, Vol. 7 (1), pp. 71–83.

Medhurst , Kenneth (1972) *Allende's Chile* (London: Hart-Davis MacGibbon).

Meller, Patricio (1996) *Un Siglo de Economía Política Chilena (1890–1990)* (Santiago, Editorial Andrés Bello).

Meneses, Augusto (1973) "Las JAP: Servicio a la Comunidad o Control Político," *Revista Mensaje*, No. 219 (June), pp. 266–268.

Menges, Constantine C. (1966) "Public Policy and Organized Business in Chile: A Preliminary Analysis," *Journal of International Affairs*, Vol. 20 (2), pp. 343–365.

Mera, Jorge, Felipe González and Juan Enrique Vargas (1978) *Los Regímenes de Excepción en Chile Durante el Período 1925–1973* (Santiago: Academia de Humanismo Cristiano).

Merryman, John Henry (1969) *The Civil Law Tradition: An Introduction to the Legal Systems of Western Europe and Latin America* (Stanford: Stanford University Press).

Millar, René (1972) "Significado y Antecedentes del Movimiento Militar de 1924," *Historia*, No. 11, pp. 7–102.

Molina, Sergio (1972) *El Proceso de Cambio en Chile* (Santiago: Editorial Universitaria).

Monteón, Michael (1982) *Chile in the Nitrate Era* (Madison: University of Wisconsin Press).

Montt, Pedro (1891) *Exposition of the Illegal Acts of Ex-President Balmaceda, Which Caused the Civil War in Chile* (Washington, DC: Gibson Bros., Printers and Bookbinders).

Moore, Stanley (1963) *Three Tactics* (New York: Monthly Review Press).

Moran, Theodore (1974) *Multinational Corporations and the Politics of Dependence: Copper in Chile 1945–1973* (Princeton: Princeton University Press).

Morris, James O. (1966) *Elites, Intellectuals, and Consensus—A Study of the Social Question and the Industrial Relations System in Chile* (Ithaca: New York State School of Industrial Relations, Cornell University).

Munita, Eduardo (1955) *Estudio Crítico del Recurso de Queja* (Santiago: Editorial Jurídica).

Muñoz, Oscar (1968) *Crecimiento Industrial de Chile 1914–1965* (Santiago: Editorial Universitaria).

——— (1986) *Chile y su Industrialización* (Santiago: CIEPLAN).

NACLA (1973) *New Chile* (California: North American Congress for Latin America).

Novoa, Eduardo (1963/64) "Sistema Legal y Desarrollo Económico," *Anales de la Facultad de Ciencias Jurídicas, Políticas y Sociales (Universidad Católica de Chile)*, Nos. 17–18, pp. 81–110.

——— (1968) "La Renovación del Derecho," *Revista de Derecho y Ciencias Sociales (Universidad de Concepción)*, Vol. 36 (144), pp. 3–28.

——— (1970) "Justicia de Clase?" *Revista Mensaje* (Apartado), No. 187, p. 12.

——— (1971) "Vías Legales para Avanzar Hacia el Socialismo," *Revista de Derecho Económico*, Vol. 9 (33–34), pp 27–37.

——— (1972) "El Difícil Camino de la Legalidad," *Revista de la Universidad Técnica del Estado*, No. 7 (April), pp. 9–34.

——— (1975) *El Derecho Como Obstáculo para el Cambio Social* (México: Siglo Veintiuno Editores).

——— (1978) *Vía Legal Hacia el Socialismo? El Caso de Chile, 1970–1973* (Caracas: Editorial Jurídica Venezolana).

——— (1992) *Los Resquicios Legales* (Santiago: Ediciones BAT).

Nunn, Frederick M. (1970) *Chilean Politics, 1920–1931: The Honorable Mission of the Armed Forces* (Albuquerque: University of New Mexico Press).

O'Brien, Thomas F. (1982) *The Nitrate Industry and Chile's Crucial Transition, 1870–1891* (New York: New York University Press).

Oneto, Antonio (1971) *Tratado General Sobre Reanudación de Faenas* (Santiago: Ediciones Revista Técnica del Trabajo y Previsión Social).

Orrego, Claudio (ed.) (1979) *Siete Ensayos Sobre Arturo Alessandri Palma* (Santiago: Instituto Chileno de Estudios Humanísticos), pp. 55–118.

Ortega, Luis (1984) "Nitrates, Chilean Entrepreneurs and the Origins of the War of the Pacific," *Journal of Latin American Studies*, Vol. 16 (2), pp. 337– 380.

——— (1985) "Economic Policy and Growth in Chile from Independence to the War of the Pacific," in Christopher Able and Colin M. Lewis (eds.), *Latin America, Imperialism and the State: The Political Economy of the External Connection from Independence to the Present* (London: The Athlone Press), pp. 147– 171.

Osgood, Harry (1949) "Los Intereses Salitreros Ingleses y la Revolución de 1891," *Revista Chilena de Historia y Geografía*, Vol. January–June, pp. 60–81.

Palma, Gabriel (1983) "Chile 1914–1935: De Economía Exportadora a Sustitución de Exportaciones," *Nueva Historia*, Vol. 2 (7), pp. 165–192.

—— (1985) "External Disiquilibrium and Internal Industrialization: Chile 1914–1935," in Christopher Able and Colin M. Lewis (eds.), *Latin America, Imperialism and the State: The Political Economy of the External Connection from Independence to the Present* (London: The Athlone Press), pp. 318–338.

Parrish, Charles J., Arpad von Lazar and Jorge Tapia (1970) "Electoral Procedures and Political Parties in Chile," *Studies in Comparative International Development*, Vol. 6 (12), pp. 255–267.

Pereira, Teresa (1994) *El Partido Conservador 1930–1965* (Santiago: Fundación Mario Góngora).

Petras, James (1969) *Politics and Social Forces in Chilean Development* (Berkley: University of California Press).

Petras, James and Maurice Zeitlin (1967) "Miners and Agrarian Radicalism," *American Sociological Review*, Vol. 32 (4), pp. 578–586.

Pike, Frederick B. (1963) *Chile and the United States, 1880–1962* (South Bend, IN: University of Notre Dame Press).

—— (1968) "Aspects of Class Relations in Chile, 1850–1960," in James Petras and Maurice Zeitlin (eds.), *Latin America: Reform or Revolution?* (Greenwich, CT: Fawcett Publications), pp. 202–219.

Pinto, Aníbal (1973) *Chile un Caso de Desarrollo Frustrado* (3rd edition) (Santiago: Editorial Universitaria).

Pinto, Julio and Verónica Valdivia (2001) *Revolución Proletaria o Querida Chusma?* (Santiago: Editorial LOM).

Poblete, Moisés (1926) *La Organización Sindical en Chile y Otros Estudios Sociales* (Santiago: Ministerio de Higiene, Asistencia Social, Previsión y Trabajo).

Pregger-Roman, Charles G. (1983) "The Origin and Development of the Bourgeoisie in Nineteenth Century Chile," *Latin American Perspectives*, Vol. 10 (2/3), pp. 39–59.

Przeworski, Adam, Michael Alvarez, José Antonio Cheibub, and Fernando Limongi (1996) "What Makes Democracies Endure?" *Journal of Democracy*, Vol. 7 (1), pp. 39–55.

Quiros, Gustavo (1973) "El Contenido Ideológico de la Escuela Nacional Unificada," *Política y Espíritu*, Vol. 28 (342), pp. 46–48.

Radtke, Carlos (1964) *El Poder Judicial en las Diversas Constituciones Chilenas* (Santiago: Editorial Universitaria).

Ramírez Necochea, Hernán. (1969) *Balmaceda y la Contrarevolución de 1891* (2nd edition) (Santiago: Editorial Universitaria).

Ramos, Sergio (1979) "Inflation in Chile and the Political Economy of the Unidad Popular Government," in Sandro Sideri (ed.), *Chile 1970–1973: Economic Development and its International Setting* (The Hague: Martinus Nijhoff), pp. 313– 362.

Reinsch, Paul S. (1909) "Parliamentary Government in Chile," *American Political Science Review*, Vol. 3 (4), pp. 507–538.

Remmer, Karen L. (1984) *Party Competition in Argentina and Chile— Political Recruitment and Public Policy, 1890–1930* (Lincoln: University of Nebraska Press).

Ríos, Juan Antonio (1943) *Mensaje de S.E. el Presidente de la República en la Apertura de las Sesiones Ordinarias del Congreso Nacional* (Santiago: Presidencia de la República).

Robles, Victor (1936) "Estudio Sobre el Recurso de Queja Referido a la Jurisprudencia de la Corte Suprema de Agosto 1935 a Agosto 1936," *Revista de Derecho y Jurisprudencia*, Vol. 33, pp. 145–169.

Rodríguez, Pedro J. (1964) "La Autonomía Económica del Poder Judicial," *Revista de Derecho y Jurisprudencia*, Vol. 61, pp. 71–80.

Roldán, Alcibíades (1913) *Elementos de Derecho Constitucional* (Santiago: Imprenta Barcelona).

Rosenblatt, Karin Alexandra (2001) "Charity, Rights, and Entitlement: Gender, Labor, and Welfare in Early Twentieth-Century Chile," *Hispanic American Historical Review*, Vol. 81 (3–4), pp. 555–585.

Roxborough, Ian, Philip O'Brien, and Jackie Roddick (1977) *Chile The State and Revolution* (London: Macmillan Press).

Rueschemeyer, Dietrich, Evelyne Huber Stephens, and John D. Stephens (1992) *Capitalist Development and Democracy* (Cambridge: Polity Press).

Saavedra, Pablo and Carlos Pecchi (1971) "Estudio Teórico y Práctico de los Tribunales del Trabajo y sus Procedimientos," *Revista de Derecho de Concepción*, Vol. 39 (No. 156), pp. 5–39.

Sader, Emir (1973) *Movilización de Masas y Sindicalización en el Gobierno U.P.* (Santiago: Universidad de Chile, Departamento de Estudios Socio-Económicos).

Santa María, Alfredo and Arturo Alessandri (1944) "La Legalidad del Decreto de Requisición del Uso y Goce del Matadero Municipal de Santiago," *Revista de Derecho y Jurisprudencia*, Vol. 41 (9/10), pp. 133–145.

Santa María, Raúl (1972) "La Requisición de Industrias," *Estudios Jurídicos*, Vol. (1), pp. 16–36.

Schweitzer, Daniel (1972) *Acusación Constitucional, Regimes de Emergencia y Otros Estudios Jurídicos* (Santiago: Editorial Andrés Bello).

Scully, Timothy R. (1992) *Rethinking the Centre Party-Politics in Nineteenth and Twentieth Century Chile* (Stanford: Stanford University Press).

Serrano, Sol (1979) "Arturo Alessandri y la Campaña Electoral de 1920," in Claudio Orrego (ed.), *Siete Ensayos Sobre Arturo Alessandri Palma* (Santiago: Instituto Chileno de Estudios Humanísticos), pp. 55–118.

Sierra, Enrique (1969) *Tres Ensayos de Estabilización en Chile* (Santiago: Editorial Universitaria).

Sigmund, Paul E. (1977) *The Overthrow of Allende and the Politics of Chile, 1964–1976* (Pittsburgh: University of Pittsburgh Press).

Silva-Bascuñán, Alejandro (1963) *Tratado de Derecho Constitucional* (3 Vols.) (Santiago: Editorial Jurídica).

Silva Cimma, Enrique (1968) *Derecho Administrativo Chileno y Comparado Tomo I* (3rd edition) (Santiago: Editorial Jurídica).

——— (1969) *Derecho Administrativo Chileno y Comparado Tomo II* (2nd edition) (Santiago: Editorial Jurídica).

———— (1977) *El Tribunal Constitucional de Chile (1971–1973)* (Caracas: Editorial Jurídica Venezolana).

Silva Solar and Jacques Chonchol (1970) "Development without Capitalism: Toward a Communitarian World," in Paul Sigmund (ed.), *Models of Political Change in Latin America* (New York: Prager Publishers), pp. 310–315.

Silvert, Kalman H. (1965) *Chile: Yesterday and Today* (New York: Houghton Mifflin).

Smith, Brian H. (1982) *The Church and Politics in Chile* (Princeton: Princeton University Press).

Soto, Eduardo (1972a) "Sobre la Legalidad de las Requisaciones de Industrias," *Revista de Derecho Público*, No. 13, pp. 61–80.

———— (1972b) "Vigencia de las Normas Requisitorias de Industrias y Análisis de su Aplicación," *Estudios Jurídicos*, Vol. I (2), pp. 178–207.

———— (1973) "Requisación de Industrias en la Jurisprudencia de la Contraloría General de la República," *Estudios Jurídicos*, Vol. II, pp. 233–260.

———— (1977) "La Toma de Razón y el Poder Normativo de la Contraloría General de la República" in *La Contraloría General de la República—50 Años de Vida Institucional* (Santiago: Facultad de Derecho, Universidad de Chile), pp. 165–189.

Stallings, Barbara (1978) *Class Conflict and Economic Development in Chile, 1958–1973* (Stanford: Stanford University Press).

Stevenson, John Reese (1942) *The Chilean Popular Front* (Westport, CT: Greenwood Press).

Strawbridge Jr. George (1968) "Militarism and Nationalism in Chile 1920–1932" (PhD dissertation, University of Pennsylvania).

Sunkel, Osvaldo (1959) "La Inflación Chilena: Un Enfoque Heterodoxo," *El Trimestre Económico*, Vol. 25 (4), pp. 570–599.

———— (1965) "Change and Frustration in Chile," in Claudio Véliz (ed.), *Obstacles to Change in Latin America* (Oxford: Oxford University Press), pp. 116–144.

Super, Richard R. (1975) "The Chilean Popular Front and the Presidency of Pedro Aguirre Cerda: 1938–1941" (PhD thesis, Arizona State University).

Szladitz, Charles (1984) "The Civil Law System," *International Encyclopaedia of Comparative Law*, Vol. 2, Chapter 2, pp. 26–81.

Talesnik, Gregorio (1940) *Intervencionismo del Estado y control de Precios por el Mismo* (Santiago, Escuela de Derecho, Universidad de Chile: Memoria para optar al Grado de Licenciado de la Facultad de Ciencias Jurídicas).

Tamanaha, Brian Z. (2004) *On The Rule of Law* (Cambridge: Cambridge University Press).

Thayer, William (1970) "Communitarianism and Christian Democracy," in Paul Sigmund (ed.), *Models of Political Change in Latin America* (New York: Prager Publishers), pp. 312–315.

Thiesenhusen, William C. (1966) *Chile's Experiments in Agrarian Reform* (Madison: University of Wisconsin Press).

Thome, Joseph R. (1971) "Expropriation in Chile under the Frei Agrarian Reform," *American Journal of Comparative Law*, Vol. 19, pp. 489–513.

——— (1989) "Law Conflict and Change: Frei's Law and Allende's Agrarian Reform," in William C. Thiesenhausen, (ed.), *Searching for Agrarian Reform in Latin America* (Boston: Unwin Hyman), pp. 188–215.

Tilly, Charles (2000) "Processes and Mechanisms of Democratization," *Sociological Theory*, Vol. 18 (1), pp. 1–16.

——— (2004) *Contention and Democracy in Europe, 1650–2000* (Cambridge: Cambridge University Press).

——— (2007) *Democracy* (Cambridge: Cambridge University Press).

Tomic, Radomiro (1974) "Primeros Pasos Hacia la Recuperación del Cobre: El Convenio de Washington de 1951," in Ricardo Ffrench Davis and Ernesto Tironi, (ed.), *El Cobre en el Desarrollo Nacional* (Santiago: Universidad Católica, Vice-Rectoría de Comunicaciones), pp. 131–158.

Urzúa, Germán (1968) *Los Partidos Políticos Chilenos* (Santiago: Editorial Jurídica).

——— (1984) *Diccionario Político Institucional de Chile* (Santiago: Editorial Jurídica).

——— (1986) *Historia Política Electoral de Chile (1931–1973)* (Santiago: Tamarcos-Van S.A.).

U.S. Department of Labor (1969) *Labor Law and Practice in Chile* (Washington, DC: Bureau of Labor Statistics Report No. 339).

Valenzuela, Arturo (1977) *Political Brokers in Chile* (Durham, NC: Duke University Press).

——— (1978) *The Breakdown of Democratic Regimes: Chile* (Baltimore: Johns Hopkins University Press).

——— (1984a) "Parties, Politics, and the State in Chile—The Higher Civil Service," in Ezra N. Suleiman (ed.), *Bureaucrats and Policy Making* (New York: Holmes and Meier), pp. 242–279.

——— (1984b) *Origins and Characteristics of the Chilean Party System: A Proposal for a Parliamentary Form of Government* (Paper prepared for the Workshop on Political Parties in the Southern Cone, Woodrow Wilson International Center for Scholars, Washington, DC).

——— (1994) "Party Politics and the Crisis of Presidentialism in Chile: A Proposal for a Parliamentary Form of Government," in Juan J. Linz and Arturo Valenzuela (eds.), *The Failure of Presidential Democracy—The Case of Latin America* (Baltimore: Johns Hopkins Press), pp. 91– 150.

Valenzuela, Arturo and Samuel Valenzuela (1983) "Los Orígenes de la Democracia. Reflexiones Teóricas Sobre el Caso de Chile," *Estudios Públicos*, Vol. 12 (Spring), pp. 5–39.

Valenzuela, Arturo and Alexander Wilde (1984) "El Congreso y la Redemocratización en Chile," *Alternativas*, Vol. 3 (May–August), pp. 5–40.

Valenzuela, Eugenio (1991) "Labor Judicial de la Corte Suprema," in Eugenio Valenzuela (ed.), *Proposiciones para la Reforma Judicial* (Santiago: Centro de Estudios Públicos), pp. 143–177.

Valenzuela, J. Samuel (1979) "Labor Movement Formation and Politics: The Chilean and French Cases in Comparative Perspective 1850–1950" (PhD thesis, Columbia University).

———— (1985) *Democratización Vía Reforma: La Expansión del Sufragio en Chile* (Buenos Aires: Ediciones Ides).

Vanderschuren, Franz (1973) "Political Significance of Neighborhood Committees in the Settlements of Santiago," in Dale L. Johnson (ed.), *The Chilean Road to Socialism* (New York: Anchor Books), pp. 256–283.

Varas, Guillermo (1940) *Derecho Administrativo* (Santiago: Editorial Nascimento).

Vekemans, Roger and Jorge Giusti (1970) "Marginality and Ideology in Latin American Development," *Studies in Comparative International Development*, Vol. 5 (11), pp. 221–234.

Véliz, Claudio (1971) "La Mesa de Tres Patas," in Hernán Godoy (ed.), *Estructura Social de Chile* (Santiago: Editorial Universitaria), pp. 232–240.

Vergara, Aquiles (1931) *Ibáñez, César Criollo* (Santiago: Imprenta Sud-Americana).

———— (1954) *Criba de Recuerdos Memorias—Mi Odisea Ministerial* (La Paz: N. Ed).

Vergara, Ximena and Luis Barros (1972) "La Guerra Civil del 91 y la Instauración del Parlamentarismo," *Revista Latinoamericana de Ciencias Sociales* Vol. 2, pp. 71–94.

Viera-Gallo, José Antonio (1972) "The Legal System and Socialism," *Wisconsin Law Review* (1972), pp. 754–766.

Villalobos, Sergio (1987) *Orígen y Ascenso de la Burguesía Chilena* (Santiago: Editorial Universitaria).

———— (1989) *Portales: Una Falsificación Histórica* (Santiago: Editorial Universitaria).

Volk, Steven S. (1993) "Mine Owners, Money Lenders, and the State in Mid-Nineteenth-Century Chile: Transitions and Conflict," *Hispanic American Historical Review*, Vol. 73 (1), pp. 67–98.

Von Brunn, Reinhard (1972) *Chile—Con Leyes Tradicionales Hacia una Nueva Economía?* (Santiago: Instituto Latinoamericano de Investigaciones Sociales).

Walker, Francisco (1965) *Esquema del Derecho del Trabajo y de la Seguridad Social en Chile* (Santiago: Editorial Jurídica).

Wolin, Sheldon (1996) "The Liberal Democratic Divide—On Rawls's Political Liberalism," *Political Theory*, Vol. 24 (1), pp. 97–142.

Wright, Thomas C. (1982) *Landowners and Reform in Chile* (Urbana: University of Illinois Press).

Yávar, Ernesto (1972) "La Reanudación de Faenas," *Estudios Jurídicos*, Vol. 1 (2), pp. 90–130.

Yocelevzky, Ricardo (1987) *La Democracia Cristiana Chilena y el Gobierno de Eduardo Frei (1964–1970)* (Mexico: Universidad Autónoma Metropolitana Unidad Xochimilco).

Zammit, J. Ann (1973) *The Chilean Road to Socialism* (Brighton: University of Sussex, Institute of Development Studies).

Zeitlin, Maurice (1968) "Social Determinants of Political Democracy in Chile," in James Petras and Maurice Zeitlin (eds.), *Latin America: Reform or Revolution?* (Greenwich, CT: Fawcett Publications), pp. 220–234.

——— (1984) *The Civil Wars in Chile* (Princeton: Princeton University Press).

Zeitlin, Maurice and James Petras (1967) "Miners and Agrarian Radicalism," *American Sociological Review*, Vol. 32 (4), pp. 578–586.

——— (1970) "The Working-Class Vote in Chile: Christian Democracy versus Marxism," *British Journal of Sociology*, Vol. 21 (1), pp. 16–29.

Official Sources, Codes, Case Reporters, and Newspapers

Cámara de Diputados—*Boletín de Sesiones.*

Código Civil (1964) (Santiago: Editorial Jurídica).

Código del Trabajo (1964) (Santiago: Editorial Jurídica).

Código Orgánico de Tribunales (1957) (Santiago: Editorial Jurídica).

Código Penal (1964) (Santiago: Editorial Jurídica).

Código de Procedimiento Civil (1964) (Santiago: Editorial Jurídica).

Código de Procedimiento Penal (1964) (Santiago: Editorial Jurídica).

Contraloría General de la República, Boletín de Jurisprudencia.

Contraloría General de la República, Memoria Annual.

Constitución Política de la República de Chile (1958) (Santiago: Editorial Jurídica).

Diario Oficial.

Diario de Sesiones del Senado.

El Mercurio.

El Siglo.

Fallos del Mes.

Revista de Derecho y Jurisprudencia.

Index

Recurso de queja: see complaint
   proceeding
Red Week, 60–1
Republican Confederation of Civic
   Action, see CRAC
Republican Militia, 78, 230
Republicanism, 33
Requisitions, 122–3, 207, 210–14
Rights:
   and possessory actions, 218
   and requisition decrees, 207
   and social inclusion, 163–7
   and Statute of Democratic
      Guarantees, 192–3
   denied to agricultural workers,
      81, 93–4
   denied on political grounds, 133
   extension of, to agricultural
      workers, 161–3
   extension of, to subordinate
      groups, 237
   women and, 98–9
Ríos, Juán Antonio, 79
   and Contraloría, 121
   and presidentialism, 104
Rule of law, 8, 31, 202, 217
Rural unions, 4, 92–4, 162–3
Russia, 29, 46

Santa Cruz, Andrés, 23
Santa María, Domingo, 18, 37, 42
Santiago, 58, 60
Sardinia, 29
SNA, see *Sociedad Nacional de
   Agricultura*
Social exclusion, 152
Social security, 67, 167
Socialism:
   and communitarian society, 153
Socialist Party:
   and dual strategy, 179–81, 196
   and Frei administration, 167, 169
   and rural unions, 162
   and workers' participation, 198–9
   creation of, 83

Socialist Republic, 65
Socialist Workers' Party, 96
Sociedad Nacional de Agricultura
   (SNA), 91–3, 160
Society for Equality, 36
Soviet Union, 2, 101
State Security Act (1948), 86, 113,
   133
State Security Act (1958), 114–15,
   122, 124
Statute of Democratic Guarantees:
   and Allende, 177–8
   and legality debate, 191–3
Strikes:
   and Allende administration, 178,
      194–5
   and Frei administration, 163
   and parliamentary republic, 60
Supreme Court, 3, 35, 65, 203,
   222, 225, 226, 235–6, 239
   and administrative justice,
      139–45, 219–20
   and cassation powers, 68, 136
   and class bias, 205
   and complaints proceeding,
      135–9
   and ecclesiastical tribunals, 35, 39
   and enforcement of judgments,
      223–4
   and impeachment proceedings, 39
   and judicial independence, 138
   and judicial review of legislation,
      110, 131–5, 201
   and property rights, 218–19, 221
   and requisition decrees, 218
   as head of the judiciary, 135–6,
      215
   composition, 68
   establishment of, 128
   exchange of letters with Allende,
      223–4
Switzerland, 2

Talca, 22
Tarapacá, 49